Eliot and Beckett's Low Modernism

Other Becketts – Series List

Published

Creative Involution: Bergson, Beckett, Deleuze
S. E. Gontarski

Beckett's Thing: Painting and Theatre
David Lloyd

Samuel Beckett and the Terror of Literature
Christopher Langlois

Samuel Beckett's How It Is: *Philosophy in Translation*
Anthony Cordingley

Posthuman Space in Samuel Beckett's Short Prose
Jonathan Boulter

Beckett and Embodiment: Body, Space, Agency
Amanda M. Dennis

Eliot and Beckett's Low Modernism: Humility and Humiliation
Rick de Villiers

www.edinburghuniversitypress.com/series/ORBT

Eliot and Beckett's Low Modernism
Humility and Humiliation

Rick de Villiers

Edinburgh University Press is one of the leading university presses in the UK. We publish academic books and journals in our selected subject areas across the humanities and social sciences, combining cutting-edge scholarship with high editorial and production values to produce academic works of lasting importance. For more information visit our website: edinburghuniversitypress.com

© Rick de Villiers, 2021, 2023

Edinburgh University Press Ltd
The Tun – Holyrood Road
12(2f) Jackson's Entry
Edinburgh EH8 8PJ

First published in hardback by Edinburgh University Press, 2021

Typeset in 11/13 Adobe Sabon by
IDSUK (DataConnection) Ltd

A CIP record for this book is available from the British Library

ISBN 978 1 4744 7903 5 (hardback)
ISBN 978 1 4744 7904 2 (paperback)
ISBN 978 1 4744 7905 9 (webready PDF)
ISBN 978 1 4744 7906 6 (epub)

The right of Rick de Villiers to be identified as the author of this work has been asserted in accordance with the Copyright, Designs and Patents Act 1988, and the Copyright and Related Rights Regulations 2003 (SI No. 2498).

Contents

	Series Editor's Preface	vi
	Acknowledgements	vii
	Abbreviations and Conventions	viii
	Introduction	1
1	Fat Fingers and Private Truths: Between Manners and Morals in *Eeldrop and Appleplex*	27
2	Pudenda of the Psyche: Embarrassment in *More Pricks than Kicks*	60
3	Mr Eliot's Sermons and Sermonising: Participation, Good Will and Humility in *Murder in the Cathedral*	93
4	A Defence of Wretchedness: *Molloy* and Humiliation	125
5	Assuming the Double Part: Irony as Humility in *East Coker*	149
6	*How It Is* and the Syntax of Penury	178
	Conclusion: Humility's Edges	211
	Bibliography	215
	Index	243

Series Editor's Preface

In 1997 Apple computers launched an advertising campaign (in print and on television) that entreated us to 'Think Different', and Samuel Beckett was one of Apple's icons. Avoiding Apple's solecism, we might modify the appeal to say that *Other Becketts* is a call to think differently as well, in this case about Beckett's work, to question, that is, even the questions we ask about it. *Other Becketts*, then, is a series of monographs focused on alternative, unexplored or under-explored approaches to the work of Samuel Beckett, not a call for novelty per se, but a call to examine afresh those of Beckett's interests that were more arcane than mainstream, interests that might be deemed quirky or strange, and those of his works less thoroughly explored critically and theoretically, the late prose and drama, say, or even the poetry or criticism. Volumes might cover (but are not restricted to) any of the following: unusual illnesses or neurological disorders (the 'duck foot, goose foot' of *First Love*, akathisia or the invented duck's disease or panpygoptosis of Miss Dew in *Murphy*, proprioception, or its disturbance, in *Not I*, perhaps, or other unusual neurological lapses among Beckett's creatures, from Watt to the Listener of *That Time*); mathematical peculiarities (irrational numbers, factorials, Fibonacci numbers or sequences, or non-Euclidian approaches to geometry); linguistic failures (from Nominalism to Mauthner, say); citations of or allusions to contrarian aesthetic philosophers working in a more or less irrationalist tradition (Nietzsche, Bergson or Deleuze, among others), or in general 'the simple games that time plays with space'. Alternative approaches would be of interest as well, with foci on objects, animals, cognitive or memory issues, and the like.

S. E. Gontarski, Florida State University

Acknowledgements

Writing a book is a humbling experience, not least because it's made possible by the unearned generosity of others. The ideas developed here had their start in my doctoral work at Durham University, where Pat Waugh and Jason Harding were unfailing in their warmth, expertise, and encouragement. Since then, the evolution of this project owes more than I can say to Arthur Rose and our near-weekly conversations. Not with greater care – nor with more necessary pushback – has anyone read my work over the last two years. Another special debt is owed to Matthew Feldman, who is ever-unstinting with his time and advice.

This book has also benefited hugely from exchanges with Marc Botha, Francesca Bratton, Fraser Riddell, Steven Matthews, John Pilling, Marco Bernini, John Haffenden, Mika Vale, Tom Smith, John Nash, Andries Wessels and my colleagues in the Department of English at the University of the Free State. To the UFS librarians, Henriette van den Berg and ESAP, my heartfelt thanks.

I'm honoured to be part of the *Other Becketts* series and grateful for Stan Gontarski's support along the way. To the EUP staff – Jackie Jones, Ersev Ersoy and Susannah Butler – thank you for all your patient assistance.

Parts of this book have appeared elsewhere in slightly different form: a shorter version of Chapter 3 in *Literature and Theology* 34.2 (2020); Chapter 4 in the *Journal of Modern Literature* 42.4 (2019); and a small section from Chapter 5 in the *New Cambridge Companion to T. S. Eliot* (2017).

To my parents, Gus and Hettie, and my sister, Lindi, whom I cannot thank sufficiently for their love and unceasing encouragement: ek het nie die woorde om te sê hoeveel ek julle waardeer nie – veral nie in Engels nie. And lastly, my deepest gratitude to Michelle, without whose sacrifice and love this book would not be. I humbly dedicate it to her.

Abbreviations and Conventions

T. S. Eliot

CP1	*The Complete Prose of T. S. Eliot: The Critical Edition, Volume 1: Apprentice Years, 1905–1918*
CP2	*The Complete Prose of T. S. Eliot: The Critical Edition, Volume 2: The Perfect Critic, 1919–1926*
CP3	*The Complete Prose of T. S. Eliot: The Critical Edition, Volume 3: Literature, Politics, Belief, 1927–1929*
CP4	*The Complete Prose of T. S. Eliot: The Critical Edition, Volume 4: English Lion, 1930–1933*
CP5	*The Complete Prose of T. S. Eliot: The Critical Edition, Volume 5: Tradition and Orthodoxy, 1934–1939*
CP6	*The Complete Prose of T. S. Eliot: The Critical Edition, Volume 6: The War Years, 1940–1946*
CP7	*The Complete Prose of T. S. Eliot: The Critical Edition, Volume 7: A European Society, 1947–1953*
CP8	*The Complete Prose of T. S. Eliot: The Critical Edition, Volume 8: Still and Still Moving, 1954–1965*
CPP	*The Complete Poems and Plays*
L1	*The Letters of T. S. Eliot, Volume 1: 1898–1922*
L2	*The Letters of T. S. Eliot, Volume 2: 1923–1925*
L3	*The Letters of T. S. Eliot, Volume 3: 1926–1927*
L4	*The Letters of T. S. Eliot, Volume 4: 1928–1929*
L5	*The Letters of T. S. Eliot, Volume 5: 1930–1931*
L6	*The Letters of T. S. Eliot, Volume 6: 1932–1933*
L7	*The Letters of T. S. Eliot, Volume 7: 1934–1935*
L8	*The Letters of T. S. Eliot, Volume 8: 1936–1938*
P1	*The Poems of T. S. Eliot, Volume 1: Collected and Uncollected Poems*
P2	*The Poems of T. S. Eliot, Volume 2: Practical Cats and Further Verses*

Samuel Beckett

BDL	The Beckett Digital Library
CC	Comment c'est, How It Is and / et L'Image: A Critical-Genetic Edition / Une edition critic-genetique
CDW	The Complete Dramatic Works
Com etc.	Company; Ill Seen Ill Said; Worstward Ho; Stirrings Still
CP	Collected Poems
CSP	The Complete Short Prose, 1929–1989
Dis	Disjecta: Miscellaneous Writings and a Dramatic Fragment
DN	Beckett's Dream notebook
Dream	Dream of Fair to Middling Women
EB	Echo's Bones
Eleutheria	Eleutheria
HII	How It Is
L1	The Letters of Samuel Beckett, Volume 1: 1929–1940
L2	The Letters of Samuel Beckett, Volume 2: 1941–1956
L3	The Letters of Samuel Beckett, Volume 3: 1957–1965
L4	The Letters of Samuel Beckett, Volume 4: 1966–1989
MC	Mercier and Camier
MPTK	More Pricks Than Kicks
Mur	Murphy
PTD	Proust and 'Three Dialogues with Georges Duthuit'
TN	Three Novels: Molloy, Malone Dies, The Unnamable
TNSB1	The Theatrical Notebooks of Samuel Beckett, Volume 1: Waiting for Godot
W	Watt

Reference

OED	The Oxford English Dictionary (online edition)

General

Unless otherwise stated, all biblical references are to the King James Version.

Though no distinction is made between abbreviations referring to Eliot's and Beckett's respective volumes of letters, this should be clear from the context.

Introduction

During the Sermon on the Mount scene in *Monty Python's Life of Brian*, there is some confusion as to who exactly will inherit the earth. Standing at the rear of the multitude, a group of squabblers is dumbfounded that one particular Greek should be the lucky heir. Soon it dawns on them that they had misheard: 'Oh, it's the *meek*! Blessed are the *meek*! Oh, that's nice, isn't it? I'm glad they're getting something, 'cause they have a hell of a time.'[1] What heightens the irony of the scene is the apocryphal emphasis placed on humility. Christ blesses not only the meek, but also 'those of gentle spirit'. These are equivalent renderings of the same verse (Matt. 5:5), not separate categories of sanctity. And so, by doubling up on what is at best an ambient endorsement of selflessness, the skit can double down on its wry exhibition of self-interest. Bored with the blessings heaped on the peacemakers and other quiet souls, Brian's mother suggests going to a stoning instead. Another man makes merry with the size of his neighbour's nose, to which the neighbour responds with a boiling spirit: 'I said one more time . . . mate and I'll take you to the fucking cleaners.' And, at the moment we are meant to hear the Lord's encouragement for those who take insults in good grace, bad words are traded for blows.

However impish and irreverent, the scene opens onto two concerns that animate this book. In the first instance, it invites thinking about both the power and dispossession at the heart of humility. Are the meek those of self-effacing disposition or are they the downtrodden of society? Are they the humble or the humiliated? The distinction is not easy to make, given that humility and humiliation have an awkward, often unacknowledged intimacy. The former may be a queenly, cardinal or monkish virtue; it could attest to a diffident spirit or a slavish cast of mind. It has been framed as a component of magnanimity, an enabling awareness of human limitation, a religious ideal. Much less equivocally, humiliation conjures bleak associations. It implies violence against autonomy and points to a state at the extreme end of shame. Yet between the two words is common ground. A shared etymology links them to lowliness (*humilis*) and, further down, to the earth (*humus*). And in ascetic traditions painfully aware of humanity's quintessence – 'dust thou art, and unto dust shalt thou return' (Gen. 3:19) – humiliation cultivates humility. The second concern is with humility's mimetic potential, whether this virtue that dare not speak its own name can somehow be made legible in the work of art. While the Monty Python scene is patently not interested in representing humility, it suggests an avenue by which we can arrive at the comportment's inference: responses to humiliation. In the case of Big Nose, his injured dignity prompts an injurious response. But humiliation can also be humbly met.

With this ambivalence and these two concerns in mind, I turn to T. S. Eliot and Samuel Beckett. Granting their imperfect likeness, this book nevertheless recognises between the two writers a common if differently handled interest in the low and the lowly. They share a fascination with suffering. Both are driven by an endless carrying 'on', whether towards 'lessness' or the extinction of personality. And in crowding their works with those having a hell of a time, they recuperate something of the affinity between humility and humiliation. Elaborating on this affinity, this study develops a framework for complementary performances of humility across three categories: the affective, the ethical and the aesthetic. It emphasises, first and foremost, the singularity of the work of art in nuancing the relation between humility and humiliation. But it also sheds light on the authors' debt to a theological tradition within which lowliness is a constitutive aspect of subjectivity. This filiation pits 'low modernism' against interpretations that play up humility's affirming aspects. And, in drawing out these parallels and oppositions, I contend that Eliot and Beckett have shaped our modern minds in a particularly unmodern way.

Two Subtraction Stories

There are two assumptions behind this claim. First, by bringing humility and humiliation into closer contact, Eliot and Beckett evince an attitude unaccommodating of modernity's ideals about self-sufficiency and human flourishing. Disobliging towards social utility and progress, this attitude brings out sharply that entrenched antipathy to civilisation many have seen as a central feature of modernism. Recall the myriad complaints against Eliot's ascetic brand of Christianity: that it was deeply unhealthy, medieval rather than modern, antiquated as well as anti-social.² In its turn, Beckett's beyond-the-pale *via negativa* may be indexed by the 1969 Nobel Committee's doubts about awarding him the prize for literature.³ His art was deemed incompatible with the spirit of Nobel's will, which stipulates that recipients' work should exhibit an 'idealistic tendency' and confer 'the greatest benefit to humankind'.⁴ The reading public, it seems suggested, deserve to have set before them examples of strength and uplift.⁵

This brings us to the second point about our unmodern attunement: if we grant lowness as a concern for these two writers around whom towering cultural edifices have been erected, we must also grant that these edifices testify to our transcendence of the 'modal difficulty' implied in the first point. Modal difficulties, as George Steiner conceived of them, confront us with the limits of our critical tolerance. We may understand a work's intellectual complexity yet be unable to reconcile its sensibility with our own, since it 'challenge[s] the inevitable parochialism of honest empathy'.⁶ But absorbed as it is into the culture industry, modernism's lowness no longer seems to present the hurdle to taste and decency that once it did. Think of that proliferating marker of assimilated abasement, the 'fail better' tattoo, or of pop star Harry Styles's smiling pose with a copy of *The Waste Land*.⁷ As a more scholarly gauge of this transcendence we may take the 2004 'Low Modernism' special issue of *Critical Quarterly*. There, the editors remark that '[m]any of the key texts of so-called "high" modernism are entangled in all that is low: obscene bodies, animals and objects; masturbation, shit and piss'.⁸ Put in decidedly un-euphemistic terms, the reclamation is also a provocation. On the one hand is the assertion of corporeal humility's thematic significance for modernism; on the other hand, the subtle suggestion that this theme's neglect could be explained by a critical squeamishness that hesitates before the exploration of 'shit and piss', let alone its naming.⁹ The vanquishing of modernism's modal difficulties seems implied in the distance – in freedom of expression, in sexual politics, in LGBTQIA+ rights – between our moment and the moment of the obscenity cases brought against D. H. Lawrence and James Joyce, of the scandals caused by Djuna Barnes's *Nightwood*, of the censorship that long dogged Beckett. That these issues are now the province of literary history could, unhumbly, be taken to supply the measure of a moral and intellectual emancipation from earlier codes of inhibition and decorum.

The previous two paragraphs highlight a paradox key to this book: that we can stomach and even turn extreme degradation in Eliot, Beckett and other modernists into an object of analysis, while also maintaining that humiliation, by definition, is something that most people do not desire.[10] This paradox – this unmodern making of our modern mind – inheres in the simultaneous telling of two 'subtraction stories', Charles Taylor's term for those ideological positions arrived at by casting aside 'confining horizons, or illusions, or limitations'.[11] The first story, fleshed out more fully below, centres on the secular conception of humility as a social virtue. Whether in the guise of modest behaviour or as a mode that drives communal endeavour, humility is an enabling and voluntary motion of assent. It is a comportment that encourages accurate self-assessment and disallows both boasting and deprecation. It implies at once the recognition of our shared limitations and the effort to transcend them. Subtracted from this account is not only the moral prostration that a penitent might feel before an overawing divinity, but humility's historical overlap with humiliation.

The second story also involves humility. It refracts through a critical trend which, disabused of modernism's overhyped claims of strength, turns its gaze towards aesthetic weakness – towards powerlessness, passivity and shame.[12] Indeed, 'make it weak' is the call to disarmament in a recent *Modernism/modernity* special issue.[13] The revised Poundian imperative is both *of* and *for* modernism. *Of* modernism in that a sense of vulnerability and insufficiency runs through the modernists' anxious, compensatory reworkings of tradition.[14] But *for* modernism insofar as 'modernism' is itself taken as a provisional marker by which to grab a protean bundle of works, writers and interests. In fine, scholarship's recent swerve towards the low and weak follows a methodological injunction to cast off modernism's vaunted associations with the high and strong.

Eliot and Beckett's Low Modernism brings these subtraction stories together. Its primary concern is with humiliation's capacity to make humility legible in the work of art: how embarrassment gives onto a recognition of otherness, how sacrifice becomes the image of obedience, how textual penury facilitates a letting-go of intertextual riches. In pursuing these questions, this study offers a theory of mimetic humility by involving modernist literature in the conception of a virtue that has almost exclusively been defined by theology, philosophy and medieval studies.[15] At the same time, it keeps in view those discourses that have rejected humiliation as hostile to a post-Enlightenment understanding of humility. By heeding the ideals that have led to humility's secular reinvention – community building, the redress of structural injustice, the safeguarding of human dignity – we might wonder at the relative ease that has come to subtend uneasy elements in Eliot and Beckett. How does one read the tortures and cruelties in Beckett and still glimpse in these a supposed affirmation of humanity's resilience? Can the deeply anti-social, anti-humanist streak that runs through Eliot be squared with the blessedness of the meek? The conjunction of the two subtraction stories necessitates the recognition that, at times, the humility–humiliation nexus we find in Eliot and Beckett troubles the honest empathy of modernity. At other times, however, this alignment speaks to those impulses that Lionel Trilling saw lurking 'somewhere in the mind of every modern person' – impulses towards suffering, surrender and self-undoing.[16] My aim is to bring that 'somewhere' out of the margins and into a critical clearing.

Performances of Humility

The difficulty in getting to this clearing, however, is locked up in humility's elusiveness. On the one hand, it is a virtue known not to know itself. A long theological tradition holds that humility can remain intact only so long as it is not regarded as something achieved or summited.[17] Forever guarding against finality, humility must be endless. On the other hand, humility seems absent when too obviously present. Think of Belacqua who determines to 'efface himself altogether' (*MPTK*, 155) only to impress those around him, or of *Murder in the Cathedral*'s Thomas Becket spurred to earthly sacrifice by thoughts of eternal recompense. The opacity of humility's motives means that we are apt to regard its bowings-down as bent on personal gain.

Such suspicion perhaps seems implied in the phrase 'performance of humility'. Gripped by the pincers of misgiving, it suggests attunement to the stratagems behind self-lessening. This might be a necessary precaution against critical hagiography, particularly when approaching writers whose concern with humility is firmly established in their own work and in scholarly discourse. Given how widely and sometimes peremptorily Eliot treats the subject in his writings, an unkindly reader might be tempted to reverse his pronouncement on Byron: it is difficult to say whether Eliot was a humble man, or a man who liked to pose as a humble man.[18] In Beckett's case, the sceptic looks warily on those well-worn narratives about the author's saintly acts, or wonders with Nietzschean distrust if the embrace of impotence – reified by scholarly consensus as *the* Beckettian thing – could be a means of asserting strength.[19] Is there not something eminently assured in the deprecation of '*Posthumous Droppings*', the title Beckett playfully proposed for a volume by which posterity might come to know his lesser works?[20] Thinking of performances of humility encourages discernment between sanctimony and sincerity, between the 'pharisee's tarantara' and the 'publican's whinge' (*Dis*, 68).

But responding to the performance of humility goes beyond a bad-faith hermeneutics of suspicion. Instead, it means keeping alive an indeterminacy by which humility's dynamism is made perceptible. For an accounting of lowliness must pursue the dialectical tensions that enable the onwards-and-downwards trajectory wherein humility assumes an infinitely specular, infinitely mobile relation to itself. Not in the spirit of Pyrrhonism, then, but with a suspension of belief, I want to outline three ways in which this iterative intensity can be understood, three theories that cast in relief humility's making and unmaking. Two of these – the Aristotelean and humanistic models – make up the first subtraction story discussed above which sees humiliation as excessive and unnecessary to modern notions of humility. The third account, Christian religious humility, takes the two forms of lowliness to be deeply imbricated. What follows does not pretend to be a comprehensive account of theories on humility. Nor are the designations necessarily representative of the way in which the virtue theorists, philosophers and theologians engaged below label their own work. Rather, these categories emerge in proportion to their congruence or incompatibility with what I am calling Eliot and Beckett's low modernism.

In the Aristotelean or realistic account, as the latter term suggests, humility is regarded as a just estimation of self-worth: the humble person neither overvalues his merit nor succumbs to self-deprecation. The pursuit of this mean has its basis in Aristotle's 'great-souled' or magnanimous man. As depicted in the *Nicomachean Ethics*, this is a figure who shuns both vanity and expressions of inferiority, expects acknowledgement level with his (decidedly *his*) virtue, and is motivated by honour and not altruism.[21] He likes to be a benefactor, though resents being a beneficiary. Most importantly, his accurate self-assessment is anchored in respect for truth; he therefore takes fair measure of his worth and works.[22] By contrast, both the boaster and self-deprecator fall foul of the mean at opposite ends. The boaster exaggerates his merit, while the self-deprecator wilfully underrates himself. The evil of these two lessers is self-deprecation ('smallness of soul'), judged the more grievous affront for its vulgarity.[23]

From this brief sketch, it should already be clear that Aristotelian magnanimity ill fits Christian understandings of humility. Despite Thomas Aquinas's attempt to consolidate them as complementary aspects of reason and temperance, the two qualities remain incongruent.[24] Beckett would have known this from his philosophy primers. Archibald Alexander's *A Short History of Philosophy* sees Aristotle's 'aristocratic' list of virtues as 'marred by significant omissions', most notably humility.[25] And from Arnold Geulincx's *Ethics* – a work Beckett recommended 'most heartily' (*L1*, 329) to his friends and whose axiom of morals ('wherein you have no power, therein you should not will') he identified as key to much of his work (*L2*, 427, 669) – Beckett copied the sure and succinct dismissal: '*Humility foreign to the ancients*'.[26] Though slight, Geulincx's treatment of the *Nicomachean Ethics* conveys his fundamental disagreement with the idea of virtue as the perfection of good habits or as a 'disposition' towards moral excellence.[27] He is pointedly critical of the ancients 'abysmal ignoran[ce]' of humility, and is generally dismissive of the utilitarian purposes that govern their moral philosophy.[28]

Eliot would have been even more intimately familiar with the pragmatics of Aristotelean self-assessment. He read Aristotle in the original and in its entirety, and was well-versed in virtue theory of the late nineteenth and early twentieth centuries.[29] Henry Sidgwick, whose ethics Eliot treated sceptically in a graduate paper, was alarmed both by the cognitive dissonance that humility seems to require, and also by its potential to short-circuit civic duty.[30] For Sidgwick, true humility demands weighing up one's worth in order to worthily weigh in:

> [I]f our merits are comparatively high, it seems strange to direct us to have a low opinion of them. It may be replied, that though our merits may be high when compared with those of ordinary men, there are

always some to be found superior, and we can compare ourselves with these . . . But surely in the most important deliberations which human life offers, in determining what kind of work we shall undertake and to what social functions we shall aspire, it is often necessary that we should compare our qualifications carefully with those of average men, if we are to decide rightly. And it would seem just as irrational to underrate ourselves as to overrate . . .[31]

Another roughly contemporaneous version of this realism is Hastings Rashdall's, who argues that humility should transcend its traditionally 'non-utilitarian' and 'non-teleological character'.[32] Despite rejecting the 'revolting picture' of the original magnanimous man, Rashdall's theory operates on the same assumption of giftedness as the *Nicomachean Ethics*. The difference is that while Aristotle attributes this giftedness to an inborn aristocratic superiority, Rashdall more humbly credits luck, grace or a good upbringing. And although the public duty of his humble individual is not dispassionate like the great-souled man's, it is still activated by an awareness of elevated status and self-sufficiency. Such a view explains in part why Eliot saw parallels between Rashdall's thought and Unitarianism, the faith of his own family that Eliot denounced as 'bad preparation for brass tacks like birth, copulation and death, hell, heaven and insanity' (*L3*, 228). Rashdall's position also explains why Eliot, long before his own conversion, ridiculed the theologian's attempts to water down the demands of Christian self-abnegation.[33]

Given the apparent incompatibility between magnanimity and humility, virtue ethics has generally favoured the term 'modesty' in its retrieval of truthful self-assessment.[34] Modesty more readily speaks to publicly coded conduct and less obviously leans on a lowly regard of the self. It is a civilised trait of those highly gifted individuals who accept their due in good grace while declining to trumpet their own achievements. Adopting a modest but evaluative conception of self allows us to appreciate our accomplishments in relation to others' and so direct our talents where most needed. With this comes the avoidance of false humility. Like Sidgwick, Norvin Richards rejects negative self-valuations and suggests that it would be specious for the 'rather splendid among us' to subject ourselves to unwarranted abasement.[35] In his turn, Aaron Ben-Ze'ew proposes a comparative framework that allows us to regard our worth as similar to – though not the same as – that of others.[36] And, more recently, Steven Connor has claimed for humility a concomitant 'magnificence', since the act of giving way presupposes 'grandeur, authority, or power'.[37]

Though turning himself to noble ends, the great-souled man does not have humble beginnings.

Such privilege is unknown to Beckett's moribunds: lowliness is their station in life, not a goal to which they can aspire.[38] For instance, when Watt is struck by a maliciously cast rock and carries on without fuss, the narrator remarks that 'he deserved no credit for this' (W, 25). We are to infer that Watt's self-minimising manner can neither be understood as disrupting the *lex talionis*, nor as the ingathered force of indignation. Such 'credit' is due either to those who turn the other cheek or those who, in the ominous words of 'Sonnet 94', 'have power to hurt and will do none'.[39] This general incompatibility notwithstanding, we find in Beckett also a more pointed rejection of Aristotelean magnanimity. As mentioned earlier, the magnanimous man likes to do good deeds but cringes at the prospect of the charitable gesture. Indebtedness, after all, marks the inferior, which is why the *megalopsychos* 'repay[s] benefits with interest'.[40] Beckett travesties this moral economy in various ways. I return to this matter in Chapter 4, though it is worth mentioning a few examples here. Malone is grateful that his 'aphony' (TN, 263) has spared him the humiliation of being able to ask someone for a favour. In *Rough for Theatre I*, a man is horrified by the prospect of being done 'a service for nothing' (CDW, 231) and seeks immediately to restore an equitable relation of exchange. Perhaps the most bleakly humorous example occurs in *Watt*, with the exchange of kisses between the antihero and his patrician paramour, Mrs Gorman:

> From time to time, hoisting his weary head, from waist to neck his weary hold transferring, Watt would kiss, in a despairing manner, Mrs Gorman on or about the mouth, before crumpling back into his post-crucified position. And these kisses, when their first feverish force began to fail, that is to say very shortly following their application, it was Mrs Gorman's invariable habit to catch up, as it were, upon her own lips, and return, with tranquil civility, as one picks up a glove, or newspaper, let fall in some public place, and restores it with a smile, if not a bow, to its rightful proprietor. So that each kiss was in reality two kisses, first Watt's kiss, velleitary, anxious, and then Mrs Gorman's, unctuous and urbane. (W, 120)

In a clear effort to resist the dues of love, Mrs Gorman repays Watt's awkward affection with the lofty meekness of the great-souled. Her genteel alchemy transforms intimacy into courtesy, fumbling into refinement, vulnerability into self-sufficiency. These oppositions are clinched in the half-rhyme heard between 'anxious' and 'unctuous'. Grotesque though they seem, Watt's kisses are attended by the awful daring of a moment's surrender, the heart-stopping uncertainty of giving yourself away. But Mrs Gorman's kisses politely decline love's egality: they are 'unctuous' not only because smug, but also because they effect an unguent separation between giving and getting, between the haves and the have-nots.

Such a separation is alien to humanistic understandings of humility. If modesty is personified in the great-souled man, then humanistic humility's exemplar is Prometheus: not the defiant hero hailed by Romanticism, but that democratising figure in Plato's *Protagoras*. In this version of the myth, Prometheus pilfers fire and practical wisdom from the gods so that humans, in their naked and vulnerable state, might stand a chance of survival.[41] His efforts are impelled by necessity rather than by vaulting ambition or a desire for plenitude. Indeed, the word that differentiates humanistic humility from the realistic assessment account is 'incompleteness'. Mark Button, who prefers the term 'democratic humility', writes that this kind of humility 'cultivate[s] sensitivity toward the *incompleteness* and contingency both of one's personal moral powers and commitments, and of the particular forms, laws, and institutions that structure one's political and social life with others'.[42] What sets Button's theory and others like it against the Aristotelian accounts is a fundamental belief in human finitude.[43] Epistemically, such a view approaches religious humility in its negative valuation of self-worth, though it does not require belief in transcendental dependence. Practically, it deflates notions of individual self-sufficiency in order to facilitate communal endeavour and social change.

Humanistic humility is thus marked by an aspirational quality: the admission of universal limitation should not result in apathy but serve as a spur to better the status quo. Martha Nussbaum's notion of 'primitive shame', for instance, falls into this category, since it suggests our awareness of lack and fragmentation.[44] In its healthiest manifestation, primitive shame encourages positive striving: recognising our shortcomings, we are driven to overcome them. Nussbaum argues that this longing for restoration to a state of fullness may be turned into a practical value which anchors our march onwards and upwards in the belief that the type of completeness or perfection one craves 'is a type of completeness or perfection that one rightly ought to have'.[45] Or, as Norman

Foerster (one of Eliot's principal opponents in the humanism/religion debate) puts it: 'An adequate human standard calls for *completeness*; it demands the cultivation of every part of human nature . . .'[46] Such belief should not encourage a spirit of entitlement or an attitude of complacency (contra the great-souled man). Instead, it is meant to foster a kind of hopeful hardiness in spite of failures and disappointments – failures and disappointments that pave the way for progress. Ideally transmuted, a realisation of finitude enables rather than stultifies.

Humanistic humility is clearly a product of post-Enlightenment subjectivity. While it emphasises universal limitations, it asserts with equal force the inherent dignity of each individual. In short, its impulse is affirmative and its project ameliorating. Given that its theorists are chiefly concerned with promoting egalitarian forms of government and compassionate law-making, it is unsurprising that humiliation is not a complementary aspect of humanistic humility. The reduction of humility 'to a medieval state of self-mortification' is rejected, and humiliation is unequivocally seen as the intentional stripping away of human dignity.[47] So although sacrifice is an integral concept to humanistic humility, it is always underpinned by the ideals of human flourishing, self-realisation and sometimes even perfectibility.

These words bring to mind the debates around humanism that preoccupied Eliot throughout the 1920s and into the 1930s. Whether under the classicism/romanticism rubric, or in his cultural–critical jousting with Irving Babbitt, Norman Foerster, H. G. Wells and others, Eliot was wary of a too-credulous faith in the human species.[48] This may be recognised even without considering his post-conversion stance: the early prose variously disparages the humanitarian 'belief in the fundamental goodness of human nature' (*CP1*, 471), while the poetry of this period sees Emersonian enlightenment and self-reliance eclipsed in Sweeney's shadow (*P1*, 37).[49] The humanism Eliot opposed is not the kind he admired in figures like Lancelot Andrewes, or his contemporary, Paul Elmer More.[50] Rather, it is a humanism which sets itself up as an alternative to religion and positions civilisation as the highest good, as we will see in Chapter 3. Underpinning Eliot's well-documented denigration of liberalism and progress is his profound belief in original sin, a belief that was strengthened and sustained by his reading of Dante, Pascal, Stendhal, Dostoevski, Baudelaire and many other writers who were preoccupied with the problem of evil. One such other was T. E. Hulme, whom Eliot praised in the essay 'Second Thoughts on Humanism' for acknowledging that 'there is an *absolute* to which Man can *never* attain. For the modern humanist, as for the romantic, "the problem of evil disappears, the conception of sin disappears"' (*CP3*, 621). This distils Eliot's position on the subject: humanism errs in disavowing the supernatural, in harbouring hopes of perfection, in making man the measure of all things.

Beckett's misgiving about just such a measure is neatly captured in Lucky's scatological stuttering, 'the Acacacademy of Anthropopopometry' (*CDW*, 43), while his distaste for humanist striving is intimated by the Unnamable's unequivocal dissociation from Prometheus: 'between me and that miscreant who mocked the gods, invented fire, denatured clay and domesticated the horse, in a word obliged humanity, I trust there is nothing in common' (*TN*, 297). A more direct and nominally apt gauge, however, is the short essay, 'Humanistic Quietism', published in 1934.[51] Ostensibly a review of his close friend Thomas MacGreevy's *Poems*, the piece really constitutes a lapidary *ars humilis*, a theory on the art of humility. Here Beckett draws the line between pharisaic and publican poems, and also tips his hat to Eliot, however circumspectly: 'To the mind that has raised itself to the grace of humility "founded ... not on misanthropy but on hope," prayer is no more (no less) than an act of recognition' (*Dis*, 68).[52] But it is the essay's concluding words that show the countervailing quality of Beckett's own humanism:

> To know so well what one values is, what one's value is, as not to neglect those occasions (they are few) on which it may be doubled, is not a common faculty; to retain in the acknowledgement of such enrichment the light, calm and finality that composed it is an extremely rare one. I do not know if the first of these can be acquired; I know that the second cannot. (*Dis*, 69)

The confusing syntax stands in apposition to confused self-appreciation: just as the reader struggles to parse subjects and predicates, so Beckett seems unable to take fair measure of himself. The tone, too, is ambivalent. Something critical or even parodic is suggested by 'doubled', a word that belongs to the objective world of accounting and is therefore out of place in a passage otherwise marked by apophatic expression and quiet resignation.[53] In the background, the directive force of Geulincx's axiom of morals is discernible, particularly if the piece is held up to Beckett's loose translation in *Murphy*: 'to want nothing where [one is] worth nothing' (*Mur*, 107). Reabsorbed and reformulated, the imperative is not meant to assert an abject nihilism but rather a form of negative capability that allows one to inhabit a position of lowliness without an irritable reaching after 'light, calm and finality'. Gesturing towards something almost diametrically opposite to humanistic humility, 'humanistic quietism' implies a radical imperfection which can neither be overcome nor ever fully known.

It is within the third framework – religious humility, and specifically Christian humility – that such radical imperfection is admitted. As a totality, Christian humility is marked by the inversion of a worldly calculus: 'And whosoever shall exalt himself shall be abased; and he that shall humble himself shall be exalted' (Matt. 23: 12). The Gospel verse not only promotes a countercultural attitude but also a countercultural imperative. To modern readers, the King James's use of the verb 'humble' here obscures its synonymity with 'humiliate' – a dissociation that sets in after the Enlightenment, as the *OED* reflects. There is an aptness about the fact that many accounts of humility start with the word's etymology. In thinking through its roots, we necessarily consider the soil of its making. The effect is vertiginous: we have to dig deep in order to make the connection between our contemporary understanding of humility and earlier notions that tie it to abasement. An example of usage from Robert Burton's *Anatomy of Melancholy* (1621) (copiously copied in Beckett's *Dream* notebook) implies the reflexive meaning of the verb 'humiliate' ('to humble or abase oneself'): 'How much we ought to ... examine & humiliate our selves, & seek to God, & call to him for mercy.'[54] This captures three aspects of Christian humility: dependency on God, inspection of oneself, and active humiliation or self-lowering. It is during the eighteenth century that 'humiliation' begins to signal an interpersonal rather than intrapersonal act: humiliation is degradation visited by one person on another. By the nineteenth century, a clear definitional gulf had arisen between 'humility' and 'humiliation', with the *OED* supplying the following: 'I think "humiliation" is a very different condition of mind from humility. "Humiliation" no man can desire; it is shame and torture.'

The undesirability of humiliation is at the core of Christian humility: not doing as one likes but as commanded. It is for this reason that the virtue centres on the notion of kenosis: the Godhead's humble submission to a humiliating incarnation. The scriptural basis for kenosis is Philippians 2: 5–7: 'Christ Jesus . . . Who, being in the form of God, thought it not robbery to be equal with God: But made himself of no reputation, and took upon him the form of a servant, and was made in the likeness of men.' In addition to supplying the inimitable example of humility, Christ's kenosis endows the concept of humiliation with twofold significance. It implies a degradation of being (the Word become flesh) but also material suffering: low birth, poverty, death on a cross. For Kierkegaard, the recognition of the first point – kenosis as radical ontological displacement – dwarfs any consideration for the personal humiliations Christ would endure on earth. However, some theologians regard the kenotic mode to be equally determined by Christ's bodily and material humiliations.[55] So while the incarnation is a unique event (what Eliot calls 'supermiraculous' [CP4, 351, n. 24] and thus unrepeatable), Christ's sufferings as a human being supply the template for holy living and holy dying. It is in suffering – not triumph – that Estragon identifies with Christ ('All my life I've compared myself to him' [CDW, 51]); it is through bodily affliction that the narrator of Watt sees a likeness between the title character and Bosch's depiction of 'Christ Mocked' (W, 139).[56]

Like the realistic and democratic accounts, religious humility implies self-knowledge – only here it is distinguished by intense scrutiny, both of one's individual weakness and also of the deficiencies inherent to all humanity. As such, it qualifies the Delphic imperative to know oneself as a unique soul and as a member of the species. Taken together, these two aspects of self-knowledge form part of what is variously called cognitive, imperfect or rational humility.[57] Superficially, imperfect humility appears to amount to a combination of the realistic and democratic accounts of introspection. Inspection of oneself shares with Aristotelian theories an evaluative perspective, though here comparisons are exclusively negative.[58] Hence the seventh step of St Benedict's ladder of humility urges the sinner to not only 'denounce himself as inferior to all and more worthless, but also believe it in his inner consciousness, humbling himself and saying with the prophet: "But I am a worm and not a man, a shame of men and an outcast of the people".'[59] Similarly, while admitting that all humanity is 'weak and frail', Thomas à Kempis urges his reader to 'hold . . . no man more frail than thyself'.[60] Or, in the ever-unsatisfied comparatives of Beckett's

Worstward Ho (*Com etc.*, 95): 'Say that best worse. With leastening words say least best worse. For want of worser worst. Unlessenable least best worse.'

The second part of self-knowledge is a general awareness of human fallibility. In this regard it appears to correspond with humanistic humility. But where the latter instrumentalises human weakness by turning it into a means for upward mobility, religious humility treats it as the grounds for further abasement. Jeremy Taylor, whose *Holy Living and Dying* both Eliot and Beckett read closely, claims that humanity's manifold feebleness should inspire a negative self-regard:

> 1. The spirit of a man is light and troublesome. 2. His body is brutish and sickly. 3. He is constant in his folly and error, and inconstant in his manners and good purposes. 4. His labours are vain, intricate, and endless. 5. His fortune is changeable, but seldom pleasing, never perfect. 6. His wisdom comes not till he be ready to die, that is, till he is past using it. 7. His death is certain, always ready at the door, but never far off.[61]

Imperfect humility, however, has a 'perfect' or 'affective' counterpart, which emphasises the affirmative reinforcement of divine love. As Jane Foulcher explains, '[i]t is in the "inpouring of love" that allows the movement from a cold, rational understanding of the humiliating truth about oneself to a warm, affective, and ultimately liberating reality where one is no longer afraid to be known'.[62] The author of the *Cloud of Unknowing* typifies perfect humility as permanent since its source is everlasting. It also induces a self-forgetfulness that is attendant on humility (Mary of Bethany is exemplary because her imperfect humility is supplemented and even overwhelmed by perfect humility).[63] In getting to grips with her own inferiority, the sinner humbles herself; by contemplating the greatness of God, the believer forgets herself. Humility then transforms from thinking less *of* oneself to thinking less *about* oneself.

From self-knowledge there is a clear trajectory to self-lowering – an aspect alien to both the realistic and democratic theories. 'Once we have understood that we are nothing,' says Simone Weil, 'the object of all our efforts is to become nothing.'[64] In this translation from the epistemic into the ethical – from knowledge to sacrifice – humiliation shifts from being a baseline condition to a measure by which that baseline condition is rendered yet more visible. In extreme cases this means self-mortification: hair-shirts, self-flagellation, fasting, prostration and other shows of penance. But most writings on humility urge detachment. Geulincx, for instance, advocates 'disregard for the self', which requires the acceptance of affliction rather than the active pursuit of self-harm.[65] Again, Christ's life stands as paragon: turning the other cheek, living in poverty, enduring extremes of physical and mental affliction – all are instances of humbly accepting humiliation. And, in appreciating the revelation and realisation of humility that comes with such afflictions, humiliation is endowed with positive potential.[66] Weil again: '[i]t is impossible to forgive whoever has done us harm if that harm has lowered us. We have to think that is has not lowered us, but has revealed our true level.'[67]

Pseudo-Couplings

It is against the background of these positions and performances that I read humility and humiliation in Eliot and Beckett. The rest of the book follows a loosely chronological trajectory with the chapters paired according to three categories: the affective, the ethical and the aesthetic. The first two chapters locate us at the start of the writers' careers where humility is not only in question but sometimes actively resisted. Chapter 1 posits 1917 as a watershed year in Eliot's writing. I argue that with his only short story, *Eeldrop and Appleplex*, Eliot edges away from social embarrassment towards theological shame – that is, a sense of sin. Undoubtedly the least 'canonical' of Eliot's creative works, the story embodies diffusive feelings out of which humility emerges in the lower case. That is to say that in its blurring of grave religious commentary and self-directed mockery, the story refuses to take itself too seriously. Situating *Eeldrop and Appleplex* in relation to Eliot's early poetry, I first consider moments of embarrassment and disgust, and how these affective experiences impede an appreciation of a given situation's moral reality. Contrasted with this is Eliot's valuation of private truth and fixed moral standards, both in *Eeldrop and Appleplex* and in Eliot's criticism. The short story is shown to anticipate Eliot's critique of '*bovarysme*': the effort to dramatise oneself against one's environment so as to not lose face or sink into shame – an act that resists humility.

Chapter 2 explores the relation between embarrassment and pride in Beckett's early works. Juxtaposing personal letters and selected stories from the 1934 collection, *More Pricks than Kicks*, embarrassment emerges as a marker of the superiority Beckett himself regarded as a symptom of his anxiety neurosis. After discussing certain pre-emptive strategies against embarrassment, I proceed to close readings of stories in which we see embarrassment being counteracted through Belacqua's identification with Christ – a manoeuvre that does not confer humility but rather reinforces the character's sense of proud otherness. Beckett's early and incidental embarrassment is then briefly contrasted with the later work's representation of an existential embarrassment. The latter is conceived as an aspect of humility in which the embarrassed human condition is accepted without recourse to self-protective reflexes.

The middle chapters approach humility and humiliation through an ethical lens. Chapter 3 focuses on specific theological reiterations that define Eliot's understanding of Christian humility between 1927 and 1935. It grapples with humility as a component of Christian sacrifice and reflects on the relation between belief and action. The sermon of *Murder in the Cathedral* serves as a structuring device to discuss these statements, both because many of these theological statements are vicariously rehearsed in Thomas Becket's Christmas sermon and also because no other work by Eliot so pointedly dramatises the proximity between humility and spiritual pride. The chapter closely discusses the influence of the seventeenth-century divine, Lancelot Andrewes, and the nineteenth-century philosopher, F. H. Bradley – two authors who played a determining role in Eliot's conception of humility and his scepticism about human good will. It also expounds the significance of a hitherto unexamined biblical source for the sermon's verses of scripture that further threads the continuity between grace, humility and good will. In circling around recurring phrases and influences, I trace a conceptual genealogy behind the play's sermon and offer a revaluation of *Murder in the Cathedral* as the creative culmination of Eliot's ongoing engagement with secular humanism and, by extension, humanistic humility.

Chapter 4 worries the ethics of approaching others' humiliation. Here, humiliation manifests as an individuating property in Beckett's writing: the thing that 'mobilises' his creatures and also confers identity. In the first instance, this invites meta-critical reflection on the dangers of overly familiar narratives and concepts in Beckett studies. With close reference to *Molloy*, humiliation is subsequently explored as an ontologically determining phenomenon that should preclude the conflation and consolidation of private suffering. A final section draws more broadly on Beckett's mistrust of charity and posits humility as an important ethical criterion when dealing with the suffering of others.

The last two chapters are concerned with aesthetic humility. Where the earlier discussions address different ways in which humility might be represented, I am here specifically interested in the poetics of humility: how does a literary text humble itself? By engaging works produced at the height of the writers' respective powers and fame, these chapters confront the fact that a residuum of power is retained in the act of self-lowering. Any performance speaks to a measure of agency even where that agency drives towards its own diminishing. And in this regard, humility implies a paradoxical performance of subjectivity. Chapter 5 therefore tests Eliot's claim that 'humility is endless' (*P1*, 188) against the parodic and ironic procedures of *East Coker*. It explores the ways in which the poetry can be said to question its own assumptions and undermine its own importance. Humility is thus closely allied with the poet's self-ironising confrontation with his own work. In particular, Eliot's allusive relationship with Yeats configures as part of a master–apprentice dialectic that at once critiques Eliot's early works and unsettles the late work as a basis for such critique. Chapter 6 proceeds along similar lines, asking how a 'syntax of penury' is operational in *How It Is*. Broadly, this question pertains to Beckett's engagement with his own writing and delineates a scepticism in *How It Is* about old foundations and new turnings. The chapter considers three aspects of the novel: its impoverished style, its self-critical appropriation of earlier works in the Beckett canon and what we are to make of the text's endless cruelties. I argue that the novel's textual penury facilitates humility in its resistance to a totalising poetics of impotence.

Lest this overview and its categorical correspondences suggest more than a complementary association between the authors, I conclude by offering a final caveat about the separation between Eliot and Beckett in this book. In his biography of Beckett, Anthony Cronin provides a suggestive if erroneous point of contact between the two authors: that *Dream of Fair to Middling Women*'s allusion to the English mystic, Julian of Norwich, arrived via *Little Gidding*.⁶⁸ Notwithstanding the fact that Beckett's novel was written in 1931 and Eliot's poem a decade later, this alternative textual archaeology telescopes something of the differences and affinities between the two authors. In *Little Gidding*, Eliot weaves the English mystic's 'Sin is Behovely' into the purgatorial yet affirmative vision of his poem (*P1*, 207). Much less reverentially, Beckett transplants the phrase into a profane context of sexual desire in *Dream* (9), while in his '*Dream* Notebook' he went a step further, editorialising Julian's stigmatic experience as 'Eschatological catamenia' (*DN*, 59) – that is, menstrual flow. What brings Eliot and Beckett together through this allusion is a fundamental belief in fallenness: sin and its wages are behovely, inescapable. What divides them is the way in which they assert their view of humanity's lowly position. For Eliot, it is mostly a question of one's relation to God; for Beckett, it is a matter of self-emptying. Though of a similar species, the way up and the way down are not the same.

Notes

1. *Monty Python's Life of Brian*, dir. Terry Jones (1979; UK: Paramount Home Entertainment, 2003), DVD, my italics.
2. I return to these objections in Chapter 3.
3. A recently released report on the 1969 Nobel Committee's deliberations shows that the strongest opposition to Beckett's nomination came from Anders Österling. He asserts that even when given the broadest possible interpretation, Nobel's will limits the criteria to works of literature that 'can be used to help and benefit humanity' – an 'element . . . missing in Beckett's work'. Anders Österling, 'Yttrande av Herr Österling', in 'Utlåtande av Svenska Akademiens Nobelkommitté, 1969', compiled by Anders Ryberg, 10–11, Swedish Academy Archive. https://www.svenskaakademien.se/sites/default/files/nobelkommittens_utlatande_1969.pdf. My thanks to both Madeleine Broberg from the Swedish Academy, who supplied me with this report, and to Ellinor Mattsson for her kind assistance with the translation.
4. Alfred Nobel, 'Testament', 27 November 1895. https://www.nobelprize.org/alfred-nobel/full-text-of-alfred-nobels-will-2/.
5. After his arrest on the apparent charge of offending public decency, Molloy (*TN*, 20) remarks: 'It is indeed a deplorable sight, a deplorable example, for the people, who so need to be encouraged, in their bitter toil, and to have before their eyes manifestations of strength only, of courage and of joy, without which they might collapse, at

the end of the day, and roll on the ground.' I return to Beckett's disruption of normative conceptions of the good and beautiful in Chapter 4.
6. George Steiner, *On Difficulty and Other Essays* (Oxford: Oxford University Press, 1978), 40.
7. Truncated into a motto, the phrase is taken from Beckett's *Worstward Ho*: 'Ever tried. Ever failed. No matter. Try again. Fail again. Fail better' (*Com etc.*, 81). Swiss tennis player Stan Wawrinka has the full quotation tattooed on his left forearm. For the picture of Harry Styles and his copy of *'The Waste Land' and Other Poems*, see https://twitter.com/styleslookbook/status/1199782010643976193.
8. Rachel Potter and David Trotter, 'Low Modernism: Introduction', *Critical Quarterly* 46.4 (2004): iii.
9. The authors continue: 'The idea that the obscene or low bits of modernism are disconnected from the world challenges one model of interpretation, which sees modernist texts as defined by their imposition of cultural hierarchies onto the low facts of modern life.' Potter and Trotter, 'Low Modernism', iii–iv.
10. The modern definition of humiliation is discussed below in the section on Christian humility under 'Performances of Humility'.
11. Charles Taylor, *A Secular Age* (Cambridge, MA: Belknap Press of Harvard University Press, 2007), 22.
12. To name a few studies representative of this turn: Anthony Cuda, *The Passions of Modernism: Eliot, Yeats, Woolf, and Mann* (Columbia: University of South Carolina Press, 2010); Arthur Rose, *Literary Cynics: Borges, Beckett, Coetzee* (London: Bloomsbury, 2017); Ben Hutchinson, *Lateness & Modern European Literature* (Oxford: Oxford University Press, 2016); Justus Nieland, *Feeling Modern: The Eccentricities of Public Life* (Urbana and Chicago: University of Illinois Press, 2008); Barry Sheils and Julie Walsh, *Shame and Modern Writing* (Routledge, 2018).
13. Paul Saint-Amour, 'Weak Theory, Weak Modernism', *Modernism/modernity* 25.3 (2018): 443.
14. In this regard, Marianne Moore's understanding of humility as defence is instructive: 'Humility . . . is armor, for it realizes that it is impossible to be original, in the sense of doing something that has never been thought of before.' Moore, 'Humility, Concentration, and Gusto', in *The Complete Prose of Marianne Moore*, ed. and intro. Patricia C. Willis (New York: Viking, 1986), 420–1.
15. Jeredith Merrin's fine study, *An Enabling Humility: Marianne Moore, Elizabeth Bishop, and the Uses of Tradition* (New Brunswick: Rutgers University Press, 1990), deserves mention, though it is not concerned with formulating humility as an aesthetic category.

16. Lionel Trilling, 'On the Teaching of Modern Literature', in *The New York Intellectuals Reader*, ed. Neil Jumonville, 223–42 (New York: Routledge, 2007), 241.
17. This can be gauged by considering three very different points of view. For Martin Luther, humility can never know itself as such without transforming into pride – a result predicated on eventual stasis and satisfaction, and thus not endless (*The Annotated Luther, Volume 4: Pastoral Writings*, ed. Mary Jane Haemig [Minneapolis, MN: Fortress Press, 2016], 334–5). For Gabriel Marcel, Eliot's contemporary, it can remain intact only so long as it is not regarded as a 'possession' (*Being and Having*, trans. Katharine Farrer [Westminster: Dacre Press, 1949], 159). And the author of the *Cloud of Unknowing* – from whose chapter on 'a stirring to meekness' Eliot directly quotes in *Little Gidding* (*P1*, 208) – asserts that human efforts at humility ('imperfect humility') can never find fulfilment without divine Love ('perfect humility') (see James Walsh, 'Introduction', *The Cloud of Unknowing* [New York: Paulist Press, 1981], 64–7).
18. 'It would be difficult to say whether Byron was a proud man, or a man who liked to pose as a proud man . . .' (*CP5*, 432).
19. See 'Arrow' 31 in *Twilight of the Idols*: 'A worm will twist back on itself when it is stepped on. In the language of morality: *humility*.' Friedrich Nietzsche, *The Anti-Christ, Ecce Homo, Twilight of the Idols*, ed. Aaron Ridley and Judith Norman; trans. Judith Norman (Cambridge: Cambridge University Press, 2005), 160.
20. Beckett (*L2*, 446) writes to Jérôme Lindon in 1954 about the republication of *Mercier and Camier*: 'I really could not bear it if that text were released in my imitation lifetime. It can always take its place, if you really want it, in a volume to be entitled *Posthumous Droppings*, together with all the false starts for example . . .' Christopher Ricks identifies the a similarly proud downplaying in Beckett's title, *Film*, and in Eliot's decision to label some of his works as 'Minor Poems'. See Ricks, *Decisions and Revisions in T. S. Eliot* (London: British Library and Faber and Faber, 2003), 14.
21. Aristotle, *Nicomachean Ethics*, trans. and ed. Roger Crisp (Cambridge: Cambridge University Press, 2004), 32, 68.
22. Aristotle, *Nicomachean Ethics*, 33.
23. Aristotle, *Nicomachean Ethics*, 72.
24. 'Humility restrains the appetite from aiming at great things against right reason while magnanimity urges the mind to great things in accord with right reason. Hence it is clear that magnanimity is not opposed to humility: indeed they concur in this, that each is according to Right reason.' Aquinas quoted in Howard J. Curzer, 'Aristotle's Much Maligned Megalopsychos', *Australasian Journal of Philosophy*

69.2 (1991): 148. For further discussion of irreconcilability of humility and ancient virtue, see also Alasdair MacIntyre, *After Virtue: A Study in Moral Theory*, Third Edition (Notre Dame: University of Notre Dame Press, 2007), 149. Equating ancient Cynicism and Christian humility, Michel Foucault points to an exception and draws parallels between Christian humility and Cynic humiliation. See *The Courage of the Truth (The Government of Self and Others II): Lectures at the Collège de France, 1983–1984*, ed. Frédéric Gros, trans. Graham Burchell (Basingstoke: Palgrave Macmillan, 2011), 262. Possibly one of the most striking compromises between humility and magnanimity occurs in a sermon by one of Augustine's most famous translators, E. B. Pusey, who equates the former with the foundations of a beautiful building ('sunk deep, unseen, unhonoured, in the earth') and the latter with the structure's 'high glorious canopy'. *'Blessed Are the Meek': A Sermon, Preached at the Opening of the Chapel of Keble College* (London: Rivingtons, 1876), 20–1.
25. Arch. B. D. Alexander, *A Short History of Philosophy* (Glasgow: James Maclehose and Sons, 1907), 74–5.
26. Arnold Geulincx, *Ethics: With Samuel Beckett's Notes*, trans. Martin Wilson; ed. Han van Ruler, Anthony Uhlmann and Martin Wilson (Leiden: Koninklijke Brill NV, 2006), 337, 311.
27. Beckett took down Geulincx's argument against the understanding that virtue results from a certain disposition. See Geulincx, *Ethics*, 318–19.
28. Geulincx, *Ethics*, 167.
29. At Oxford in 1914, Eliot read Aristotle under the tutelage of Harold Joachim, one of the day's most formidable scholars of ancient Greek philosophy. During this period 'Aristotle entered [Eliot's] bloodstream', Robert Crawford remarks. Crawford also notes that Eliot attended all of Joachim's lectures on the *Nicomachean Ethics*. Crawford, *Young Eliot: From St Louis to* The Waste Land (London: Jonathan Cape, 2015), 215. Eliot offered to send his notes on these lectures to his former Harvard professor, J. H. Woods (see *L1*, 74, 91, 98).
30. Cf. Tony Milligan's much more recent discussion of the 'moral-cognitive failure' in both over- and underestimation. 'Murdochian Humility', *Religious Studies* 43.2 (2007): 220. And for an outlier among theories of modesty, see Julia Driver's ignorance account: 'The Virtues of Ignorance', *The Journal of Philosophy* 86.7 (1989): 373–84. For Eliot's graduate paper on Sidgwick, see *CP1*, 147–64.
31. Henry Sidgwick, *The Methods of Ethics*, Seventh Edition (London: Macmillan and Co., 1907), 334–5.
32. Hastings Rashdall, *The Theory of Good and Evil: A Treatise on Moral Philosophy*, Volume 1 (Oxford: Clarendon Press, 1907), 204.

33. Rashdall would later oppose Christian humility with more force: 'There is something singularly grotesque in the notion of a man being humble because, though he could not see any essential beauty or excellence in it, he had received a supernatural communication of the fact that he ought to be humble.' Hastings Rashdall, *Conscience and Christ: Six Lectures on Christian Ethics* (New York: Charles Scribner's Sons, 1916), 249. Eliot's review of this book constitutes the most acerbic piece of writing he would do for the *International Journal of Ethics*; see *CP1*, 428–9.
34. See, for instance, G. Alex Sinha, 'Modernising the Virtue of Humility', *Australasian Journal of Philosophy* 90. 2 (2012): 265; Daniel Statman, 'Modesty, Pride and Realistic Self-Assessment', *The Philosophical Quarterly* 42.169 (1992): 429. See also Nancy E. Snow's 'selective glimpse' of modesty accounts: 'Theories of Humility: An Overview', in *The Routledge Handbook of the Philosophy of Humility*, ed. Mark Alfano, Michael P. Lynch and Alessandra Tanesini (Abingdon: Routledge, 2020), 9–25. And for the separation between humility and modesty in early modern contexts, see Jennifer Clement, *Reading Humility in Early Modern England* (New York: Routledge, 2015), 3: '[H]umility differs from modesty and meekness in that it is usually invoked as a virtue that helps the soul understand its relationship to God first of all, and only then to other people. In contrast, modesty and meekness tend to be primarily invoked towards other humans.'
35. Norvin Richards, *Humility* (Philadelphia: Temple University Press, 1992), 2.
36. Aaron Ben-Ze'ew, 'The Virtue of Modesty', *American Philosophical Quarterly* 30.3 (1993): 235. One of the subtlest critiques of the magnanimous man's sense of specialness occurs in William Empson's *Some Versions of Pastoral*. Towards the end of his introduction, Empson ventriloquises an artist who sets himself the task of venturing from his privileged enclave to the experience of the common man. 'I must imagine [the simple person's] way of feeling because the refined thing must be judged by the fundamental thing, because strength must be learnt in weakness . . .' When Empson again assumes his own voice, he remarks on the inescapable condescension of this attitude which serves to stratify rather than to level out. Empson, *Some Versions of Pastoral* (Harmondsworth: Penguin, 1966), 22–3.
37. Steven Connor, *Giving Way: Thoughts on Unappreciated Dispositions* (Stanford: Stanford University Press, 2019), 7.
38. Even if Beckett's characters are not possessed of sufficient agency to enact Aristotelean magnanimity, Beckett himself was. Having received from James Joyce the paltry payment of 250 francs and five

old ties for several hours of taxing proofreading, Beckett made no fuss: 'It is so much simpler to be hurt than to hurt' (*L1*, 574).
39. William Shakespeare, *The Complete Sonnets and Poems*, ed. Colin Burrow (Oxford: Oxford University Press, 2002), 569.
40. Beckett was not above dramatising the pusillanimous also. In *Waiting for Godot*, Vladimir's thoughts about helping the fallen Pozzo are shown up as cynical and exploitative: he offers aid '[i]n anticipation of some tangible return' (*CDW*, 74).
41. After Prometheus' theft, humans still require two essential qualities to govern civilly; Zeus eventually obliges: 'To all [give shame and justice] . . . and let all have a share. For cities would never come to be if only a few possessed these . . . And establish this law as coming from me: Death to him who cannot partake of shame and justice, for he is a pestilence to the city.' Plato, *Protagoras*, in *Complete Works*, ed. by John M. Cooper (Indianapolis: Hackett Publishing Company, 1997), 758.
42. Mark Button, '"A Monkish Kind of Virtue"? For and Against Humility', *Political Theory* 22 (2005): 841, my emphasis.
43. Two book-length studies that fall into this camp are Julie E. Cooper, *Secular Powers: Humility in Modern Political Thought* (Chicago: The University of Chicago Press, 2013); and Jeanine Grenberg, *Kant and the Ethics of Humility: A Story of Dependence, Corruption and Virtue* (Cambridge: Cambridge University Press, 2005).
44. Martha Nussbaum, *Hiding from Humanity: Disgust, Shame, and the Law* (Princeton: Princeton University Press, 2004), 336.
45. Nussbaum, *Hiding from Humanity*, 184.
46. Norman Foerster, *American Criticism: A Study of Literary Theory from Poe to the Present* (Boston: Houghton Mifflin Company, 1928), 241, author's emphasis. Eliot considered Foerster to be humanism's 'fugleman' (*CP4*, 227) and that his book *American Criticism* 'states the general humanistic position' (*L4*, 284).
47. Grenberg, *Kant and the Ethics*, 190. For a notable exception, see Paul Saurette, *The Kantian Imperative: Humiliation, Common Sense, Politics* (Toronto: University of Toronto Press Incorporated, 2005).
48. I discuss Eliot's ongoing engagement with humanism in Chapters 1 and 3.
49. Compare also Eliot's early attack on the 'fallacy of Progress' and the 'fallacy of the Relativity of Knowledge' in *CP1*, 94–5.
50. See *CP2*, 819; *CP1*, 406–8.
51. Turning also to nominally relevant scholarship, it is telling that none of the essays collected in *Samuel Beckett: A Humanistic Perspective*, ed. Morris Beja, S. E. Gontarski and Pierre Astier (Columbus: Ohio State University Press, 1983), offers an outright link between Beckett and humanism.

52. Beckett quotes from Thomas MacGreevy's *Thomas Stearns Eliot: A Study* (London: Chatto and Windus, 1931), 16. Recognising Eliot's religious sympathies though overlooking the hold his New England upbringing had on him, MacGreevy writes that 'even in [Eliot's] earlier poems there were traces of a capacity for self-criticism, for humility, that penitential Catholic virtue, founded not on misanthropy but on hope, that is so utterly alien to the puritanical mind'.
53. My view here differs from that of Andy Wimbush, who argues that Beckett 'wants the poet to be sufficiently aware of his or her own worth and priorities, while still being able to see where both these things might be enhanced ("doubled")'. 'Humility, Self-Awareness, and Religious Ambivalence: Another Look at Beckett's "Humanistic Quietism"', *Journal of Beckett Studies* 23.2 (2014): 215.
54. Though the final listing under this primary sense occurs in 1776, the word had already undergone a change that signals passive and enforced rather than active and self-inflicted suffering. In these examples after 1621, 'humiliate' is no longer unequivocally used as a reflexive verb. For a fuller discussion of usage, see William Ian Miller, *Humiliation: And Other Essays on Honor, Social Discomfort, and Violence* (New York: Cornell University Press, 1993), 175–6.
55. '"[K]enosis" becomes a metaphor for Christ's humiliation.' David R. Law, *Kierkegaard's Kenotic Christology* (Oxford: Oxford University Press, 2013), 60.
56. Mary Bryden astutely remarks that it is 'in a context of pain, violence, and victimisation that a distinction emerges in Beckett's work between the figure of God, and that of Christ. Rather than being blurred with the Father, in a triumphalist Godhead, Christ is overwhelmingly discerned in kenotic mode: emptied, made destitute, and available for suffering of the worst kind.' Mary Bryden, *Samuel Beckett and the Idea of God* (New York: St. Martin's Press, 1998), 140.
57. See Jane Foulcher, *Reclaiming Humility: Four Studies in the Monastic Tradition* (Collegeville, MN: Liturgical Press, 2015), 150–1.
58. As Button remarks, 'the humble do not simply acknowledge their limitations or resist overestimating their moral qualities but hold a positively negative view of the self and of the self's moral powers without God'. '"A Monkish Kind of Virtue"?', 844.
59. Benedict of Nursia, *The Rule of St Benedict* (London: SPCK, 1931), 27.
60. Thomas à Kempis, *The Imitation of Christ*, in *The Harvard Classics: The Confessions of St Augustine* and *The Imitation of Christ by Thomas A Kempis*, trans. William Benham (New York: P. F. Collier and Son, 1909), 207.
61. Jeremy Taylor, *Holy Living and Dying: With Prayers Containing the Whole Duty of a Christian, and the Parts of Devotion Fitted to All*

Occasions, and Furnished for All Necessities (London: G. Bell and Sons, 1913), 74.
62. Foulcher, *Reclaiming Humility*, 197.
63. Anonymous, *The Cloud of Unknowing*, ed. James Walsh (New York: Paulist Press, 1981), 154–5.
64. Simone Weil, *Gravity and Grace*, trans. Emma Crawford and Mario von der Ruhr (New York: Routledge, 2002), 34.
65. Geulincx, *Ethics*, 29.
66. Cf. Avishai Margalit, *The Decent Society*, trans. Naomi Goldblum (Cambridge, MA: Harvard University Press, 1996), 12: 'The lesson Christians are supposed to learn from Jesus' humiliating journey is to consider humiliating behavior as a trial rather than a sound reason for feeling humiliated.'
67. Weil, *Gravity and Grace*, 6.
68. Anthony Cronin, *Samuel Beckett: The Last Modernist* (London: Flamingo, 1997), 112.

I

Fat Fingers and Private Truths: Between Manners and Morals in *Eeldrop and Appleplex*

During a brief summer stay in Marburg in 1914, Eliot writes to Conrad Aiken with a typical blend of the bawdy and the self-conscious (*L1*, 44–7). He asks for a blue suit to be sent on from London so that he may appear suitably '*herrlich*' when lunching with his Lutheran hosts, records stuttering and sweating through conversations in German, and produces two cartoon sketches: one of a 'Herr Professor' in whose presence the sweats and stutters occur, and one of a bow-tied, cigar-smoking Bolo – antihero of Eliot's improper rhymes. The drawings supplement eight lines of ribald verse and faux-scholarly speculation about a supposed double entendre in the lines 'Will you take [hyena] tail / Or just a bit of p(enis)?' Such playful indecency then leads Eliot to a bashful thought:

> I find that I have only one (torn) pair of pajamas [*sic*], and my dictionary does not give the word for them. *Que faire?* The dictionary, however, gives the German equivalent for *gracilent* and *pudibund*. You might do something with that, but I lack the inspiration. (*L1*, 47)

Perhaps the reason Eliot felt unable to use these words, whether in letter or in spirit, is that he had already exhausted their significance. *Gracilent*, catching 'slim' and also 'graceful' in its meaning, is caught up in the mood of several early poems: variously we encounter slender arms and hands, fine porcelain, and gestures 'light and deft'.[1] *Pudibund*, with its connotations of modesty and even prudishness, belongs to a world of New England propriety and Unitarian principles. It is a word compatible with Eliot's blush at the state of his pyjamas and also with Prufrock's anxious withdrawals.

As Eliot approached the 'intensely serious' (*L1*, 441) poetry he was to write in the latter half of the decade, there was a marked downturn in prudent evasions, both in life and art. Within a year of the letter to Aiken, he had abandoned prospects of an academic career in order to pursue his literary ambitions in London. More momentous still was his sudden marriage to Vivien Haigh-Wood on 26 June 1915 – an act Eliot would later explain by claiming that he 'wanted to burn my boats and commit myself to staying in England'.[2] Anyone familiar with Eliot's biography knows that the union was marred almost from the beginning by financial worries, mental and physical lapses, and the hurt of betrayal. Out of these experiences issued a poetry that went beyond the pains of social awkwardness. Missteps were traded for sin, and Prufrock's circumspection was supplanted by the indelicate directness of Sweeney.[3] With the publication of *Ara Vus Prec* [sic] in 1920, Eliot flaunted chronology and placed the most recent work ahead of his first collection's careful and cautious 'observations'. The relegation betrayed his feelings about the earlier poems: they were '*réchauffée*' (*L1*, 209), the reheated remains of a worn-out poetic mode.[4] But read another way, the table of contents – running without interruption from 'Gerontion' to 'La Figlia Che Piange' – suggests a contiguity between Eliot's poetry of manners and his poetry of morals.

My aim in this chapter is to extrapolate two types of humility from this uneasy alignment. The first is a religious humility which, in rejecting social codes and embracing absolute laws, entails the experience of a singularising dread. The second is an aesthetic humility that recognises the impossibility of adequately representing that dread. What results is a kind of mimetic embarrassment: the work of art that would assert an incommunicable moral prostration must do so by inference and indirection. This may mean owning up to ineffability and pursuing a kind of negative poetics that defines the untranslatable experience against that which it is not.

Eliot has frequent recourse to these methods, particularly in his dramatic works. There, the apprehension of a spiritual reality is set against the backdrop of social anxieties and sympathies that are at once the foil to and opportunity for another reality's emergence. In tracing this mimetic embarrassment, however, I fix my attention on a text that prefigures the drama and also stands at the tipping point between Eliot's poetry of manners and morals: *Eeldrop and Appleplex* (1917). Demarcating a shift from faux pas to moral infraction, I take this much-neglected text as the hinge between Prufrock and Sweeney. Generically, it hovers between polemic and *autre*biography, between an overflow for various 'thoughts and feels' (*L2*, 215) and a dialogue looking ahead to the later drama. Critically, it has been relegated to Eliot's marginalia. This liminality is important. Neither 'Poetry nor Criticism' (*L2*, 215), nor a text that generates much scholarly interest, *Eeldrop and Appleplex* falls outside the classifiably 'Eliotic' and exhibits the tonal diffuseness that makes it, on Christopher Ricks's reading, 'honourably uneasy'.[5] It is honourably uneasy because it critiques ugly prejudices while involving itself in those ugly prejudices; honourably uneasy, since the characters preach what they do not practise. Through this liminality – this ambiguity – *Eeldrop and Appleplex* enacts humility in the lower case: taking moral questions seriously, it duly fails to take itself so.

In the first section of the chapter, my concern is with how care of social convention limits appreciation of another's conduct to the realm of nice behaviour. In spite of the title characters' claims to probe the uniqueness of each soul, their prejudices make them complicit in the very bourgeois mentality they reject. Embarrassment, disgust and disgrace thus emerge as affective impediments to the recognition of moral upheaval. After this I turn to two unnoted intertextual sources that help us constellate the bygone orthodoxy Eeldrop sees as the *sine qua non* of tragedy. Their rendering – deliberately partial and obscure – brings into view the abovementioned theological humility while also keeping it out of reach. In the last two sections I consider the story as harbinger of elements in Eliot's later writing: morally compromising unions between men and women, ethical postures that negate humility, literature's troubled accommodation of the unsayable.

Generalised Men: Embarrassment, Disgust and Disgrace

Eeldrop and Appleplex are Eliot's own pseudo-couple. And, like Beckett's, they show a certain Manichean complementarity. While Eeldrop has a predilection for theology, Appleplex is a materialist; where Eeldrop stands aloof making mental notes on people's tautological expressions and their ways of spitting, Appleplex mingles with the lower classes and records his discoveries in large ledgers. But if their interests and methods divert, they are united in their quest to 'apprehend the human soul in its concrete individuality' (*CP1*, 526). Retreating periodically to a rented flat in an 'evil neighbourhood ... of silence' (525), they conduct what might be described as moral investigations. From their view onto the local police station, they observe scenes of squalor and misery which are foreign to their suburban lives. Occasionally their encounters lead them to an opaque understanding of another reality. This is the case when they meet a 'fat Spaniard' and a man named Bistwick, both of whom seem to have been in unhappy marriages. Their plight – the 'ruin of a life' (*CP1*, 527) – is elided with that of the notorious Gopsum murderer, a man whose actions have put him beyond the pale of social categories and sympathies. In the story's second part, Eeldrop and Appleplex discuss a figure named Edith, subjecting her to the very pigeonholing they claim to avoid.

Eliot felt ambivalent about his 'dialogue'. Following its publication in the May and September issues of *The Little Review* of 1917, he was uncertain whether it warranted further trouble.[6] But as late as 1923 the story held sufficient interest for him to mention it to three different correspondents.[7] Whatever Eliot's attitude towards the story, some of its preoccupations resonate within his life and work at the time. Eeldrop, after all, resembles his maker in several respects. Like Eliot, who wrote his doctoral thesis on F. H. Bradley and keenly read the works of Julian of Norwich, St John of the Cross and other mystics, Eeldrop is 'a sceptic, with a taste for mysticism' (*CP1*, 525–6). He, too, is a bank clerk, and the suburb which he and Appleplex scrutinise resembles the Eliots' surroundings at 18 Crawford Mansions.[8] As for correspondences with other works, the story initiates a tragicomic tone that carries into the quatrain poems, and its oblique interest in eschatology seems a product of the theological reviewing Eliot was doing at the time. At the same time, as I have said, the story does not take itself very seriously, since the duo's self-importance undercuts the earnestness of their claims without completely voiding them. On the one hand, their quest seems silly, even pretentious; on the other, it bears the signature of grave moral inquiry.

An early example of this tension emerges when Eeldrop suggests two ways of understanding the Spaniard, Bistwick, and the murderer. The first involves classification according to social structures and codes, while the second entails glimpsing an individuating reality on which public interests can cast no light. It is the quest for the second type of insight that drives Eeldrop and Appleplex into wicked suburbs:

> Both were endeavoring to escape not the commonplace, respectable or even the domestic, but the too well pigeon-holed, too taken-for-granted, too highly systematized areas, and – in the language of those whom they sought to avoid – they wished 'to apprehend the human soul in its concrete individuality.' (*CP1*, 526)

This insight, however, does not lend itself to positive expression. What the characters learn about one man cannot be transferred to another, nor can it be 'recalled in words' (526). And so, in order to limn the contours of their observations, they must define this knowledge against the kind of experience and thinking they wish to avoid. In other words, Eeldrop and Appleplex attempt to pit the gravity of tragedy against decorum's transience and triviality. But impeded as they are by their snobbishness, these attempts are not wholly successful.

Eeldrop's vague appreciation of the first subject's 'unique soul' is preceded by a disgusted sketch of that subject's public self: a fat Spaniard with poor table manners and questionable fashion sense.[9] Between asking why the man constituted 'an object of interest' and the eventual, self-congratulatory declaration that he (Eeldrop) and Appleplex managed to 'detach [the Spaniard] from his classification', Eeldrop indulges in exactly such classification. It is apparent that Eeldrop feels the man's behaviour to be lacking in delicacy: 'he made unpleasant noises while eating'; 'his way of crumbling bread between fat fingers made me extremely nervous'; '[h]e was oppressively gross and vulgar' (*CP1*, 526). These particulars are sufficient for Eeldrop to cast the Spaniard as a 'type' and to distance himself tacitly from this type.

At play here is a psychologically complex attempt at othering. While Eeldrop's description of the Spaniard is marked by nervousness and disgust and thus constitutes a visceral response of self-protection, there occurs at the same time a process of abjection which involves Eeldrop in what repulses him. Martha Nussbaum explains that a key function of disgust is to reinforce boundaries and keep 'problematic substance[s] at arm's length'.[10] The practical value of disgust therefore lies in averting a specific kind of physical danger. At an ontological level, however, disgust creates distance between the subject and what it finds repulsive: it is a strategy to stave off decay and animal mortality. What necessitates this strategy in the first place is an undesired affinity between us and the object of our disgust. 'In an aversion to animals,' writes Walter Benjamin, 'the predominant feeling is fear of being recognized by them through contact. The horror that stirs deep in man is an obscure awareness that in him something lives so akin to the animal that it might be recognized.'[11] Building on Benjamin's insight, Giorgio Agamben sees disgust as a site of conflict where the subject becomes implicated in a warring movement: identification with and detachment from the loathsome object. 'The man who experiences disgust recognizes himself in an alterity that cannot be assumed – that is, he subjectifies himself in an absolute desubjectification.'[12]

These terms – subjectification and desubjectification – are otherwise dichotomised as 'self-possession' and 'self-loss', and though Agamben employs them in the grave context of his study on Auschwitz testimony, they nonetheless have application in much less serious situations and operate in ways far from 'absolute'. Many of Eliot's early poems are preoccupied with the fragile balance between poise and its opposite – 'My self-possession gutters' is a line emblematic of this tension (*P1*, 13). Eeldrop's reaction to the conduct of the Spaniard balances on the same knife-edge since he suffers discomfiture on account of his companion's unrefined eating habits. On the one hand, this unease stems from the porous boundaries that disgust establishes: subconsciously sensing a danger of proximity or even likeness, Eeldrop feels the need to record his repugnance for the man. On the other hand, Eeldrop's nervousness is conditioned by his awareness of being in public and, more to the point, being seen in the company of the Spaniard. In this light, Eeldrop's remarks are a declaration that, though the Spaniard might remain oblivious to his own vulgarity, Eeldrop himself recognises the indecorous crumbing of the bread as such. As Erving Goffman observed, embarrassment is not always felt by the person guilty of a social misstep, and this lack of social sensitivity often leads those in the presence of the offender to blush on his or her behalf.[13]

In 'Hysteria', a similar kind of embarrassment-by-association occurs. Eliot's only collected prose-poem centres on the awkwardness of a speaker who feels implicated in the boisterous laughter of his female companion. Her 'hysteria' becomes his own as he allows the microscopic to become cosmic: mere teeth evolve into stars, and the woman's throat becomes a menacing void.

> As she laughed I was aware of becoming involved in her laughter and being part of it, until her teeth were only accidental stars with a talent for squad-drill. I was drawn in by short gasps, inhaled at each momentary recovery, lost finally in the dark caverns of her throat, bruised by the ripple of unseen muscles. (*P1*, 26)

The sense of claustrophobia underscores the speaker's apprehension of a boundary collapse between himself and the woman. Yet, in embarrassment – as in disgust – the experience of identification coincides with the impulse to resist it. Ostensibly a loss of face is at stake; implicitly, an emasculating loss of control. The title word, with its etymological and historical gender-bias, threatens to qualify not only the convulsively laughing woman, but also the male speaker. His 'decision' to stop the 'shaking of her breasts' simultaneously asserts an effort to reclaim control and to maintain what is the most obvious difference between himself and the woman: their gender. This specious redirection of focus – away from the actual embarrassing act (laughter) to an unrelated aspect of the agent who is responsible for the embarrassing act – constitutes an *ad feminam* attack comparable to the *ad hominem* attack which Eeldrop subliminally levels at his companion. The fact that the man has poor table manners has nothing to do with his nationality, yet Eeldrop regards the detail as proof of his belonging to a 'type' to be encountered in 'any town of Provincial Spain' (*CP1*, 526). Disgust then signals Eeldrop's subconscious desire to dissociate himself from the Spaniard; embarrassment prompts his need to declare an awareness of impropriety. Stereotyping is a third step in separation. Just as the short story invites one to infer the subtly elided facts that Eeldrop is neither vulgar nor Spanish, the prose-poem reveals its speaker's unconscious attempt to establish a similarly illogical connection between hysterical behaviour and having breasts. In 'Hysteria' the speaker is driven not only to maintain self-possession but to achieve this through control of the other. To use Agamben's words, he subjectifies himself in desubjectification.

When the story shifts to its second case, Bistwick, the awkward position of his relatives also depends on their proximity to the source of improper conduct. Having impulsively married his mother's housemaid – 'one of the low' (*P1*, 63) – Bistwick has scandalised his family; they suffer what Nick Salvato calls the 'cringe of mutual embarrassment'.[14] Unlike Eeldrop's embarrassment (which is superficial and short-lived), the family's sense of taint rests on a deeper, more intimate connection – hence the word 'disgrace' (*CP1*, 527). Disgrace need not only be felt by a person responsible for disgraceful behaviour, but by anyone who shares a close connection. In *The 'Art' of Rhetoric*, Aristotle writes that

> [m]en also feel shame when they are connected with actions or things which entail disgrace, for which either they themselves, or their ancestors, or any others with whom they are closely connected are responsible. In a word, men feel shame for those whom they themselves respect; such are those mentioned and those who have any relation to them.[15]

Likewise, David Hume recognised intimate association with a disreputable person as sufficient grounds for the experience of disgrace. In his account of the indirect passions in *A Treatise of Human Nature*, he argues that we may experience pride or shame not only on the basis of our inherent qualities or defects, but also through our relation to other people or things: 'The passions . . . comprehend whatever objects are in the least allied or related to us. Our country, family, children, relations . . .; any of these may become a cause of pride or of humility [shame].'[16] What brings these two disparate perspectives together is a concern for public opinion. Aristotle reflects that we experience dishonour before those we esteem. Hume directly links his theory to the gaze of others: in the first instance, the object (or person) who gives rise to pain or pleasure and the subsequent shame or pride must be obvious to others; second, societal norms are significant in affecting our experience of the object as agreeable or disagreeable.[17] These two stipulations have bearing on Bistwick's situation. That the 'generous-minded and thoughtful outsider' (*CP1*, 526) grasps the infelicity of the situation indicates its obviousness; that the relatives are disgraced indicates the breach of a norm, at least within their circles.

Norms, as Gabriel Taylor explains, may be conditioned in three ways: first, by what a person might expect in relation to external circumstances (financial or social, for example); second, by the individual's capacities or defects (thus what they believe they can or cannot achieve); third, by one's awareness of the expectations of others.[18] The last norm in particular is teased out in those two poems that deal with the scandals of kin and close associates, 'Aunt Helen' and 'Cousin Nancy'. In 'Aunt Helen' the reader encounters similar tensions hinted at in Bistwick's story: there is the contrast between upper and lower classes, decorum and impropriety, poise and baseness. But what is missing from the poem is a note of indignity; in fact, the tone is arch and urbane. The first-person speaker witnesses the frolicking of a footman and maid with equanimity perhaps because, like the undertaker, he was accustomed to 'this sort of thing' (*P1*, 23). Yet a more likely explanation is that no norms have been disrupted. The death of Aunt Helen is respectfully observed by neighbours and the heavens, the upmarket house is kept in order and the dogs are dutifully looked after. Only a mild tremor occurs when the parrot dies: the 'But' at the beginning of line nine for a moment registers the possibility of an unscripted event. Such a trivial scare is sufficient in itself to suggest that this is not a world subject to turns, catastrophes or social contagion.

In 'Cousin Nancy' there is more of a threat to the status quo, and it is worth highlighting Eliot's anxious declaration that 'the lady in the verses is an entirely imaginary character and in no way a portrait of any of my female relations' (*L3*, 808). Violating the New England landscape and customs, the neoteric Nancy Ellicott stirs uncertainty in her aunts. Tellingly, though, this this is all they experience. Despite Nancy's disruptive modernity, the 'unalterable law' (*P1*, 24) of Arnoldian personal betterment and Emersonian self-reliance remains unchallenged, at least in the lives of the aunts. The tone is characteristically tongue-in-cheek, and one senses the friction between the jagged lines that depict the movements of Nancy and the stiff correctness of the last three lines which invoke the named guardians, Meredith and, by extension, the unchallengeable decrees of God. While this stability is undermined, it is also kept intact. The aunts are neither ruffled nor outraged but only uncertain – the luxury of those unimplicated in scandal.

Such is not the fortune of the prostitutes in 'Sweeney Erect', a poem that belongs to the same period of creative output as *Eeldrop and Appleplex* and also shares the story's opposition of morals to manners. Disturbed by the shrieks coming from Sweeney's room,

> The ladies of the corridor
> Find themselves involved, disgraced,
> Call witness to their principles
> And deprecate the lack of taste. (*P1*, 37)

'Taste' has the distinct flavour of Eliot's early poetry where the speaking voice is acutely aware of society and its rules. We are told that '*hysteria* might easily be misunderstood' (my emphasis), and that this could lead to the diminished estimation of Mrs Turner's house in the eyes of those who hide behind the line's passive construction. Putting aside the irony of a brothel worried about its reputation, the verbal nod to Eliot's earlier prose-poem and the recasting of 'involved' within a comparable context gesture at the prostitutes' reluctance to be tainted by association.

More mutedly, Bistwick drags his family name through the mud since he disrupts all three social norms. In view of his inferred standing, privilege and education (first norm), his relatives may have expected a marriage comparable to Wolstrip's, who 'consummat[es] the union of two of the best families in Philadelphia' (*CP1*, 527). This is hinted at in their 'regard for Bistwick's interests' – interests which turn out to be their own. To argue for the transgression of the second norm might seem less feasible. But when one considers that a parent may feel pride or shame in a child as product of the parent, the disgrace experienced by Bistwick's relatives is in some measure an expression of personal failure.[19]

In Bistwick's case, however, the third norm's breach carries the most weight. The relatives' 'collective feeling of family disgrace' (*CP1*, 526) confirms that public dishonour has been visited upon them. On the one hand, their disgrace is negative in character: it points to loss and failure. On the other hand, the disgrace inheres in the family's qualitatively positive association with its newest member – Bistwick's wife, the housemaid. The union is at once an expansion of the Bistwick tribe and a dilution of what they stand for. In his 1916 review of Émile Durkheim's *The Elementary Forms of the Religious Life*, Eliot wrote that totems, emblems or insignia (material tokens of communal belonging) are more than 'heraldic crests' (*CP1*, 421) signifying an association with local flora and fauna. Rather, the 'cockatoo men are cockatoos; they partake in a common nature from which other men are excluded' (421). The totem, which is eventually replaced by a name, has a dual function: first, it declares an identity with which certain positive traits are associated (which occasion pride in the family name); second, it preserves that identity through the exclusion of unwanted connections or the inclusion of desired ones. But as *East Coker* makes clear, legacies are not permanent: 'Houses live and die . . .' (*P1*, 185).

One significant difference between embarrassment and shame is duration. The fact that embarrassment cannot only be overcome but forgotten is what allows comedy to end in social integration and unity; shame's endurance and inexpugnability drive tragic heroes into a state of exile, whether actual or mental.[20] While the conditions which made an act embarrassing in the first place might change and so nullify the embarrassment, shame signals an irrevocable breach. And so, seen within the story's binary conflict between public conduct against private, moral conduct, the disgrace of the Bistwick family stands closer to embarrassment than shame. This is not to say that their experience of the situation is laughable or petty. The Eliot family's shock at the union of T. S. Eliot and Vivien Haigh-Wood was not unwarranted, nor was Eliot's own sense of familial pride negligible.[21] But the story implies that such responses, which include the shame-hypersensitivity of New England Puritanism, dwarf against the 'awful importance of the ruin of a life' (*CP1*, 527).

Dante, Péguy, and Private Truth

'In the Puritan morality that I remember,' writes Eliot in 1937,

> it was tacitly assumed that if one was thrifty, enterprising, intelligent, practical and *prudent in not violating social conventions*, one ought to have a happy and 'successful' life . . . It is now rather more common to assume that all *individual misery is the fault of 'society,'* and is remediable by alterations from without. (*CP5*, 459, my emphasis).

This personal confession occurs in the introduction to the first Harcourt Brace edition of Djuna Barnes's *Nightwood*, a work that curiously allows us to circle back to *Eeldrop and Appleplex*. I will explain this link in due course, but for now it is worth remarking on the continuity Eliot sees here between the decency promoted in his Unitarian upbringing (the Puritan morality he remembers) and a tendency to reduce individual suffering to a symptom of systemic failure. Whether affiliated with decorum or humanitarianism, good behaviour or good will, these 'philosophies' explain away misery as something epiphenomenal. They fail to show it as a horrific thing in itself, irreducible and incommunicable.

Such a determinist gloss is the very thing Eeldrop and Appleplex want to avoid. Eeldrop declares that neither family nor magnanimous onlookers are in a position to appreciate Bistwick's plight. He does so on the basis of a theory that involves three convictions:

first, that private truth is untranslatable; second, that the significance of private truth suffers in the absence of a doctrinal belief in free will and absolute laws; and third, that tragedy cannot be understood in relation to public codes and classes.

> [T]he essential is unique. Perhaps that is why it is so neglected: because it is useless. What we learned about that Spaniard is incapable of being applied to any other Spaniard, or even recalled in words. With the decline of *orthodox theology and its admirable theory of the soul*, the unique importance of events has vanished. A man is only important as he is classed. Hence there is no tragedy, or no appreciation of tragedy, which is the same thing. (*CP1*, 526, my emphasis)

The passage is crucial for an appreciation of the text's separation of public and personal transgression, and for grasping the respectively ensuing states of embarrassment and shame. The terse, tripartite observation is at once diagnostic and remedial. While Eeldrop laments the lapse of conditions which would enable the apprehension of the 'human soul in its concrete individuality' (526), his and Appleplex's investigations constitute an effort to recover such conditions.

The first conviction outlined above – that private truth cannot be transferred to other contexts – recalls certain remarks in Eliot's philosophical writings. The earliest iterations about 'private truth' occur in two graduate essays, 'Degrees of Reality' (1913) and 'The Validity of Artificial Distinctions' (1914), written at Harvard and Oxford respectively. The same idea returns in the conclusion of his PhD dissertation on Bradley, completed in 1916 – a year before the publication of *Eeldrop and Appleplex*:

> I remember a phrase of Eucken's, a phrase which had a certain *entrain* about it: *es gibt keine Privatwahrheiten* (there are no private truths). I do not recall the context, and am not concerned with the meaning which the phrase had there; but I should reverse the decision, and say: All significant truths are private truths. As they become public they cease to become truths; they become facts, or at best, part of the public character; or at worst; catchwords. (*CP1*, 377)

The phrasing is almost identical to that of the earlier essays and further corresponds in a general feeling of dissatisfaction. All three contexts suggest a deep scepticism about the categories and taxonomies by which philosophy attempts the ordering of knowledge and experience. In *Eeldrop and Appleplex*, this dissatisfaction is directed at social contingencies that might aid understanding of a situation's general significance, though only at the cost of its singular significance. As feelings of self-value (such as embarrassment) stand in the way of appreciating this significance, so do feelings of humanitarian sympathy – at least in Eeldrop's view. Antipathetic to those notions of humanistic humility I discussed in the Introduction, he is impatient with the reduction of sin to social ills. For him, moral actions can only be explained under the aspect of eternity:

> The important fact is that something is done which cannot be undone ... For the man's neighbors the important fact is what the man killed her with? And at precisely what time? And who found the body? For the 'enlightened public' the case is merely evidence for the Drink question, or Unemployment, or some other category of things to be reformed. But the mediaeval world, insisting on the eternity of punishment, expressed something nearer the truth. (*CP1*, 527)

The 'mediaeval' worldview mentioned above joins up with Eeldrop's reference to 'orthodox theology and its admirable theory of the soul'. The latter phrase, I want to argue, points to one of two overlooked sources that reinforce the story's preoccupation with absolute moral standards. Here, Eeldrop nods to Dante's formulation of the Aristotelian conception of the soul in Canto 16 of the *Purgatorio*, a passage that had special significance for Eliot. In the bilingual Dent edition of *The Divine Comedy* that he used during his undergraduate days, he underscored lines from the section – a means of emphasis applied very infrequently across the book.[22] Elsewhere in his writing, the section is alluded to six times, including his 1929 essay on Dante in which he supplies his own prose translation:

> From the hands of Him who loves her before she is, there issues like a little child that plays, with weeping and laughter, the simple soul, that knows nothing except that, come from the hands of a glad creator, she turns willingly to everything that delights her. First she tastes the flavour of a trifling good; then is beguiled, and pursues it, if neither guide nor check withhold her. Therefore laws were needed as a curb ... [The laws exist, but who applies them now?] (*CP3*, 719)[23]

The passage forms part of Marco Lombardo's discourse on free will, which is prompted by the Pilgrim's inquiry into the cause of evil. Rejecting the notion that vice and virtue are bound by external forces, Lombardo affirms that the individual soul is personally responsible for its own actions: 'light has been giv'n to you for good and evil, / with Free Will . . . Hence, if the present world go wrong, the cause / is in yourselves, and should in you be sought.'[24] Given these concerns, the oblique reference to this medieval theory of the soul represents a desirable countermeasure to the generalised and vacillating ways in which individuals are weighed up. Eeldrop's disgusted painting of modern life depicts the individual as his or her own source of satisfaction. The practical, radiating value of a life returns upon itself in an economy of public self-fulfilment. As Eeldrop remarks: 'this cataloguing [according to social function or position] is not only satisfactory to other people for practical purposes, it is sufficient to [people] themselves for their "life of the spirit"' (*CP1*, 527). But in a system founded upon absolute laws and personal accountability, the individual soul has recourse neither to social institutions (which supply relative standards of judgement) nor to social categories (which supply a relative identity). Put differently, Eeldrop's 'orthodox theology' may be understood as a doctrine that sees subjectivity uniquely determined in relation to values that are common to all humanity. His desire is for a humility in the face of absolute judgement.

The second source that insists on this kind of moral prostration returns us to Eliot's appreciation of *Nightwood*. I mentioned that between the Harcourt Brace introduction and *Eeldrop and Appleplex* is a shared opposition to social 'philosophies' as a means of explaining misery. A still more pertinent connection is established in the blurb which Eliot wrote anonymously for the novel's Faber edition of 1936:

> [T]he characters suffer rather than act: as with Dostoevski and George Chapman, one feels that the action is hardly more than the shadow-play of something really taking place on another plane of reality. It is concerned with *le misérable au centre de sa misère*, and has nothing to offer to readers whose temperament attaches them to either an easy or a frightened optimism. (*CP5*, 460, fn. 2)

Most immediately, the tension between acting and suffering brings to mind *Murder in the Cathedral*.[25] Eliot also rehearses the doubleness he often associated with Chapman and Dostoevsky.[26] But it is the French phrase, thrown off with casual familiarity, that leads us back to *Eeldrop and Appleplex* and, in particular, 'the centre of misery . . . engulfed in his cell' (*CP1*, 523). Not obvious in the least, the source for the French phrase and for Eliot's loose translation in 1917 is an obscure essay by the French poet and critic, Charles Péguy – a fact that, to my knowledge, has gone unnoticed.

Published in 1902 in the *Cahiers de la Quinzaine* (the journal which Péguy edited for fifteen years), 'De Jean Coste' mounts a defence of a now-forgotten novel, Antonin Lavergne's *Jean Coste: ou l'instituteur de village*. Dispassionately detailing its protagonist's descent from a state of material destitution to spiritual misery, *Jean Coste* is a sobering indictment of the poverty that pervades France at the turn of the century. Initially it failed to find a publisher on the grounds that its bleak portrait strained credulity ('*trop noir*' was the verdict).[27] Péguy then took it upon himself to publish the novel in a 1901 issue of the *Cahiers*, following it up with his essay the next year. While there is no evidence to suggest that Eliot read the Lavergne novel, he was well acquainted with Péguy's work, as he demonstrated in a *New Statesman* review whose composition coincided with the first etchings of *Eeldrop and Appleplex* in 1916.[28] In the same year, he also prescribed three of Péguy's books for his extension lectures, one of which (*Œuvres choisies, 1900–1910*) contained 'De Jean Coste'.

In the section that supplies Eliot with his partial lifting, the essay takes a theological turn and diverts from its more pointed socialist commentary. While 'De Jean Coste' foregrounds the dehumanising effects of poverty, it is adamant that penury does not equate to spiritual wretchedness. 'The poor man,' Péguy writes, 'is separated from the wretch by a gulf in quality, in nature.'[29] He goes on to suggest that failure to recognise this separation is akin to the conflation between modesty and humility – in other words, a confusion between contingent rules and fixed laws.[30] Pre-empting Eeldrop, Péguy attacks the 'extrinsic observer' who thinks that misery might be eradicated if the belief in hell and other morbid religious ideas were quelled.[31] We read that the wretch's experience cannot be explained by the 'sociologist', that his life is 'universal bondage' and 'living death'.[32] At this point, the essay reaches a crescendo of despair:

> *The wretch is in his misery, at the centre of his misery* . . . his domain is the playground of the prisoner . . . [W]hen a man like Jean Coste

is in ... the hell of misery, the thing that pushes him over the edge might be an extrinsically insignificant event ... [though for him] it is a capital event, an event of infinite consequence.[33]

In addition to these verbal echoes, 'De Jean Coste' resonates with other features of *Eeldrop and Appleplex*. There is overlap in the texts' critique of secular subtraction stories that jettison eschatology, and so too in their framing of apparently inconsequential misdemeanours as moral acts.[34] Each also offers a deeply sardonic take on humanistic humility, or what Eliot elsewhere calls the 'false humility of evolutionism' (*CP5*, 196–7). 'The wretches,' Péguy scoffs, 'can at least be consoled by the fact that through their particular temporary miseries, humanity is marching deliberately, assuredly, towards an era of definitive happiness.' And yet, despite these correspondences, the truncation and translation of the phrase that invokes 'De Jean Coste' seem to ensure a certain distance from the source text. While the essay's understanding of misery as an impenetrable and irrevocable hell is certainly apposite to Eeldrop's claims, it registers as something of a vanished presence.

Theorists of intertextuality stress the difference between allusion and source. An allusion is the deliberate invocation of a text that is meant to enrich interpretive possibilities; a source may be involved in the initial stages of imaginative creation but is not directly woven into the fabric of the final product.[35] Both the Péguy and the Dante fall somewhere between these two categories. They are part of *Eeldrop and Appleplex*, but only in a spectral capacity. Given that the Dante reference indexes the disappearance of the very context it recalls, the story seems to admit its own inability to conjure the moral correlative necessary for tragedy. As we have seen, the disappearance of 'orthodox theology' means that 'there is no tragedy, or no appreciation of tragedy, which is the same thing'. The Péguy fragment renders this loss even more sharply, since its invocation of an unchangeable state stands beyond even the recognition of Eeldrop and Appleplex. It is the narrator who remarks on the 'centre of misery engulfed in his cell' while the title characters go off cataloguing crimes and indiscretions in exactly the systematised way they reject. The obscurity and vagueness of the characters' insights are thus of a piece with the obscurity and vagueness of the sources.

What further complicates the intertextual status of the Péguy phrase is its synthesis with another intellectual context. While 'cell' is of course literal and refers to the jailing of the 'center of misery', it obliquely evokes the monadic philosophy of F. H. Bradley. *The Waste Land* introduces the same ambiguity around a site of confinement: 'We think of the key, each in his prison / Thinking of the key, each confirms his prison' (*P1*, 70). As Eliot's 'Notes' make clear (*P1*, 76–7), the lines simultaneously point to Count Ugolino's imprisonment in *Inferno* 33, as well as Bradley's discomfiting view of consciousness in *Appearance and Reality*. In the section to which Eliot refers us, Bradley writes that

> the whole world for each is peculiar and private to that soul . . . No experience can lie open to inspection from outside; no direct guarantee of identity is possible. Both our knowledge of sameness, and our way of communication, are indirect and inferential.[36]

The synthesis of Péguy and Bradley thus has a metonymic relation to the two types of humility in *Eeldrop and Appleplex*. On the one hand is a religious humility: the recognition of eternal values and states – aspects that are reinforced both through *Purgatory* 16, 'De Jean Coste', and a great deal of Eliot's reviewing of the time.[37] On the other hand, the text presents mimetic humility – or, more accurately, mimetic humiliation – through its inability to represent the 'unique importance of events'. We have here the intimation of tragedy in excess of its saying.

'In a different world from ours': Ugly Unions, Ethical Posturing and Untranslatable Tragedy

Eeldrop claims that tragedy cannot be understood in classes and categories or, to use Eliot's terms in *Knowledge and Experience*, according to 'facts' and 'catchwords'. But the feline ironies of the story make it difficult to know why exactly the Spaniard's confession is tragic and thus beyond the sociologically diagnosable. The point at which Eeldrop brings tragedy into his three-part equation is also the point at which the first case gives way to the second. The transition between the Spaniard's individuating truth ('I was married once myself') and the unhappy marriage of Bistwick seems to place them on a continuum. The text proffers a gambit. We are invited, despite any contextual clarity, to see the 'ruin' marriage has wreaked on these two lives. We are perhaps also tempted to speculate that Eeldrop is unhappily married given the dire terms in which he reflects on the two cases. And, because of the resemblance between creature and creator, we might think Eeldrop's bias a product of Eliot's own tortured marital life – a situation thrown into still sharper relief by the unveiling of the Emily Hale correspondence.[38] These speculations are drawn out by *Eeldrop and Appleplex*, by its 'honourably uneasy' Rorschach qualities. Indeed, one of its remarkable effects is eliciting from readers that which it explicitly opposes: an irritable reaching after socio-biographical facts and reasons to make sense of situations which transcend those very facts and reasons.[39] Against this impulse, I explore in this penultimate section the text's apophatic insistence, its refusal to codify experiences beyond the reach of words. In doing so, I consider its relation to some of Eliot's later writing on the subject of tragedy.

The proximity between the Spaniard and Bistwick intimates that tragedy may take hold even in banal situations such as unhappy marriages. The tragedy here adumbrated by Eeldrop belongs to the kind Eliot would later identify in Thomas Middleton's (and William Rowley's) *The Changeling*: not that of the 'naturally bad' but of the 'irresponsible and undeveloped nature, caught in the consequences of its own action'.

> In every age and in every civilization there are instances of the same thing: the unmoral nature, suddenly trapped in the inexorable toils of morality – of morality not made by man but by Nature – and forced to take the consequences of an act which it had planned light-heartedly. Beatrice is not a moral creature; she becomes moral only by becoming damned. Our conventions are not the same as those which Middleton assumed for his play. But the possibility of that frightful discovery of morality remains permanent. (*CP3*, 123–4)

The passage corresponds with *Eeldrop and Appleplex* both in its separation of temporary, man-made laws and enduring 'Natural' laws, and also in the belief that any act can have lasting moral consequences. Here, too, the weight of *Purgatory* 16 is felt. The 'undeveloped nature' of Beatrice correlates to the newly created soul which is 'simple' and 'unaware'. Dante depicts the naïve soul turning to pleasures and trivialities (what 'Animula' calls the 'changing lights and noise' [*P1*, 105]) without proper concern for the consequences; Beatrice, as characterised by Eliot, pursues her interests 'light-heartedly'. As her actions inaugurate a morality that 'remains permanent', so the actions of Eeldrop's subjects have indelible significance for the individuals involved: '[t]he important fact is that for the man the act is eternal' (527).

Most significant of all, *The Changeling* also pivots on life-destroying unions. Acting upon her hatred for Alonzo (her fiancé) and her desire for Alsemero, Beatrice sets in motion a series of tragic events. She enlists the help of the murderous De Flores (whom she also detests) in order to dispose of her betrothed and so remove the main impediment in her pursuit of Alsemero. But De Flores leverages the assassination for sex. The union between them is as much moral as physical. Beatrice's desperate attempts to avoid being discovered as a compromised woman are futile, which the pseudo-comic elements of disguise and trickery highlight. With the play's climax already occurring when the murder is committed in Act III, all subsequent machinations on Beatrice's part serve only to delay the inevitable. She can neither escape the consequences of her actions, nor can she find solace in her social standing. De Flores is unsparing in his assessment:

> Look but into your conscience, read me there,
> 'Tis a true book, you'll find me there your equal:
> Push, fly not to your birth, but settle you
> In what the act has made you, y'are no more now . . .[40]

Joined in sin and shame, De Flores and Beatrice belong to a different order of existence. Their perverse union is a mockery of the prelapsarian world envisioned by Alsemero at the play's opening, and it severs them from the community to which they belonged. De Flores is instantly alive to the change: 'She that in life and love refuses me, / In death and shame my partner shall be' (III, iv, 154–5). Though Beatrice takes longer to realise personal culpability, she gradually wakes to the fact of her damnation.[41]

To appreciate Eliot's fascinated horror at *The Changeling* is to recognise two things: the affinity he saw between it and other great tragedies, and the play's divergence from the stoic morality of Elizabethan drama. He claims it as a work of 'profound and permanent moral value' (*CP3*, 129), remarkably situating it above any other Elizabethan play except those of Shakespeare. It is admitted to the company of Aeschylus, Sophocles, Corneille, Racine and Shakespeare, whose 'greatest tragedies are occupied with great and permanent moral conflicts' (*CP3*, 125). Constellated within

Eliot's writings on Elizabethan dramatists, the comparison with Greek playwrights is significant. In 'Seneca in Elizabethan Translation', also of 1927, the Renaissance is typified as 'much more Latin than Greek' (*CP3*, 200). The Romans, Eliot sneers, were 'simpler creature[s]' (199) than the Greeks. Their primary duty was toward the state, and thus their 'virtues were public virtues'. The Greeks also paid due respect to the state, but their civil consciousness was supplemented by 'a strong traditional morality' founded on a direct relation with the gods in which the state did not have an intermediary role. Thus, in Greek tragedy the staged morality is an extension of morality as 'woven through and through the texture of their tragic idea' (200). In contrast, Roman plays such as those of Seneca are informed by a performative ethics: 'moral habits' are substituted by 'moral attitudes and poses', by public codes and conventions.

Another essay that centres on such posturing is 'Shakespeare and the Stoicism of Seneca' (1927). Commenting on Othello's final speech, Eliot famously reads the protagonist's self-dramatisation – his 'pose' as a pathetic figure maligned by circumstance – as the most 'terrible exposure of human weakness':

> What Othello seems to me to be doing in making this speech is *cheering himself up*. He is endeavouring to escape reality, he has ceased to think about Desdemona, and is thinking about himself. Humility is the most difficult of all virtues to achieve; nothing dies harder than the desire to think well of oneself. Othello succeeds in turning himself into a pathetic figure, by adopting an *aesthetic* rather than moral attitude, dramatizing himself against his environment. He takes in the spectator, but the human motive is primarily to take in himself. I do not believe that any writer has ever exposed this *bovarysme*, the human will to see things as they are not, more clearly than Shakespeare. (*CP3*, 248)[42]

Along with Othello's last words (which Eliot quotes), the passage brings us back to *Eeldrop and Appleplex*. First, Othello's efforts to 'dramatize himself against his environment' is an effort to transfer his actions into the public realm and position himself in relation to circumstances that will render him an object of sympathy; in Eliot's story, the 'enlightened public' (*CP1*, 527) sees the Gopsum murder as a regrettable consequence of the 'Drink Question, or Unemployment'.[43] Second, Othello reminds the audience of his service to the state; Eeldrop ruefully remarks that people are important only according to their function in society (government officials are his first example). Lastly, both texts disparage Nietzsche as a symbol of a perverse self-sufficiency. The essay casts Nietzschean morality as a 'late variant' (*CP3*, 255) of Roman stoicism and thus as the antithesis of Christian humility, while in the short story (*CP1*, 527–8) Nietzsche is provocatively labelled a 'mob-man' whose philosophy of individualism inspires the following of those with the least character.

Eliot was not alone in drawing connections between Nietzsche and stoicism, nor in seeing their conjunction as fundamentally incompatible with humility.[44] As James Matthew Wilson has pointed out, 'Shakespeare and the Stoicism of Seneca' shows the influence of the German philosopher Max Scheler, particularly his *Ressentiment*.[45] I want to suggest that Scheler's essay, 'Humility', provides an even more compelling parallel. There is an uncanny correspondence in his claim that '[h]umility is the most delicate, most hidden . . . of Christian virtues'.[46] Scheler also sees humility as utterly antithetical to the 'moral pride held by the Roman stoics', since such pride allows a subject to suffer no diminution of self-esteem in the face of moral failing.[47] To the detriment of 'self-knowledge and recognition', the stoic clings to a flattering image of himself despite evidence to the contrary.[48] As evidence of this self-dramatising process, Scheler invokes *Beyond Good and Evil*: '"This I have done," my memory tells me. "This I could not have done," my pride stubbornly insists. Finally memory gives in.'[49]

Nietzsche's aphorism recapitulates in different terms Othello's aesthetic pose when he casts his present shame in relief with his former achievements. It also stands opposed to what Michel Foucault regards as the *cri de coeur* of the penitential abasement that gives onto humility: *ego non sum, ego*.

> This formula is at the heart of *publication sui*. It represents a break with one's past identity. These ostentatious gestures have the function of showing the truth of the state of being of the sinner. Self-revelation is at the same time self-destruction.[50]

But the self-sufficient stoic is not vulnerable to the vicissitudes of fate or the demands of an external reality. This is Nietzsche's position in *Daybreak*: 'There is a *cheerfulness* peculiar to the Stoic: he experiences it whenever he feels hemmed in by the formalities he himself prescribed for his conduct; he then enjoys the sensation of himself as dominator.'⁵¹ Having recently spent a solitary Christmas Eve in the company of Nietzsche's complete works, Eliot might well have had this passage in mind when he suggested that 'Nietzsche is the most conspicuous modern instance of cheering oneself up' (*CP3*, 249).

Of course, Eliot's unfinished play, *Sweeney Agonistes*, also contains a reference to 'cheering up' and likewise involves the murder of a woman. But where Othello 'succeeds' in becoming a figure of pity through his self-dramatisation, the murderer–acquaintance of Sweeney is exiled in a world of silence beyond sympathy. Having '[done] a girl in' (*P1*, 124), the man is unable either to self-delude or self-indulge. Though Sweeney recounts buying him a drink 'to cheer him up', this temporary measure of comfort fails to release the man from his private truth. It has often been remarked that *Eeldrop and Appleplex* provides the rough material for this theme in *Sweeney Agonistes*, since the Gopsum murderer similarly finds himself on an alien and isolating plane of existence.⁵² Recasting Lady Macbeth's words, Eeldrop intimates that the man appears resigned to the indelibility of his actions:

> The important fact is that for the man the act is eternal, and that for the brief space he has to live, he is already dead. He is already in a different world from ours. He has crossed the frontier. The important fact is that something is done which cannot be undone – a possibility which none of us realize until we face it ourselves. (*CP1*, 527)

The two murderers of Eliot's creation tacitly represent an antithetical attitude to Othello's self-determination and hubris. If Othello's attempt at 'cheering himself up' signals the desire to think well of himself, if his posture aligns with Nietzschean stoicism and pride, then the murderers in *Eeldrop and Appleplex* and *Sweeney Agonistes* are resigned to an inescapable reality: they see things as they are.

Such unflinching acceptance of culpability is the essence of Christian humility or, in a term more apposite to tragedy, shame. This is not to say that Othello is without shame; in fact, it is shame that drives him to present mitigations for his character – that is, *bovarysme*. The experience of shame and the simultaneous need to quell it is also what leads a figure like Oedipus to self-mutilation. In the *Convivio*, Dante remarks that shame is an emotion which afflicts the soul but reflects in the eyes. This is why

Oedipus blinds himself, 'lest . . . inward shame should outwardly appear'.[53] But both Othello's and Oedipus's admissions of shame are still entangled in the desire to think well of themselves. Agamben illuminates this in *The End of the Poem* when juxtaposing the blind Oedipus and the shamed Pilgrim of *Purgatory* 30 and 31.[54] The latter undergoes a purgation of guilt in humbly baring (and bearing) his shame completely; the former is unable to embrace the burden of guilt or shame to the extent that he is *'personally innocent'*. The difference Agamben identifies between them is 'penitential humiliation' – a penitential humiliation that prepares the ground for humility.[55]

In Eliot's analysis of Othello's final speech, in *Sweeney Agonistes*, in *Eeldrop and Appleplex*, and even in the introduction to *Nightwood*, there is a tension that hinges on the choice between translating the burden of suffering into general terms or embracing a private truth, however awful. Understood in Kierkegaardian dichotomies, which provide a suggestive parallel, the choice is between the ethical and the religious stages of existence. In *Fear and Trembling*, Kierkegaard juxtaposes Agamemnon and Abraham as respective representatives of these stages.[56] Though both are required to commit horrifying acts of sacrifice, they are distinguished on the basis of speech.[57] Agamemnon suffers personal loss in sacrificing Iphigenia but can assuage it by rendering his actions in the language of public service. Abraham, however, is bound in silence. As a knight of faith, he must act and abide in solitude. While the ethical stage allows escape from the inner life via a legal system and other public institutions, the religious stage offers no repose.[58] Agamemnon, Jephthah and Lucius Junius Brutus – tragic heroes of the ethical – justify their deeds in terms of duty or some other explicable criterion. They, like Othello, 'succeed in turning [themselves] into . . . pathetic figure[s]'. Or, in the language of *Eeldrop and Appleplex*, they become 'generalized men'. Even Aeneas, a figure whose piety Eliot would celebrate as the prototype of Christian humility, attempts to evade personal guilt by invoking the decrees of fate.[59] But Abraham has no recourse to explanation and cannot expect sympathy. He typifies the Christian heroism Kierkegaard praises in *The Sickness unto Death* since he 'venture[s] wholly to become [himself] . . . alone before God'.[60] This solitude is what constitutes both the dread and humility of his situation. And because he refrains from returning to the security of the ethical, his truth remains private, personal and singular. As Lord Claverton remarks in *The Elder Statesman*:

> It's harder to confess the sin that no one believes in
> Than the crime that everyone can appreciate.
> For the crime is in relation to the law
> And the sin is in relation to the sinner . . . (*CPP*, 573)

Without overstating an affinity, the correspondence between Kierkegaard's ethical or universal and Eliot's 'general' may be narrowed to this: any translation of the private into the public obscures authentic subjectivity from the subject itself.[61] Subjectivity or 'unique being' is not defined against societal structures; rather, it trembles – always in tension – between a moment's surrender and the 'awful daring' (*P1*, 70) that attends it in the scheme of eternity. This moment in *The Waste Land* dramatises the conflict between the general and the private. The general can be expressed in obituaries or cemented in wills or pithily captured in epitaphs. But private truth – belonging to the province of the religious stage – is locked in silence and irretrievability: an 'age of prudence', of proper conduct, of self-dramatisation can never retract the consequences of a moral act. This much is asserted in *Eeldrop and Appleplex*. Individuating truths cannot be recalled in words, nor do they allow access to those who are in 'different worlds from ours'.

Eeldrop's Afterlife

Drumming up material for a new project in 1935, Ezra Pound asked 'Paaason Eliot' to revivify *Eeldrop and Appleplex*.[62] After due consideration, Eliot gave a friendly but firm 'no'.

> I have finally found those two bits of juvenilia . . . [and] read them with keen relish and appreciation *it is very pleasant to think that I could write so charmingly and wittily at the age* but they will only be republished podesta literally over my Dead body and that charming compound libel on Katherine Mansfield and Brigid Patmore is out of date podesta out of date the old age is out & time to begin a new these chops from a joker's workshop I mean chips need not be repeated and never shall be. (*L7*, 712, my emphasis)

Eliot's reason for refusal centres on the sketch of Edith in Part II, the figure in whom he had mischievously fused aspects of the named Bloomsbury acquaintances. And apart from being done to others' harm, such satire was *passé*. This 'juvenilia' was written not merely when the author was of a younger age. It was written *at* the age – that age which Pound himself said

> demanded an image
> Of its accelerated grimace,
> Something for the modern stage,
> Not, at any rate, an Attic grace.⁶³

But this moment now superseded, *Eeldrop and Appleplex* could only seem *réchauffée*. Eliot did not hope to turn again.

And yet, was the new time really so different from the old? In the letter's playful phrasing is a telling though probably unintended echo of Eliot's misgivings about John Donne – another 'Paaason' known to have renounced his former ways. Unable to take seriously either Donne's early 'scoffing attitude towards the fickleness of women' (*à la* Eeldrop?) or his later religious devotion, Eliot wrote in 1931:

> *It is pleasant in youth to think* that one is a gay dog, and *it is pleasant in age to think* that one was a gay dog; because as we grow old we all like to think that we have changed, developed and improved. (*CP*4, 373, my emphasis in italics, Eliot's underlined)

This elision is not meant to impute to Eliot the charge of stasis or even *bovarysme* he levelled at Donne. Rather, it is meant to suggest that his early preoccupation with the tension between public and private realities would remain central to his art.

This is most apparent in the drama, pre-empted in form and content by the 'dialogue' that is *Eeldrop and Appleplex*. I have already remarked on the early text's correspondence with *Sweeney Agonistes*, the unfinished play whose title character acknowledges a plane of existence beyond the reach of words. *Murder and the Cathedral* concludes with the Four Knights' direct appeal that we, the audience, should situate the assassination within its proper social context; having recourse to the language of duty, honour and the greater good, the Knights ask us 'reasonable people' (*CPP*, 277) to see them in their role as instruments of the state. After this point in Eliot's dramatic career, the impasse between knowledge of the absolute and a correlating expression would play out in the drawing room – a space congenial to the social, the domestic, and those faces prepared to meet other faces. The drawing room is also the backdrop against which he would bring into relief an unhomely spiritual isolation.

In *The Death of Tragedy*, George Steiner sees Eliot's experiments in doubleness as a failure. Though he admits that the overlay of classical tragedy and suburban politesse has its effect, the merger of these horizons reveals as incommensurable the sighting and the saying of dread.

> What, in fact, has Eliot done? Unable to bring the rational, drawing-room version of the myth to a sufficient pitch of terror, he has drawn the curtains of the modern window to show beyond it the ancient daughters of the night. He performs a sleight-of-hand, shifting from one convention to another, in the hope of creating by association the tragic shock which he could not elicit from his own play ... No amount of theatrical ingenuity will make the Furies look natural in the sharp, thin light of the modern world.[64]

What Pound had described in lament in 'Hugh Selwyn Mauberley', Steiner here states as matter of fact: neither Attic grace nor Attic horror translates to the twentieth-century stage. He pre-empts his later theory of modal difficulty to suggest that an honest empathy must sometimes admit past and present to be irreconcilable, admit that there are limits to the unmodern making of our modern mind.[65] This is not because the earlier intellectual context is beyond our grasp, but because the unity of feeling and belief behind ancient drama does not transfer to the dislocated experience of modernity.[66]

Steiner's assessment centres on *The Family Reunion*, the play that perhaps stands closest to *Eeldrop and Appleplex* in letter if not in spirit. Harry Monchensey is a composite of Bistwick and the Gopsum murderer. His unhappy marriage is not only the cause of familial disgrace but also the source of incommunicable tragedy. Having 'pushed' his wife into the Atlantic Ocean (or having imagined to do so), his experience is 'unspeakable, / Untranslatable', and he must therefore 'talk in general terms / Because the particular has no language' (*CPP*, 294). Moments before rehearsing this motif from 1917, Harry echoes Eeldrop:

> But how can I explain, how can I explain to [you]? ...
> All that I could hope to make you understand

> Is only events: not what has happened.
> And people to whom nothing has ever happened
> Cannot understand the *unimportance of events*. (*CPP*, 293, my emphasis)

Generous-minded family members will ask: did he push his wife? And precisely at what time? These, however, are mere details, not the thing itself. Onlookers cannot understand the 'unimportance of events', nor 'the unique importance of events'. If Eliot reshuffled the terminology ('happening to' replacing 'events'), the significance of a singularising moral experience remained the same: it cannot be put into the common tongue. But it is in spirit, as I suggested, that *Eeldrop and Appleplex* differs from the play. Unlike *The Family Reunion*, which seeks out continuity with its classical model, the story telescopes medieval theology only to heighten the remoteness of that world. Where the play insists on an inexpressible horror in poetic monologues and choric declamations, the short story makes do with fragments of conversation, means indirect and inferential. The biggest clash is in tenor: *The Family Reunion* is a serious play about serious issues; *Eeldrop and Appleplex* is an almost-serious story about serious issues.

In this regard, *The Cocktail Party* seems a truer heir to the lower-case humility of the 1917 text. Not only does it draw a clear separation between manners and morals – 'kinks' and 'sin' (*CPP*, 415) – but it allows this separation to emerge through a mode that is gently mocking at times, at times gravely serious. 'It will do you no harm to find yourself ridiculous' (363), the Unidentified Guest tells Edward early on. The advice is meant to urge the protagonist beyond his social anxieties, beyond his *bovarystic* desire 'to think well of [himself]' (302). That he fails to heed the advice is what makes his earnestness mildly absurd:

> I have learned some things about myself . . .
> And they are not things that could be put into words;
> They lie much deeper than you can see
> And are much more humiliating discoveries
> Than anything that you could find the words for.[67]

If this reasserts a key tenet of *Eeldrop and Appleplex*, one must not overlook the fact of its assertion. In the end, Celia's martyrdom is the thing that shows up the drawing room as unsuited to the horror it was made to accommodate. The force of this event lies in its absence, in its reliance on mere reporting. The moment of spiritual agony takes place off-stage and beyond the possibility of self-dramatisation and, indeed, dramatisation itself. The effect is twofold: to heighten the play's comedic quality by diminishing its tragedy, but also to admit that certain experiences are out of the writer's reach. These were chops learnt in the old joker's workshop.

Notes

1. See *P1*, 232, 244, 28. For 'gracilent', the *OED* gives 'slender, thin', while its adjectival form ('gracile') could mean 'gracefully slender'. 'Pudibund' may signal something that 'is the subject or cause of shame' or, less dramatically, 'modest, bashful, prudish'.
2. *L1*, xix. The letter was released upon the unsealing of the Hale correspondence; it can be accessed in full here: https://tseliot.com/foundation/statement-by-t-s-eliot-on-the-opening-of-the-emily-hale-letters-at-princeton/?fbclid=IwAR1qjObn4ZvMeJIgKcUhlWsxysw-oOAkaivpaJqd4lXKZ1_AOfC9HhHAwTI.
3. I discuss the moral seriousness of the quatrain poems elsewhere. See Rick de Villiers, 'Banishing the Backward Devils: Eliot's Quatrain Poems and "Gerontion"', in *The New Cambridge Companion to T. S. Eliot*, ed. Jason Harding (New York: Cambridge University Press, 2017), 55–70.
4. For her excellent discussion of Eliot's feelings towards his first collection, see Anne Stillman, '*Prufrock and Other Observations*', in Harding, *New Cambridge Companion*, 41–54. It is worth noting Stillman's reference to a 'quite sumptuous' edition of *Ara Vos Prec* in which '*Prufrock* is printed before *Poems* (1920)' (52). Donald Gallup, however, lists only the 1919 edition in which the more recent poetry is followed by the older; *T. S. Eliot: A Bibliography* (London: Faber and Faber, 1952), 4–5. Ricks and McCue confirm this: 'Unlike all later gatherings by TSE of his poems, both *Ara Vos Prec* and *US 1920* printed the newer poems, beginning with *Gerontion*, in a section before those from *Prufrock*' (*P1*, 463).
5. Christopher Ricks, *T. S. Eliot and Prejudice* (London: Faber and Faber, 1994), 115. This indeterminacy of tone also chimes with Sianne Ngai's discussion of tonal diffuseness in 'canonically minor' works. See *Ugly Feelings* (Cambridge, MA: Harvard University Press, 2005), 12.
6. For an idea of Eliot's vacillation, compare his letters to John Quinn in 1918 and 1919 (*L1*, 253, 373).
7. See *L2*, 215, 223; *CP1*, 532, n. 3. For the story's piracy in *Two Worlds Monthly* in 1926, see Robert Spoo, *Without Copyrights: Piracy, Publishing, and the Public Domain* (Oxford: Oxford University Press, 2013), 77.

8. For Eliot's description of their surroundings at 18 Crawford Mansions, see *L1*, 501.
9. James Longenbach identifies the model for the 'fat Spaniard' as a Spanish priest named Maria de Elizondo with whom Eliot and Pound dined, and who also makes an appearance in Pound's *Pisan Cantos*. See *Modernist Poetics of History: Pound, Eliot, and the Sense of the Past* (Princeton: Princeton University Press, 1987), 154.
10. Nussbaum, *Hiding from Humanity*, 88.
11. Walter Benjamin, *One-Way Street and Other Writings*, trans. Edmund Jephcott and Kingsley Shorter (London: NLB, 1979), 50.
12. Giorgio Agamben, *Remnants of Auschwitz: The Witness and the Archive*, trans. Daniel Heller-Roazen (New York: Zone Books, 1999), 106–7.
13. See Erving Goffman, *Interaction Ritual: Essays on Face-to-Face Behavior* (New York: Pantheon Books, 1967), 99–100.
14. Nick Salvato, *Obstruction* (Durham, NC: Duke University Press, 2016), 44.
15. Aristotle, *The 'Art' of Rhetoric*, trans. John Henry Freese (London: William Heinemann, 1926), 219.
16. David Hume, *A Treatise of Human Nature*, ed. L. A. Selby-Bigge (Oxford: Oxford University Press, 1978), 279, spelling modernised. Though this section in the *Treatise* deals explicitly with the terms 'pride' and 'humility', the latter is substitutable in modern usage for 'shame'.
17. Aristotle, *Rhetoric*, 215; Hume, *Treatise*, 291–3.
18. Gabriele Taylor, *Pride, Shame, and Guilt: Emotions of Self-Assessment* (Oxford: Clarendon Press, 1985), 40.
19. Taylor, *Pride*, 29.
20. On the transience of embarrassment, see Nussbaum, *Hiding from Humanity*, 204.
21. For a suggestion of the Eliot family's reaction to Eliot and Vivien's marriage, see Theodora Eliot Smith's letter to her mother in which she deprecates the 'clan attitude' of the family (*L3*, 250–1).
22. See Henry Ware Eliot's letter to his brother on 12 September, 1935 (*L7*, 759).
23. I supply the last line (from Dante Alighieri, *The Divine Comedy of Dante Alighieri: The Italian Text with a Translation in English Blank Verse and Commentary, Volume 2: Purgatorio*, trans. Courtney Langdon [Cambridge, MA: Harvard University Press, 1920], 16.97. Hereafter *Pur*), which is not included in Eliot's translation in 'Dante'. For Eliot's other references to *Pur* 16, see: *CP1*, 407, 539; *CP2*, 233, 617; 'Animula' in *P1*, 105. Particularly important for a fuller contextualisation of *Eeldrop and Appleplex* is Eliot's unsigned review of Paul Elmer More's *Aristocracy and Justice*.
24. Alighieri, *Purgatorio*, 16.75–83.

25. See *CPP*, 245: 'They know and do not know, that action is suffering / And suffering is action.'
26. For a discussion of Eliot's interest in the double plane of reality, particularly as manifest in Chapman and Dostoevsky, see Steven Matthews, *T. S. Eliot and Early Modern Literature* (Oxford: Oxford University Press, 2013), 130–8.
27. Charles Péguy, 'Préface de L'Éditeur', in Antonin Lavergne, *Jean Coste: ou l'instituteur de village* (Paris: Éditions des Cahiers, 1902), vi. In an *Egoist* issue of 1914, shortly after Péguy's death in the battle of Marne, Richard Aldington makes mention of *Jean Coste*'s troubled publishing history and Péguy's personal investment in the novel. See Aldington, 'Charles Péguy and His Work', in *The Egoist: An Individualist Review* 20.1 (Oct 1914): 386–7.
28. Eliot writes to Harriet Monroe on 28 September 1916, and mentions an 'attempt in prose' (*L1*, 169) which, presumably, he was thinking of sending to Monroe's *Poetry*. A month earlier, he informed Conrad Aiken of the 'long review on Péguy' (*L1*, 158) that would be published in October (see *CP1*, 483–5). For a discussion of the literary networks that led to Eliot's engagement with Péguy, see Jennifer Kilgore-Caradec, 'T. S. Eliot and Charles Péguy', in *T. S. Eliot, France, and the Mind of Europe*, ed. Jayme Stayer (Newcastle-upon-Tyne: Cambridge Scholars Publishing, 2015), 129–45.
29. Charles Péguy, 'De Jean Coste', in *Oeuvres Complètes de Charles Péguy, 1873–1914: Oeuvres de Prose*, intro. Maurice Barrès (Paris: Nouvelle Revue Française, 1920), 48. All translations are my own.
30. Péguy, 'De Jean Coste', 48–9.
31. Péguy, 'De Jean Coste', 55.
32. Péguy, 'De Jean Coste', 59, 60.
33. Péguy, 'De Jean Coste', 60–1, my emphasis.
34. I refer to Charles Taylor's 'subtraction stories' in my Introduction. Péguy ('De Jean Coste', 55) criticises those who argue that human suffering would be remedied 'if we start by ridding it of [eternal suffering]'.
35. See Eleanor Cook, *Against Coercion: Games Poets Play* (Stanford: Stanford University Press, 1998), 100; Christopher Ricks, *Allusion to the Poets* (Oxford: Oxford University Press, 2002), 3–4; Leonard Unger, *Eliot's Compound Ghost: Influence and Confluence* (University Park: Pennsylvania State University Press, 1981), 4–5.
36. F. H. Bradley, *Appearance and Reality* (London: Swan Sonnenschein and Co., 1899), 346–7. Engulfed in the cell of untranslatable experience, the Bradleyan subject experiences a monadic reality different to the one which Beckett's Murphy aspires to in his hero worship of Mr Endon. Murphy idealises the 'windowless . . . monad[s]' (*Mur*, 109) of the patients' padded cells.

37. While many of Eliot's philosophical and theological reviews between 1915 and 1917 have application in this regard, two might be singled out: that of More's *Aristocracy and Justice* (*CP1*, 406–8) and of Rashdall's *Conscience and Christ* (*CP1*, 428–9). The former, as mentioned, contains a reference to *Purgatory* 16 and shows Eliot in strong agreement with More's calls for restraint and his suspicion of humanitarian efforts. The latter shows Eliot's deep disdain for what he sees as Rashdall's reduction of eschatology and his embrace of a loosely Unitarian value system.
38. For one of the fullest accounts to date, see Paul Keegan, 'Emily of Fire & Violence', *London Review of Books* 42.20 (22 Oct 2020). https://www.lrb.co.uk/the-paper/v42/n20/paul-keegan/emily-of-fire-violence.
39. The small scattering of critical readings commonly foregrounds the biographical and pseudonymous nature of the story. Most readers equate Eeldrop with Eliot, Appleplex with Pound. James E. Miller's account represents, by far, the most sustained biographical reading; see Miller, *T.S. Eliot: The Making of an American Poet, 1888–1922* (University Park: The Pennsylvania State University Press, 2006), 283–90. Michael North varies the theme by suggesting Aiken as a contender for Appleplex. North, 'The Dialect in/of Modernism: Pound and Eliot's Racial Masquerade, *American Literary History* 4.1 (1992): 73.
40. Thomas Middleton and William Rowley, *The Changeling*, ed. N. W. Bawcutt (Manchester: Manchester University Press, 1977), III, iv, 127–30.
41. The key passage here is V, iii, 149–58. Eliot quotes from it twice in the Middleton essay, and its cadence and content imprint on 'Gerontion'.
42. 'Bovarysme' derives from the self-deceptions of Gustave Flaubert's eponymous heroine, *Madame Bovary*, though Eliot was also aware of Jules de Gaultier's philosophical development of the idea. Eliot's remarks on Othello, however, require no special explanation beyond the gloss he provides in the given quotation.
43. This is an example of the liberal 'New Morality' Paul Elmer More resists in *Aristocracy and Justice*: social sympathy that obscures moral consequence. See *Aristocracy and Justice: Shelburne Essays*, Ninth Series (Boston: Houghton Mifflin, 1915), 209–11.
44. See also: Irving Babbitt, *Democracy and Leadership* (Boston: Houghton Mifflin Company, 1962), 22: 'I am [bent] on separating [Stoical and Christian ethics] and insisting on their final incompatibility . . .' Also Martha Nussbaum, 'Pity and Mercy: Nietzsche's Stoicism', in *Nietzsche, Genealogy, Morality: Essays on Nietzsche's On the Genealogy of Morals*, ed. Richard Schacht (Berkeley: University of California Press, 1994), 139–67.

45. James Matthew Wilson, '"The Rock" against Shakespeare: Stoicism and Community in T. S. Eliot', *Religion and Literature* 43.3 (2011): 61.
46. Max Scheler, 'Humility', trans. Barbara Fiand, *Aletheia. An International Journal of Philosophy*, 2 (1981): 210.
47. Scheler, 'Humility', 210–11.
48. Scheler, 'Humility', 212.
49. Scheler, 'Humility', 213. Referring to the same passage in Nietzsche (via Ernest Jones), Beckett's philosophy notes gloss it as 'defensive amnesia'. Beckett, 'Psychology Notes', 10971/8/22, Trinity College Dublin. Hereafter, TCD MS 10971.
50. Michel Foucault, 'Technologies of the Self', in *Technologies of the Self: A Seminar with Michel Foucault*, ed. Luther H. Martin, Huck Gutman and Patrick H. Hutton (Amherst: University of Massachusetts Press, 1988), 44.
51. Friedrich Nietzsche, *Daybreak: Thoughts on the Prejudices of Morality*, ed. Maudemarie Clark and Brian Leiter, trans. R. J. Hollingdale (Cambridge: Cambridge University Press, 1997), 143, my emphasis.
52. See, for instance, Grover Smith, *T. S. Eliot's Poetry and Plays: A Study in Sources and Meaning* (Chicago: The University of Chicago Press, 1956), 117; and Matthews, *T. S. Eliot and Early Modern*, 117, n. 55.
53. Dante Alighieri, *Convivio* (London: J. M. Dent, 1903), 180–1.
54. Giorgio Agamben, *The End of the Poem: Studies in Poetics*, trans. Daniel Heller-Roazen (Stanford: Stanford University Press, 1999), 15–16.
55. Cf. Saurette, *Kantian Imperative*, 9–10. Saurette's analysis of humiliation in the works of Kant offers a fascinating point of comparison: '[I]n the crucial third chapter of the first book of Kant's *Critique of Practical Reason*, humiliation makes a rather surprising appearance . . . "The moral law unavoidably humiliates every human being when he compares with it the sensible propensity of his nature. If something represented *as a determining ground of our will* humiliates us in our self-consciousness, it awakens *respect* for itself insofar as it is positive and a determining ground."'
56. Søren Kierkegaard, *Fear and Trembling* and *The Book on Adler*, trans. Walter Lowrie (New York: Everyman's Library, 1994), 49–51, 68–9.
57. Cf. Jacques Derrida, *The Gift of Death*, trans. David Wills (Chicago: The University of Chicago Press, 1995), 59–61. Derrida writes that the 'first effect or first destination of language involves depriving me of, or delivering me from, my singularity'.
58. Cf. Emmanuel Levinas, *Proper Names*, trans. Michael B. Smith (Stanford: Stanford University Press, 1996), 67. Levinas writes that

the ethical stage is 'a stage at which the inner life is translated in terms of legal order, carried out in society, in loyalty to institutions and principles and in communication with mankind'.
59. See Eliot, *CP7*, 634: 'When [Aeneas] sees Dido he tries to excuse himself for his betrayal. *Sed me iussa deum* – but I was under orders from the gods . . .'
60. Søren Kierkegaard, *The Sickness unto Death: A Christian Psychological Exposition for Upbuilding and Awakening*, trans. and ed. Howard V. Hong and Edna H. Hong (Princeton: Princeton University Press, 1980), 5.
61. Though long after the writing of *The Waste Land*, it is likely that Eliot had acquaintance with Kierkegaard via Theodor Haecker's *Soren Kierkegaard und die Philosophie der Innherlichkeit* (1913). See *L5*, 159.
62. Ezra Pound and Stanley Nott, *One Must Not Go Altogether with the Tide: The Letters of Ezra Pound and Stanley Nott*, ed. Miranda B. Hickman (Montreal: McGill-Queen's University Press, 2011), 135.
63. Ezra Pound, 'Hugh Selwyn Mauberley', in *Collected Poems* (London: Faber and Faber, 1975), 98–9.
64. George Steiner, *The Death of Tragedy* (New York: Oxford University Press, 1980), 327–9.
65. For both my discussion of what I call the 'unmodern making of our modern mind' and Steiner's modal difficulties, see my Introduction.
66. In terms strikingly close to Eliot's in 'Seneca in Elizabethan Translation', Steiner explains that 'the mythology of Greek drama was the expression of a complete and traditional image of life'. The ancient poet had the benefit of sharing with his audience 'the same habits and beliefs', but when these no longer obtain 'the corresponding mythology goes dead or spurious'. *Death of Tragedy*, 329.
67. These words occur in an early draft of the play. Quoted in E. Martin Browne, *The Making of T. S. Eliot's Plays* (Cambridge: Cambridge University Press, 1969), 208. Also apposite in relation to *Eeldrop and Appleplex* is one of Edward's other famous speeches: 'What is hell? Hell is oneself, / Hell is alone, the other figures in it / Merely projections. There is nothing to escape from / And nothing to escape to. One is always alone . . . / It was only yesterday / That damnation took place. / And now I must live with it / Day by day, hour by hour, for ever and ever' (*CPP*, 397).

2

Pudenda of the Psyche: Embarrassment in *More Pricks than Kicks*

Belacqua was an embarrassment to his creator. It is well-known that Beckett's first novel, *Dream of Fair to Middling Women*, was universally rejected by publishers and had to be repackaged as a collection of short stories, *More Pricks than Kicks*. The initial title, 'Draff', hinted at his feelings about recycling Belacqua's curriculum vitae: it constituted waste, offal, the festering sore of a dream deferred. Then there was the added insult of having to write another story so as to improve the likelihood of sales, only for the eventual product to be turned down. Apart from questions of artistic pride, Beckett was sensitive to the way in which the unflattering depictions of friends and family in *More Pricks* would be received.[1] He was also attuned to the book's reception in respectable circles. Touching up his own résumé in 1937 for a prospective lectureship, he referred to the collection only as 'Short Stories' (*L1*, 524), thereby removing the sting of innuendo.

Beckett's feelings about *More Pricks* did not soften over time. In *Krapp's Last Tape*, Krapp reflects on that 'stupid bastard I took myself for thirty years ago' and recalls with bitter irony his early artistic output which resembles young Sam's: 'Seventeen copies sold, of which eleven at trade price to free circulating libraries beyond the seas. Getting known' (*CDW*, 222).[2] Letters from the late 1950s and early 1960s also bear out Beckett's distaste for the collection and his active resistance to its republication. Though he was nearly persuaded to breathe new life into these 'embarrassed respirations' (*L1*, 83), the task proved impossible: 'I have broken down half way through galleys of More Pricks than Kicks . . . It was a ghastly mistake on my part to imagine . . . that this old shit was revivable' (*L3*, 633).[3]

Belacqua was indeed an embarrassment. But the character and his misadventures were also a crucible for Beckett's engagement with embarrassment, both as the stuff of excruciating comedy and as a feeling of self-value rooted in narcissism, paranoia and pride. As such, *More Pricks* stands as a crucial text in coming to terms with Beckett's humility, albeit in negative shape. Belacqua's attempts at face-saving provide a key to understanding how the inappropriate becomes appropriate in the later writing, how embarrassment evolves from a forcefully resisted dislocation into an accepted state of humiliation. I argue that Beckett's propensity for embarrassment is integrally connected with the feelings of superiority he sought to overcome during the mid-1930s. Furthermore, as his preoccupation with lessness, self-effacement and humility grows from *Murphy* onward, his literary treatment of conventional embarrassment undergoes an inversely proportional diminishing. This is not to say that embarrassment disappears from the sometimes-blushing body of work, only that it becomes divested of personal properties and incidental titters so as to adopt an existential character that abolishes, as Adorno observed, 'a canon for what should be laughed about'.[4]

This chapter deals with different but related types of Beckettian embarrassment. In the first two sections I pay attention to the statements and strategies related to a proactive variety. I explore how defensiveness, pre-emption, and autoimmunisation in *More Pricks* and contemporaneous letters serve to mitigate ostensible embarrassability while simultaneously inflicting a form of self-mortification. The third and fourth sections consider embarrassment of a reactive kind, particularly as indexed by Belacqua's easy recourse to indignation and identity obfuscation when threatened by unexpected exposures. Finally, the early writing is cast in relief with the existential embarrassment of the later work in order to trace a trajectory from proud self-sufficiency to humble vulnerability.

'Flagrant concealment': Beckett's Pre-emptive Embarrassment

In one of Beckett's lesser-known plays, *Rough for Theatre II*, an unsent billet-doux by a certain character reveals him to be 'morbidly sensitive to the opinion of others' (*CDW*, 242). Duly, a warning is issued about 'letters to admiratrixes': 'No need to take everything literally' (246). Mindful of the caveat but also of embarrassment's persistence in Beckett's writing, it is helpful to dwell on the two collected letters to Nuala Costello, his love interest in 1934.[5] The correspondence illuminates – even redoubles in the manner characteristic of embarrassment's echo chamber – the representation of awkward situations in *More Pricks than Kicks*. Not unlike the clumsily courting Beckett, Belacqua calls on defensive and proleptic strategies to preserve his inflated sense of self, particularly when undone by the discomfiting presence of women.

Before drawing out these parallels, I want to foreground three working hypotheses.[6] First, that a deliberate flaunting of the inappropriate may serve as an ereutophobic (fear of blushing) tactic that diminishes the transparency of embarrassability without necessarily diminishing embarrassment itself. Analogous is Belacqua's fidgeting with his glasses, a gesture suppressive and declarative in equal measure: 'He . . . clutch[ed] his enormous glasses (a precautionary measure that he never neglected when there was the least danger of his *appearing* embarrassed, appearing in italics because he was always embarrassed) . . .' (*MPTK*, 69).[7] The second hypothesis is that embarrassment, through its active magnification, can serve to preserve autonomy and transform social mortification from an unexpected event into a premeditated outcome. And third, that the same self-exposures meant to confer agency may also betoken unmotivated misdemeanours intended to draw rebuff and, therefore, to relieve general feelings of anxiety. These aspects intersect in *More Pricks than Kicks* and may be consolidated under one of Belacqua's handy oxymorons, 'flagrant concealment' (*Dream*, 148). The collection's flagrant concealments are made more visible by the Costello correspondence. Not only are comparable types of embarrassment performed in the two letters, but they also help situate Beckett's deep and disabling social anxiety in relation to his reading of contemporary psychology. Like nerves in patterns on a screen, a morbid sensitivity constellates through these loutish letters.

Witness the second missive to Costello where insecurity, indignation and erudition burn brightly together:

> How can you [? be] so little equitable, when I obviously suffer from the acutest paraesthesia to all that is said and written to and of me. When I hear a small boy giggle two liberties off I redden to the rotten roots of my white hair. The slightest unkindly cut is a dagger stuck in my heart, another dagger. So please never say anything to me that you <u>know</u> I couldn't care to hear. (*L1*, 207–8; 10 May 1934)

With this naked declaration, Beckett locates his blushing within broader neurotic behaviour. 'Paraesthesia', as he knew from his studious reading of Ernest Jones's *Papers on Psycho-Analysis*, is the abnormal physical sensation of prickling or formication.[8] Jones lists it as one of the physical manifestations of morbid anxiety or anxiety neurosis, a condition that compounds feelings of 'panic, terror, anguish, and apprehension'.[9] In extreme cases, sufferers experience 'indescribable dread'; in milder cases, anxiety neurosis expresses itself in 'slight abashment, awkwardness, embarrassment'.[10] Given the wry tenor of Beckett's letters to Costello, it is tempting to write off the clinical reference as comic exaggeration. Yet paraesthesia would persist as a phantom tingle in Beckett's later writing. In 'The End', the narrator's extremities feel 'as though they were full of ants' (*CSP*, 89), which sensation is closely linked with his fear of jumping from a cliff – a fear with a biographical spring that Beckett compulsively reworked, often stressing the unsettling gaze of onlookers.[11] There is also Winnie and Willie's laughter at the word 'formication' (*CDW*, 150) in *Happy Days*, laughter that is initially synchronised but then nervously out of step.[12]

The early to mid-1930s was a period of great mental duress for Beckett. Personally, the successive deaths of his cousin Peggy Sinclair and, most devastatingly, his father in 1933 left him deeply distraught. Professionally, he had to deal with his distaste for academia and the failure of *Dream of Fair to Middling Women*. Physically, he was worn down by numerous ailments: cysts, corns, dental problems, his racing 'bitch of a heart' (*L1*, 69). As a way of combatting psychogenic problems he undertook analysis under Wilfred Bion between 1934 and 1936, while also reading contemporary psychology in an attempt at self-diagnosis – whence his discovery of paraesthesia.[13] During this period, Beckett came to grasp some of the factors underpinning his mental, physical and even spiritual frailty. His insights are detailed in a significant letter to Thomas MacGreevy which marks a tipping point in Beckett's life and career. It limns the quietist leanings that would come to underpin his unique Christian–agnostic humility, while also exhibiting his capacity for unsparing self-inspection.[14] Indeed, the letter is a profound statement of *anagnorisis* in which Beckett cedes a morbidity behind his 'disparagement of others & myself', behind '[t]he misery & solitude & apathy & the sneers [that] were elements of an index of superiority & guaranteed the feeling of arrogant "otherness"' (*L1*, 258–9; 10 March 1935). These self-realisations, however, are recorded a year after Beckett's first letter to Costello. And if they constitute a mea culpa pointing towards humility, the Costello correspondence reads as an *apologia* for awkward, if not arrogant, otherness.

Dressed in oblique jokes and showy learnedness, the first letter's syntax is saltatory and unforgiving, while its arch references include Dante's scheme of judgement, pre-Socratic philosophers and the ineffectiveness of cold water as blushing inhibitor. What further characterises the letter is its defensiveness. Take the opening gambit: 'It's a great handicap to me in all my anabases and stases that I can't express myself in a straightforward manner, and that I cannot behave in a way that has the most tenuous *propriety* of relationship to circumstance' (*L1*, 184–5, my emphasis). Beckett punctuates this self-deflation with a glancing comparison between himself and Yahweh: 'One is not what one is not.' While the quip makes mild excuse for the bombast to follow, it also affirms an aggressive rigidity – hence the sly tautology that aligns Beckett with the inscrutable Almighty of Exodus.[15]

The rest of the letter, too, follows a proleptic line. Beckett corrects an error of usage in a previous (uncollected) letter, repeating the right word ('alights', 186) four times in an impishly self-flagellating manner. He then produces a mischievous 'poemetta' about Oedipal drives. Embedded in a letter already littered with psychoanalytic shibboleths, the verse offers little in the way of repression. Of course, the tongue-in-cheek tenor should not be overlooked, and on the plane of playfulness we see a young writer eager to impress with his worldly wisdom: he is as *au fait* with the tears of Heraclitus as with the treatments of Harley Street practitioners. But at a deeper level there is something self-defeating, even self-destructive, in fixating on his 'mother's breast' while addressing his would-be lover. By dint of egregious overshare, revelation and insulation emerge as complementary impulses. Rather than effect intimacy and expose what Murphy calls the 'pudenda of my psyche' (*Mur*, 30), the correspondence serves to estrange. Vulnerability, through its defiant parading, is transmuted Olympian into imperviousness.[16]

> Can you imagine a quarry in ebullition. I have now ceased to wish to amuse you. Forgive me. Now whereas this interesting neolithic effervescence had hitherto been so forgiving as to confine itself roughly to my centre of inertia & environs, it has lately begun to embrace me

without fear or favour from sinciput to planta. It takes my mind off my corns, no small favour I assure you . . . Pardon our emotion. Unseasonable with Commonwealth day so nigh. (*L1*, 208; 10 May 1934)

What exactly Costello might have said to prompt this response is not known, though it seems safe to infer her objection to Beckett's morbid enumeration of personal health concerns. In reply, Beckett becomes openly hostile, not only calling an end to his epistolary prancing but also hurling at Costello the same kind of unrepentant 'Forgive me' that Hamm would later level at Clov in *Endgame* (*CDW*, 95, 98). Enlarging his embarrassment, Beckett conflates the pains of his corns with what the narrator of 'First Love' calls the pains of 'the mind, those of the heart or emotional conative' (*CSP*, 33). Unlike that narrator, Beckett sees his 'omnidolence' not as a vain dream of self-abnegation but as a means of vengeful self-affirmation.

One of the learned references to shed light on such counterintuitive defence is the name of Karin Stephen, casually dropped in the first letter (*L1*, 186). Beckett had recently read Stephen's psychoanalytic study (which he refers to only by its subtitle, *The Wish to Fall Ill*) and took abundant if selective notes. Notwithstanding the flagged Oedipal issues, these transcriptions look ahead to much in the later work: sucking obsessions, scatological impulses, mutilation fantasies. But Beckett's most immediate and sustained interest was the means whereby anxiety may be allayed when 'omnipotent fantasies [threaten] to erupt'.[17] This is perhaps not surprising given references in the early writing to Belacqua's fragile ego: his 'precarious ipsissimosity' (*Dream*, 113), a 'break-down in . . . self-sufficiency', the 'sorry collapse of my little internus homo' (*MPTK*, 32). Stephen's study further details the neurotic's propensity for revenge when anticipating rejection, the pride that drives his avoidance of humiliation, and a concomitant 'need to escape retribution and to forestall it'.[18] In this composite sketch Beckett would have glimpsed a likeness: one who 'behaves as if he had a bad conscience', one 'divided against himself'.[19]

> The neurotic situation turns on acceptance of the reality of disappointment. The neurotic has never outgrown pain of realising his own limitations, he is intolerant of frustration, incapable of risking failure & putting up with what he can get. Fearing disappointment excessively, he reacts with excessive violence to the least hint of frustration, then fears his own violent reaction & represses both desire & rage.[20]

As Matthew Feldman observes, Beckett's reading of Stephen reinforced his narrowly Freudian conception of the unconscious, but also deepened (alongside Jones, as we will see) his understanding of anxiety and guilt neuroses.[21] The latter focus underpins his fascination with the neurotic's strategies against the frustration of desire. Despite the nonchalance with which Stephen is named, her study was clearly significant in offering Beckett a handle on the underlying causes behind his psychogenic symptoms, the 'puddle' beneath the 'bubble' (*L1*, 259) as he put it. What is more, *The Wish to Fall Ill* supplied him with an *ex post facto* psychoanalytic framework within which to understand some of the anti-social behaviour he had already fictionalised in his awkward antihero. If not specifically wishing to fall ill, Belacqua often acts so as to fall foul.

The short story 'Fingal' offers a case in point. Winnie asks 'sharply' about Belacqua's skin condition (impetigo) and then makes him even more self-conscious by commenting on his audacity to kiss her 'with that on [his] face' (*MPTK*, 18). Adding insult to injury, she wets a handkerchief and wipes her mouth while Belacqua 'l[ies] humbly beside her'. In answer to her question about the cause of impetigo – and in expectation of her imminent departure – he responds in a manner calculated to cause offense: 'Dirt . . . you see it on slum children.'[22] The wilful intensification of embarrassment corresponds with his physical pose: just as the attitude of relaxed reclining is at odds with an attitude of humility, so there is something contradictory in the self-denigrating comparison with slum children. Instead of placating Winnie, Belacqua's words are primed to drive her away, to fashion the foreseen desertion into an intended rather than an inadvertent consequence. In order to maintain a measure of agency, he is compelled to strike at himself.

Alongside Stephen's psychogenic coping mechanisms, the self-thwarting of this episode (and of the letter) bears relation to two other strategies of affect control. The first is what Silvan Tomkins calls 'taking a bath', which involves wilfully magnifying one's own mortification in order to lessen or even nullify the sense of powerlessness that normally attends it.[23] Such masochistic behaviour aims to heighten negative affect to the point where it erupts in a kind of relief. Tomkins offers the example of a down-and-out gambler overwhelmed by the loss of money and loss of agency that define his addiction. In a last-ditch effort to claim control, the gambler risks his entire fortune on an unlikely winner. Upon losing everything (the predicted outcome) he experiences a sense of peace. The self-destructive strategy is deployed because the gambler 'feels he cannot reduce his feelings of humiliation and loss otherwise than by magnifying them so that he is utterly consumed and finally purified, "cleaned," "bathed."' In the words of Dostoevsky's Underground Man: 'Humiliation, after all, is purification.'[24]

The second strategy is paradoxical intention, which resembles magnification but pertains to interpersonal relations. Victor Frankl defined the technique in 1939, explaining it as 'a reversal of the patient's attitude, inasmuch as his fear is replaced by a paradoxical wish'.[25] Frankl recounts the case study of a young physician who experienced great anxiety at the thought of perspiring. This anxiety was itself sufficient to trigger excessive sweating. In order to counter the somatic expression of social anxiety, the man was advised to attempt purposely sweating whenever the fear of sweating arose. The patient was apparently cured within a week because he took 'the wind ... out of the sails of [his] anxiety'. The approach, however, is limited to symptomatic treatment and does not aid discovery of an underlying cause.[26] One might also object to the view that the reversed wish – deliberate perspiration, blushing, stuttering – is an achievement, since the 'positive' results of this technique (reducing social anxiety) are contingent upon an inversion of social dynamics.[27] Where the man's sweating initially constituted an involuntary response conditioned and occasioned by the presence of others, it eventually developed into an expression of will. In 'Fingal', Belacqua also uses his own mortification to transform disappointment into a desired consequence rather than one to be suffered passively. The cognitive structure of embarrassment is essentially overturned. Where it usually implies loss of face, of power and of self-possession, embarrassment is now refashioned into a locus for the retention of these things.

Such an inversion is the object of the Polar Bear's irreverent attack in the story, 'A Wet Night'. For him, Christ's life smacks of pride, exceptionalism and deeply anti-social behaviour:

> The *Lebensbah* ... of the Galilean is the tragi-comedy of the solipsism that will not capitulate. The humilities and *retro me*'s and quaffs or sirreverence are on a par with the hey presto's, arrogance and egoism. He is the first great self-contained playboy. The cryptic abasement before the woman taken red-handed is as great a piece of megalomaniacal impertinence as his interference in the affairs of his boy-friend Lazarus. (*MPTK*, 50–1)

The key word here is 'solipsism'. It underscores the Polar Bear's belief that Christ – both through his resignation of will (*'retro me*'s') and his performance of miracles ('hey presto's') – insulates himself against the world around him.[28] Christ apparently shows no regard for established order: as his resurrection of Lazarus flaunts natural laws, so his defence of the adulteress in John 8: 1–11 thwarts Judaic law. But this view is counterbalanced by the Jesuit who explains that Christ's humility 'is beyond masochism . . . [b]eyond pain and service'; it is the humility 'of a love too great for skivvying and too real to need the tonic of urtication'. 'Skivvying' here denotes menial service and, by extension, something microcosmic and isolated; 'urtication' is a word Beckett snatched from William Cooper's *Flagellation and the Flagellants*, which pertains to the curative properties of corporeal punishment.[29] The import of the Jesuit's claim, then, is that neither Christ's humility nor his humiliations can be construed as bad-faith, self-serving practices.

One would be hard put to make the same defence of Belacqua, or of Beckett's epistolary abasement. However glancing the correspondence between creature and creator, however untidy the identification, we have in *More Pricks* and in the Costello letters comparable examples of attempts to reduce the appearance of embarrassment while also reconfiguring potential humiliation into an *intra*personal, voluntary act. Instead of arriving via the belatedness that normally characterises it, embarrassment is converted into a mode of anticipatory anxiety which disarms external censure by pre-empting it, by visiting on the morbidly sensitive subject a kind of mortification that forecloses the possibility of being humiliated by another. In short, the wind is taken out of embarrassment's sails.

Unmotivated Misdemeanours, Deliberate Tran*gres*sions

Flagging Beckett's own 'precarious ipsissimosity', then, the Costello letters appear to favour strategies of pre-emptive self-protection. Their rationale is of a piece with that underpinning the Expelled's unsightly amble: having soiled himself, he develops a bowlegged gait both to 'put people off the scent' and 'to make them think [he] was full of gaiety and high spirits' (*CSP*, 50–1). But to take the letters' pose of indifference – its *bovarysme* (see Chapter 1) – for its actualisation is to overlook the intentionally collapsing ground on which Beckett builds his defences. The same 'flagrant concealments' intended to deflate embarrassment are also legible as breaches in decorum that purposely invite correction.

The deeply self-contradicting nature of Beckett's bared embarrassments is hinted at in another oxymoron – the 'moving pause' otherwise known as 'gress' (*MPTK*, 32, 33). 'Gress' first features in the story 'Ding-Dong' where it designates a modus vivendi freed of cause and consequence. Thanks to gress, Belacqua can dart across Dublin '[e]xempt from destination' (33) and also pursue a path of self-destruction whose aetiology is simply given as '*ex nihilo*' (83). And so, as something of an unmoved mover, the gressing Belacqua 'never wearie[s] of arrogating [self-sufficiency] to himself' (32). Little wonder, then, that the word recurs in the first Costello letter when Beckett washes his hands of all propriety and identifies himself with an unfathomable deity. Here, with pointed self-referentiality, he recycles gress to declare his own desire for a cavalier being-in-the-world, for experience free from 'destination and hence from schedule' (*L1*, 186). But couched as it is in a sentence at once flapping and flexing, gress comes to assume a compensatory aspect.

Through its very assertion of untouchability, the concept is ironised as a feeble coping mechanism. This is true for both its fictional and its epistolary formulation, quoted in sequence and at length below:

> Not the least charm of this pure blank movement, this 'gress' or 'gression,' was its aptness to receive, with or without the approval of the subject, in all their integrity the faint inscriptions of the outer world. Exempt from destination, it had not to shun the unforeseen nor turn aside from the agreeable odds and ends of vaudeville that are liable to crop up. This sensitiveness was not the least charm of this roaming that began by being blank, not the least charm of this pure act the alacrity with which it welcomed defilement. But very nearly the least. (*MPTK*, 33)

> [F]rom this delicious conception of movement as gress, pure and mere gress, one arrives like a bird to its nest, though <u>nest</u> scarcely seems to be the right word in such a passage, at an elucidation of the <u>crime immotivé</u> that never occurred and never could to Gide or to any of his kidney, or indeed to any person within earshot of the ringing grooves save only to myself, who I assure you could not be induced to part with it for love or money or any other incitement whatever, on

account of its inestimable antiphlogistic properties that exceed anything of the kind I ever tried, and I have tried everything, from cold water to reduce blushing to Guinness as anterotic. (*L1*, 186)

Starting with the passage from 'Ding-Dong' and its surrounding context, it is fair to say that the bathos compares with that at the end of 'Dante and the Lobster': the subject's sensitivity during gress is as 'charming' as the lobster's death is 'quick' (*MPTK*, 14). Already at the outset of the story we are told that Belacqua was in the 'last phase' of his 'solipsism' – a fact soon followed up by noting his dread of the retributive 'Furies' (31). The suggestion of a world-unto-itself on the brink of collapse characterises the rest of the narrative. Despite gress's supposed buffering, Belacqua is utterly exposed when a woman selling theatre tickets causes him to be 'embarrassed in the last degree, but transported also' (38). The overwrought litotes at the opening of the first quoted passage is thus a red herring inviting us to see Belacqua as somehow easy-going and unruffled. But the flat, final sentence undercuts all that is supposedly charming, agreeable and welcomed. Through a canny repetition, the irony of the passage is fulfilled when Belacqua finally comes to a standstill at the story's end. Not only is 'gress' shown up as a physically unsustainable manoeuvre, but the encounter with the would-be Beatrice registers as something 'unforeseen with a vengeance, if not exactly vaudeville' (38), something from which he does attempt to turn away.

The letter's corresponding section collapses under similar pressures, both stylistically and conceptually. As charm is to Belacqua's roaming, so the avian simile is to Beckett's gress. Not only are the intimations of homecoming and security undone by a labyrinthine syntax, but an expanded definition of the liberating movement reveals it to be a deliberate provocation of censure. The key here is 'crime immotivé'. The phrase refers to the gratuitous murder that occurs in André Gide's novel, *Les Caves du Vatican* (1913), when the roguish Lafcadio pushes a stranger from a moving train without cause.[30] One reason why '*crime immotivé*' is here explicitly appropriated to the exclusion of Gide may be due to Beckett's view that the French novelist had not gone far enough in the direction of dehiscence, as John Bolin argues.[31] Another reason (fuelled less by writerly ambition than neurotic insecurity) is that Beckett's understanding of the term had recently been shaped by Ernest Jones and Karin Stephen.

As mentioned above, Jones enters the correspondence via 'paraesthesia', while Stephen is casually invoked in the paragraph following the 'gress' section. The two authors come into still closer contact via the 'Psychology Notes'. Under Stephen's name, Beckett records the 'conception of crime as the effect, not the cause, of a sense of guilt (crime immotivé), a specific act on which to fasten & so relieve the floating sense of dread'.[32] Under Jones he produces a summary of a particular 'character type': 'Those that turn criminal because of a guilty conscience. These commit some forbidden act because they have a floating sense of guilt & thereby obtain relief (acte gratuit & crime immotivé).[33] Neither Stephen nor Jones uses the exact phrase 'floating sense of dread/guilt', a fact which underscores Beckett's creative synthesis of his source material. Through this blended understanding of neurotic behaviour, the unmotivated crime re-crystallises as a surrogate act for repressed anxiety or guilt which can only be assuaged through external punishment. Since the source of this anxiety is unknown to the subject, he transgresses in order to elicit retribution that may prove generally cathartic.

The muddled relation between crime and punishment is hardly unique to Beckett's expanded understanding of gress. As early as *Proust* he had pitted magisterial forms of justice against a notion of atonement informed by Schopenhauerian pessimism: 'Tragedy is the statement of an expiation, but not the miserable expiation of a codified breach of a local arrangement, organised by the knaves for the fools. The tragic figure represents the expiation of original sin, of the original and eternal sin of him and all his "soci malorum," the sin of having been born' (*PTD*, 67). Local arrangements (possibly on par with the application of the letter's 'cold water' and 'Guinness') are scoffed at, while universal punishment is extolled.[34] What is more, the passage casts existence itself as the eternal recurrence of sin and retribution. This parasitic conjunction inflects the later works. In *Malone Dies*, Macmann finds 'the ideas of guilt and punishment confused together . . . as those of cause and effect so often are in the minds of those who continue to think' (*TN*, 233). With less equanimity, *The Unnamable* equates transgression and justice: 'this is my punishment, my crime is my punishment . . . I expiate vilely, like a pig' (*TN*, 362). Perhaps nowhere is this inverted causality expressed so poignantly as in Beckett's letter to his cousin Morris Sinclair, written just a few days before the second Costello letter:

> [I]t is highly probable that the condemned man is less afraid than I. At least he knows exactly what is at stake and exactly what he has to

attend to, and that is a greater comfort than one is generally inclined to believe. So great that many sick people become criminals solely in order to limit their fear and gain that comfort. (*L2*, 204–5, 5 May 1934)

Here we find Beckett's 'floating sense of dread' consolidated with his belief that punishment promises some kind of salve. The statement also offers a background against which to interpret the unexplained retribution that would scar so many of Beckett's moribunds. But to regard this 'confusion' merely as a symptom of a particular neurotic mind is to neglect its relation to the objectless angst that haunts Raskolnikov, Joseph K., Meursault, Roquentin and countless literary others embarrassed by crime and punishment's thrown causality.[35] Even in Eliot such confusion emerges, albeit under the rubric of a Christian existentialism:

> What we have written is not a story of detection,
> Of crime and punishment, but of sin and expiation.
> It is possible that you have not known what sin
> You shall expiate, or whose, or why. (*The Family Reunion*, *CPP*, 333)

Naturally, while Beckett's writing would come to be typified by mystifying pensums and punishments, these do not provide a retroactive gloss on the 'gress' in *More Pricks* or in the letters. And to cast the supposed relief of these texts' deliberate faux pas as 'cathartic' is to conflate the tragic with the patently comic. Beckett's word, rather, is 'antiphlogistic', which defines something with anti-inflammatory or anxiety-relaying properties.[36] He had already used it to index a kind of reinstated neutrality (*Dream*, 53) and to qualify the primary duty of a fire brigade (*MPTK*, 179). If not fires, there are blushes to quench in the letter. With his ear for puns, 'antiphlogistic' might well have resonated with the fuller syncretic definition of *crime immotivé* where punishment is the motive for a crime. And so, through the lens of Beckett's 'Psychology Notes', it becomes clear why the flogging/antiphlogistic properties of the gratuitous act are preferred over more symptomatic remedies for anxiety. While cold water and Guinness represent means of coping (or not coping) with the manifestation of anxiety – means to 'reduce blushing' and still the stirrings of erotic love – the 'gression' that becomes *trans*gression supplies a potential curative to the cause of anxiety.[37] At first, the letter to Costello appears to espouse exactly the opposite given the autoimmunisation that is effected through self-exposure. But these very self-exposures may also be seen as unmotivated misdemeanours intended to draw rebuff. So although the effects of Beckett's declared embarrassments are discrete and even antithetical, their aim is one: to diminish the dread that attends uncertainty.

Indignation and Ill-Locution

I turn now from pre-emptive to reactive embarrassment – the more common form of this awkward affect that announces, belatedly, rupture between an ideal situational self and its deficient double.[38] Specifically, my interest is in the cracks of discontinuity that become visible when words fail to provide cover for a 'mind never quite contemporaneous with itself', to borrow E. S. Burt's fine phrase.[39] Such is frequently Belacqua's predicament. Despite his apparent linguistic prowess, he often finds himself tongue-tied, obstructed and embarrassed in his quest for the *mot juste*.[40] Put out and put on the spot, Belacqua is forced to perpetrate what would become a desired end in later works: the ill-said. In *More Pricks*, however, the ill-said does not represent the deliberate actualisation of locutionary limitation but its inadvertent exposure. Put simply, Belacqua's embarrassment in and through language should be understood as an *affective* humiliation distinct from the *aesthetic* humiliation that would come to define the Beckett's gropings towards 'literature of the non-word' (*L1*, 520). A clear line thus separates the apophatic eloquence of the late poetic voice that asks 'what is the word' (*CP*, 228) from the anguish of Belacqua's ill-locutions.[41]

The most knotted example of this kind of obstruction occurs when Belacqua is faced with his limited French vocabulary in 'Dante and the Lobster'. Responding 'composedly' (*MPTK*, 12) to Mlle Glain's inquiry about the contents of the bag containing the lobster, his answer is an unabashed simplification: '"Mine" he said, "a fish."' Then, in a voice which blurs narrative statement and free indirect discourse, we are told that '[Belacqua] did not know the French for lobster, Fish would do very well. Fish had been good enough for Jesus Christ, Son of God, Saviour. It was good enough for Mlle Glain'. The passage is crucial for two reasons that I will explore in this section and the next. First, it demonstrates the relationship between embarrassment and indignation, where indignation becomes a form of resistance to the loss of control that attends embarrassment. Second, it shows how the avoidance of embarrassment is achieved through Belacqua's self-obscuring identification with a higher authority.

Indignation has a peculiar relation to embarrassment. Christopher Ricks remarks with usual wit and perspicacity that

> the one hot flush drives out the other, as fire fire, so that a common way of staving off the embarrassment one would otherwise feel is by inciting oneself to indignation. One does this when mildly wronged . . . and obliged to attract attention in public to get things put right; the smallish indignation gets factitiously stoked because you will not be ridden by embarrassment once you are hotly riding indignation.[42]

Belacqua's indignation is not voiced in the open, although it is given sufficient vent to contaminate narrative description. The words of the French teacher are delivered, we are told, 'with a blue-stocking snigger' (*MPTK*, 12), which is promptly followed by Belacqua's bristling interior epithet: 'Base prying bitch.' The two phrases suggest the compounded source of his embarrassment: he is caught off-guard by his linguistic limitations, and he is annoyed by the inquisitiveness of the woman, which prompts his vain casting for the word '*homard*' or '*langouste*'.[43] Reversing the slight in his mind, Belacqua factitiously stokes his indignation by turning a twofold insult into a three-pronged attack: 'blue-stocking' derides Mlle Glain's intellectualism, 'prying' denounces her curiosity, and 'bitch' binds the assault together in an *ad feminam* dismissal comparable to what we find in Eliot's 'Hysteria' (see Chapter 1). The resentment further swells to envelop the woman's sexuality (or lack thereof): 'The grey hairs of her maidenhead screamed at Belacqua. A devout, virginal blue-stocking, honing after a penny's worth of scandal' (*MPTK*, 12).

Strangely enough, this description invites comparison between the detested Mlle Glain and the beloved Signorina Ottolenghi. Bogged as he is in his chauvinism, Belacqua considers it impossible 'for a woman to be more intelligent or better informed' than his Italian tutor (*MPTK*, 9). His patronising estimation is further qualified by an apparent readiness to exclude aspects of her femaleness: 'There subsisted as much of the Ottolenghi as might be expected to of the person of a lady of a certain age who had found being young and beautiful and pure more of a bore than anything else' (11). The Ottolenghi is extolled for her experience and wisdom, while her physical attributes are abstracted into Belacqua's Cartesian hierarchy. But if the idealisation makes of the Ottolenghi a mature, learned woman beyond taint, it also makes her something of a 'virginal blue-stocking'. And though Belacqua remains unaware of the subtle continuity between his admiring portrait of the Ottolenghi and his vicious caricature of Mlle Glain, it nonetheless establishes a baseline for his embarrassment and consequent indignation – what is elsewhere called the 'compound of impatience and rosy pudency' (*EB*, 17).

Belacqua's reaction to Mlle Glain is exacerbated by yet another similarity with the Ottolenghi: both women touch the quick of his pride in direct challenges to his polyglottal fluency. Moments before being embarrassed by his inability to find the French for lobster, he is also embarrassed in his wish to find the English for Dante's 'superb pun':

> He assumed an expression of profundity.
>   'In that connexion [with Dante's rare movements of compassion in Hell]' he said 'I recall one superb pun anyway:
>
> "*qui vive la pietà quando è ben morta . . .*"'
>
>   She said nothing.
>   'Is it not a great phrase?' he gushed.
>   She said nothing.
>   'Now' he said like a fool 'I wonder how you could translate that?'
>   Still she said nothing. Then:
>   'Do you think' she murmured 'it is absolutely necessary to translate it?' (*MPTK*, 11–12)

The pun refers to the words of reprimand spoken by Virgil after Dante expresses his pity for the damned of the Eighth Circle: 'Here liveth piety when wholly dead / is pity. Who, then, guiltier is than he / who lets his feelings judge Divine Decrees?'[44] The play on pity/piety does not amuse the Signorina, and her persistent silence compels Belacqua to blabber on foolishly. Dante, in his turn, is expressly called 'foolish' or 'witless' by Virgil, since his pity indirectly undermines divine judgement.[45] 'Fool' also occurs in the poem, 'Text 3', in conjunction with Beckett's translation of the Dantean pun: 'pity is quick with death. / Presumptuous passionate fool . . .' (*CP*, 39). The correspondences between Dante, Beckett's poem and his short story have been sufficiently noted, and so too has the predominance of Beckett's concern with pity and pitilessness.[46] What has been overlooked, however, is the difference in tone between the respective texts. In the poem, 'fool' is transferred without irony from Dante and retains something of its pathos and judgement. The Virgilian rebuke intimates the addressee's capacity for compassion ('passionate') and his implicit questioning of eternal decree ('presumptuous'); 'fool' comprehends both these aspects. However, in 'Dante and the Lobster', Belacqua's foolishness does not stem from an open rebuff but from the need to fill an awkward, disapproving silence. It is unclear whether the phrase 'he said like a fool' is the narrator's indictment alone, or whether it signals Belacqua's self-assessment. Taken to be the narrator's voice, it implies that the question over translating the Dante line is objectively objectionable — there is thus convergence between the Ottolenghi's tacit censure and the narrator's overt ridicule. If Belacqua's self-conscious voice inflects the statement, we are alerted to the prickling of embarrassment. In the silence that follows the 'superb pun', his 'gushing' praise of Dante already appears compensatory. The subsequent utterance is a further step in that direction. Whatever the Ottolenghi's taciturnity may imply, her eventual words oppose Belacqua's wish to pursue the translation. Not long after the Ottolenghi's mute resistance, Belacqua fails to translate 'lobster'. The two moments of linguistic challenge draw into question Belacqua's ability as well as his motives.

On the one hand, Belacqua's use of the Dante line is a valid and logical response to the Ottolenghi's remark about compassion in the *Divine Comedy* and therefore stands as an example of his quick-fire wit. On the other hand, it flags his insecurity. As Daniela Caselli has observed, the pun serves the Belacqua of *Dream* as a mantric buffer when his ego is threatened:[47]

> Many a time had Belacqua, responding to the obscure need to verbalise a wombtombing or such like, murmured a syllable or two of incantation: 'La sua bocca . . .', '*Qui vive la pietà* . . .', 'Before morning you shall be here . . .', 'Ange plein . . .', 'Mais elle, viendra . . .' 'Du bist so . . .' 'La belle, la . . .' (*Dream*, 148, my emphasis).

These fragments from Dante, Beckett's own poetry, Baudelaire, Goethe and Mallarmé are shored against potential ruin from outside.[48] They verbally facilitate that special kind of solipsism, 'wombtombing', whereby the 'conflict of flight and flow and Eros' (*Dream*, 121) is nullified – much like Guinness serves as an 'anterotic' in the first Costello letter. Admittedly, the Dantean pun in the short story does not occur within a situation where gender dynamics threatens identity, but it is nonetheless part of Belacqua's calculated plan to shield himself against what he regards as the work of effete men: Manzoni, Napoleon, Pellico and Carducci.[49] By thwarting the lesson plan, Belacqua can remain as contentedly 'bogged' (3) in Dante as he is at the opening of the story. This manoeuvre not only belies his supposed concern with the ethics of pity/piety; it also reveals his self-serving motive for attempting to translate the Dante line. In other words, his intellectual curiosity is exposed as specious. This posturing includes both the conscious efforts to subvert the lesson plan and the subconscious reasons that inform them. Belacqua's dismissal of Manzoni and company as 'old maids, suffragettes' (*MPTK*, 9) relies on the same logical fallacy employed in his mental attack on Mlle Glain.

But there is another form of embarrassment that emerges in Belacqua's failure to be admitted to the desired literary-masculine network. As other commentators have shown, the story's opening paragraph already conflates the Pilgrim and Belacqua through an ambiguous use of pronouns: the 'him' addressed by Beatrice refers as much to Dante as to Belacqua.[50] The 'superb pun' would seem to be another instance of conflation or assimilation: Belacqua uses it both to keep the 'old hens' of Italian literature at bay and thus declares a literary allegiance with Dante, and also to immure himself against the outside world. But the line always belongs more to Dante than to Belacqua, and the text of 'Dante and the Lobster' suggests the pun's resistance to appropriation in several ways over and above the Ottolenghi's undercutting statement. It is placed in quotation marks, it stands between two typographic breaks that occur at no other point in the story, and, though the entire lesson is conducted in Italian, these are the only words that *appear* in Italian.

If the Dante line's non-translation enacts a kind of textual resistance to Belacqua's desired allegiance, it also signals a broader issue for Beckett as a late – or rather, belated – modernist. In his excellent study of European modernism's fraught relationship with tradition, Ben Hutchinson identifies the embarrassment of 'epochal lateness', a literary-phenomenological condition marked by 'by the extent to which the burden of acquired knowledge inhibits the freedom of modern being'.[51] This inhibition manifests through a compulsive and antagonistic reworking of the past whereby the literature of bygone eras manifests simultaneously as the vehicle of and impediment to modernism's self-actualisation. In Beckett, this dichotomy seems particularly heightened. Returning to the Costello letters for a moment, it is worth pointing out his indignant response to a reviewer's suggestion that *More Pricks* owes a debt to Joyce and Eliot. 'Is it necessary to say,' Beckett asks huffily, 'that I have never read either Leprechaun or Télégraphie Sans Egal [that is, T. S. E.], that my More Pricks is as free from Joycean portmanteaux as from allusion' (*L1*, 208). Perhaps nothing in Beckett so succinctly captures the belated modernist's strife with the past as *Watt*'s 'pereant qui ante nos nostra dixerunt' (*W*, 219; 'Let those who utter our words before us perish'). By appearing among the novel's 'Addenda', the Latin maxim becomes an afterthought aforethought, for it repeats a sentiment that itself hinges on the frustrations of iterability, on history's hauntings and the return of the expressed.[52] Moreover, by remaining untranslated and unincorporated into the novel proper, the words declare a gulf between past and present. As Jason Harding and John Nash's study on the subject makes clear, modernist non-translation often marks a 'text as a site of confrontation, not just of tongues but of interpretative dilemmas'.[53]

The full import of the Dantean line's non-translation only becomes clear when read against the non-translation of 'lobster'. Not only is Belacqua unable to supply '*homard*', but his substitution appears doubly inept for *appearing* in English. Again, as with the phrase 'like a fool', the text keeps an insoluble ambiguity alive. In the plainest reading, 'He did not know the French for lobster' suggests that Belacqua's 'fish' is actually '*poisson*'. But there is also the possibility that only the interchange between the two tutors is in French, since it alone is given in French. Further evidence is Mlle Glain's ungrammatical utterance: 'He would have *tore* it to flitters'; it is unlikely that the French teacher would make such an error in French. This means that Belacqua's response is actually in English. As such, it constitutes an act of defiance in the face of embarrassment: being surprised in his ignorance but unwilling either to admit it or deign to answer the '[b]ase prying bitch' in French, Belacqua asserts himself in his mother tongue, thus dragging the situation within the realm of his control and beyond the threat of uncertainty. With great economy, Beckett hints at his protagonist's attitude: he not only speaks, but speaks up; he not only speaks up, but speaks up composedly; and his first word is not in answer to Mlle Glain's 'what' but in answer to the 'whose' which he forcefully and proprietorially insinuates. His response hardly suggests a flustered and frantic scramble to find the right word. Rather, it attests to a chauvinist attitude that will not capitulate before the inquisitiveness of a woman who does not know her place socially, intellectually and sexually.

Humility as Sovereignty: Belacqua and Christ

Belacqua's sense of male superiority brings us to another feature of his embarrassment-avoidance: his identification with authority figures as a means of resisting external censure and of assuaging his own insecurity. This emerges as a special category of what Karin Stephen identifies as the neurotic's 'bluff': his deliberate attempt to 'disguise himself . . . from himself'.[54] Embarrassment-avoidance tactics in *More Pricks* often depend on Belacqua's hiding behind others. This is the case when the mingled narrative voice informs us that 'Fish had been good enough for Jesus Christ, Son of God, Saviour.' A curious elision occurs here, since 'fish' is surely also good enough for Belacqua who employs the word. The vanishing act is telling for two reasons. First, it suggests Belacqua's willed identification with Christ, whom he invokes in order to controvert the pretension read into a question that demands *'homard'* for an answer. This tactic approximates Beckett's statement to Costello that 'one is not what one is not', only now the defence is achieved by establishing a different criterion for unanswerability. In the letter, Beckett's resistance to pressure upon his ego is signalled by his identification with a God who refuses to explain himself.[55] But in the story, Belacqua deflects the slings of fortune by arrogating to himself both the humility and sovereignty of Christ: humility in that 'fish' is good enough for Christ's wonders, words and cryptic signification; sovereignty in the claim to a name above all names.[56]

The second point about the elision is this: as with the Dantean line's non-translation and consequent unassimilability, the text of 'Dante and the Lobster' allows only a semblance of identification between Belacqua and Christ – a semblance which is contrived by the protagonist but unstitched in the story. At the moment when Belacqua's tacit allegiances are revealed as the epiphenomena of self-interested skivvying, neither the suffering of Christ nor the suffering of the lobster is of genuine concern. As he employs the

Dante line to uphold his own agenda and as he robs the lobster of its taxonomy in order to avoid embarrassment, so he misappropriates the 'host of holy names in one name' (*DN*, 29) for his own ends, which are at once self-affirming and self-obscuring. Knowing 'fish' to be both a lie and an acknowledgement of his limitations, Belacqua invokes a name which stands beyond question. Embarrassed and indignant, he must hide himself in order to assert himself.[57]

'Love and Lethe' instances another facile identification between Belacqua and Christ. In this *More Pricks* story, Belacqua initiates a suicide pact with the nearly femme fatale, Ruby Tough. What motivates his course of action remains uncertain even to the narrator, who impatiently avers that the protagonist's 'faculty for acting with insufficient reason' is patent enough in previous episodes and should therefore 'be no longer a matter of surprise' (*MPTK*, 82). The surprise comes in, however, when Ruby fails to follow through with the plan. At this point Belacqua's gun mysteriously misfires, and the couple end up consummating a smaller death – gress unexpectedly becoming congress. Like its whimpering end, which takes an obvious stab at Eliot's 'The Hollow Men', the story's title could not be more bathetic. 'Love' is nothing more than an acquaintance of convenience, while 'Lethe' is the waters of a future anterior that will have washed away the blushes of a foiled plan. In the service of this wilful forgetting, Belacqua misappropriates a familiarly divine pleroma and invokes 'The finger of God' (91).

Before pausing to consider this particular bluff, however, it is necessary to tarry on the event that provokes it: Belacqua's slow realisation of Ruby's grand refusal. The event elicits a misogynistic reaction comparable to that in 'Dante and the Lobster', though here vexation manifests first as a bodily affront and then as cognitive upheaval: 'That indescribable sensation, compound of exasperation and relief, relaxing, the better to grieve, the coenaesthesis of the consultant when he finds the surgeon out, now burst inside Belacqua. He felt suddenly hot within. The bitch was backing out' (91). The passage is remarkable for the way in which it traces Belacqua's somatic realisation of the fact that Ruby is an autonomous agent. Because of his extreme narcissism, Belacqua seems incapable of conceiving his companion as something other than the means to his end. Callously, he 'cultivate[s]' and 'prime[s] her for the part she was to play on his behalf' (82). His courtship is conducted with such complacency and at such distance that he is hardly aware of her appearance, and this blinding self-interest even impinges on narrative description: 'Further than this hint we need not allow her outside to detain us, seeing that Belacqua was scarcely ever aware of it' (81). Indeed, that we learn anything about Ruby – her age, her sexual history, her resemblance to the 'Magdalene in the Perugino Pietà in the National Gallery of Dublin' – is due to a narrative 'lull' during which Belacqua's arrival is awaited (80). Only when he undergoes a 'coenaesthetic' experience does he begin to register Ruby's otherness.

Beckett encountered this term in the English translation of Max Nordau's controversial work of social criticism, *Degeneration* (1892), from which he copied an abbreviated definition: 'general sensibility . . . Dimly perceived cellular organic Ego not involving cerebral consciousness' (*DN*, 96, item 664).[58] Tellingly, the concept appears in a chapter entitled 'Ego-Mania' where Nordau reflects on the inability of the 'emotionally degenerate subject' to engage the outside world. Through coenaesthesis, however, the subject is confronted with a physical experience whose aetiology attests to an exterior presence:

> Coenaesthesis, the organic dimly-conscious 'I', rises into the clear consciousness of the 'Ego,' by excitations of the second order, reaching the brain from the nerves and muscles . . . [T]here must then be something else outside consciousness, and so consciousness comes, through the habit of causal thought, to assume the existence of something outside itself, of a 'not-I', or an external world, and to project into it the cause of the excitations which it perceives in the nervous system.[59]

Beckett's image in 'Love and Lethe' of an anaesthetised patient waking to the surgeon at work intimates the process by which Belacqua gradually perceives a loss of control.[60] At first, there is 'undirected feeling . . . below the limen of consciousness', as Chris Ackerley puts it.[61] The groggy patient cannot immediately filter his surroundings through sensory differentiation (hence 'indescribable sensation') but nonetheless experiences it through the sum of his bodily feelings. This is followed by the sensation of heat from within. Lastly, a leap from the embodied experience of otherness is made to a cognitive awareness of otherness. In terms of the altruistic ethics outlined by Nordau, this is a step in the right direction: 'the highest degree of development of the "I" consists in embodying in itself the "not-I," in comprehending the world, in conquering egoism, and in establishing close relations with other beings, things and phenomena'.[62]

Such relational ethics would preoccupy Beckett's later work. While *Not I* is a nominally obvious example, *Company* grapples with embarrassment as a cognitive-affective structure for the experience of alterity. At first, its manifestation seems punitive, since the hearer is unsure whether he is being spoken to or spoken of:

> Why does [the voice] never say, for example, You saw the light on such and such a day and now you are alone on your back in the dark? Why? Perhaps for no other reason than to kindle in his mind this faint uncertainty and embarrassment. (*Com etc.*, 4)

The possibility of overhearing others is quite naturally a source of discomfort; it involves exposure and objectification that the hearer is powerless to resist. Yet he gradually comes to understand that embarrassment – 'kindled' bodily like coenaesthesia – negates solitude and affirms the existence of others. He would therefore be in 'company' if the voice '[w]ere ... only to kindle in his mind the state of faint uncertainty and embarrassment mentioned above' (5).

This is not the relief Belacqua is after. As the 'principal boy' (*Dream* 11, 19, 38, 113) of the early fiction, he is more concerned with conquering the 'not-I' than with conquering his own egoism. Not only is the name-calling in 'Love and Lethe' verbally proximate to that in 'Dante and the Lobster', but so too is the structural experience of embarrassment-come-indignation that underpins it. The image of the patient under the knife relates to more than just dim organic consciousness. It speaks to the powerlessness of being acted upon, of becoming an object.[63] This disempowering divestment of one's selfhood is what the Unidentified Guest in Eliot's *The Cocktail Party* has in mind when he says to Edward that 'stretched on the table, / You are a piece of furniture in a repair shop' (*CPP*, 362). Metaphorically etherised upon the table as he is, Belacqua's suffering goes beyond mere objectification and is exacerbated by feelings of emasculation. For, in addition to the infuriating knowledge of his thwarted designs, Ruby's 'backing out' registers as a visceral trespass. The surgeon/patient image adumbrates the invasive, even threatening, role she inadvertently assumes. It also limns Belacqua's passive, female position in the dynamic – a role repeated in 'Yellow' when, literally etherised, his bandaged neck is like a 'bride's adorned' (*MPTK*, 160).[64]

Belacqua's alignment with Christ occurs at the moment when he realises that his plans are contingent rather than absolute. Following Ruby's perceived defiance and the bathetic misfiring of the gun, he adopts a sagely aloof pose by offering the phrase 'The finger of God', after which the narrative voice blurs the identities of Christ and Belacqua in its ambiguous use of pronouns.[65]

> Who shall judge of his conduct at this crux? Is it to be condemned as wholly despicable? Is it not possible that he was gallantly trying to spare the young woman embarrassment? Was it tact or concupiscence or the white feather or what? We state the facts. We do not presume to determine their significance. (*MPTK*, 91)

What reinforces the subtextual presence of John 8 is the lexicon of judgement. Moreover, the interrogatives, while feigning humble ignorance, are in keeping with the biblical narrative's focus on persecution. The passage thus presents an instance of 'megalomaniacal impertinence' in which Belacqua's embarrassed expectations are fallaciously manipulated in order to preserve the appearance that his will has been done. We read that 'It will quite possibly be [Belacqua's] boast, when Ruby is dead and he an old optimist, that at least on this occasion . . . he achieved what he set out to do' (*MPTK*, 91). In this light the 'Digitus Dei' is not a *deus ex machina* by which the couple's lives are spared, but a *deus 'internus homo'* (*MPTK*, 32) by whose design there are no unforeseen events and thus no room for embarrassment.[66] Christ (who cryptically writes in the dust) and Belacqua (who cryptically refers to Christ's writing in the dust) are entangled in their inscrutability and omniscience.

But the same opacity which invests Belacqua with a Christ-like pleroma also undercuts the roles played by the 'young wom[e]n'. The supposed 'embarrassment' stands in trivialising apposition both to Ruby's defiance of Belacqua and to the adulteress's shame in being hauled before Christ. That Ruby's autonomy would be seen as a kind of affront to notions of female decency is already hinted at in her probing questions: 'The normal woman of sense asks "what?" in preference to "why?" . . . but poor Ruby had always been deficient in that exquisite quality' (*MPTK*, 83). In the Gospel's account, the Pharisees bring the woman to Christ in order to bait him: 'This they said, tempting him, that they might have to accuse him' (John 8: 6). Correspondingly, this passage in the story centres on questions of *his* rather than *her* conduct. As with

Mlle Glain, Belacqua – in cahoots with a narrator clearly under his thumb – mentally wrests back control from an overpowering female presence through his identification with Christ.

The common ground between Belacqua's multiple instances of manipulation and posturing considered in the last two sections (the Dante line, the taxonomic injustice done to the lobster, the self-serving association with Christ) is Belacqua's resistance to situations that are beyond his control. Ultimately, his strategies to maintain the status quo are the kind of behaviour Beckett had denounced in *Proust* but which are nevertheless in keeping with his fictional hero's own fear of unknown consequences: 'our current habit of living is as incapable of dealing with the mystery of a strange sky or a strange room, with any circumstance unforeseen in her curriculum' (*PTD*, 21). The public house Beatrice, Mlle Glain, Ruby and even Nuala Costello represent circumstances unforeseen – 'unforeseen with a vengeance'. Their intrusion, their femaleness, and their otherness are threats to be parried so that the old ego may stay intact. But as with Beckett's need for 'blushing inhibitors and anterotics', Belacqua's defences of indignation and identity conflation intimate that the system is not as sufficiently sealed-off as he might wish. The last phase of his solipsism is at an end.

Beyond Embarrassment, towards Humility

Reflecting on Nagg's joke in *Endgame* (*CDW*, 102–3), Theodor Adorno writes:

> [T]he embarrassment that comes over us when someone laughs about his own words becomes existential; life is still a quintessence only as the quintessence of everything one has to be ashamed of . . . But what shame protests against has its social value: in the moments when the bourgeois act like true bourgeois, they sully the notion of humanity that is the basis for their own pretentions.[67]

Adorno does not develop a distinction between embarrassment and shame in this essay but rather uses the terms synonymously in order to characterise the subjectivity of Beckettian characters who glimpse their place in a world worse-made than a pair of trousers. Such a glimpse, though disenfranchising in its import, nonetheless signals the usefulness of embarrassment in revealing a humbled existence.

A similar realisation of this 'quintessence' prompts Winnie's and Willie's laughter in *Happy Days* when 'formication' is mentioned after the sighting of an emmet. 'I suppose,' Winnie remarks, 'some people might think us a trifle irreverent, but I doubt it ... How can one better magnify the Almighty than by sniggering with him at his little jokes, particularly the poorer ones?' (*CDW*, 150). According to *The Faber Companion to Samuel Beckett*, the joke has at least four components: 'visual (magnifying glass), linguistic (fornication), ontological (reproduction as a cosmic joke), and religious (the Magnificat ...)'.[68] But there is yet a fifth that harks back to Beckett's reading in psychology, to the links between anxiety neurosis and paraesthesia, between dread and embarrassment. As the levity comes to an end, Winnie is left wondering if she and Willie had laughed for the same reasons. In vain, she attempts to assuage her sense of isolation by quoting broken lines from Thomas Gray's 'On a Distant Prospect of Eton College': 'laughing wild ... something something laughing wild amid severest woe' (*CDW*, 150).[69]

By this point in Beckett's career, the comingling of embarrassment and tragedy was becoming a recognisable trope. Estragon's wardrobe malfunction is a case in point which represented for its author a crucial marriage of the laughable and the unhappy. On hearing that Estragon's trousers had not fallen down completely during one of the earliest performances of *En Attendant Godot*, a distressed Beckett wrote to the director:

> [Suzanne] tells me that he holds on to [his trousers] half-way down. This he must not do – it's utterly inappropriate. It wouldn't occur to him at that moment – he doesn't realise they have fallen down. As for any laughs that might greet their falling right down, to the great detriment of that touching final tableau, there's absolutely no objection to them ... The spirit of the play, in so far as it has one, is that nothing is more grotesque than the tragic, and that must be put across right to the end, and particularly at the end. (*L2*, 350; 9 January 1953)

The inappropriate becomes appropriate, even necessary, as the despair of Vladimir and Estragon reaches its highest pitch: Gogo's trousers drop down, after all, because he removes his rope-belt in order to assess its viability as a suicide weapon. The actor's intervention was thus not only inappropriate because the character fails to register what has happened, but also because such a self-protective strategy 'would not occur to him' at a moment when his very selfhood hangs in the balance. This much is suggested by Estragon's eventual equanimity when seeing his trousers around his legs. His response is merely to acknowledge the fact of embarrassment – 'True' (*CDW*, 88) – and then to pull up his trousers in order to go on rather than to save face.

The poetics of middle-to-late Beckettian embarrassment is of course circumscribed by its own decorum: it is improper to will where you have no power.[70] Though the question will be more fully addressed in Chapter 4, it is worth noting here that the Geulingian imperative is incompatible with any statement of value or power even when expressed negatively as shame or embarrassment. As Max Scheler argued, shame (and, by extension, embarrassment) is structurally similar to pride since it is also a 'feeling of self-value'. While its aspect of unworthiness may resemble humility, it does not fully partake of the self-effacement implicit in true humility:

> Shame, in contrast to humility, completely lacks awareness of unworthiness of one's self and a free subordination under the higher value felt in the love of another person ... With respect to humility we are directed in love to the higher value of *another* and become lost in the other's value.[71]

The existential embarrassment that Adorno finds in Beckett approximates Scheler's notion of humility in its opposition to acts of potentiation and affirmations of inherent worth. Put differently, embarrassment or shame (in Adorno's sense and not Scheler's) presents a means of exposing 'the moments when the bourgeois act like true bourgeois'. In Eliot, this is the deflation of *bovarysme*, which can only be achieved by realising one's position in relation to a moral absolute. In Beckett, the dismantling of pride cannot be achieved by an appeal to the transcendental. Rather, the process depends on a continual embrace of weakness, of which existential embarrassment serves both as symptom and instrument.

Generally, this is not the kind of embarrassment found in *More Pricks*. Belacqua's many moments of discomfiture are more properly classed as feelings of self-value. It is this self-value that he attempts to protect by resorting to indignation and delusions of grandeur. But the text does contain a kernel of what would later develop into Beckett's existential embarrassment: the vagabond of 'Walking Out' (*MPTK*, 97–8). Suffering the violation of

Belacqua's Kerry Blue bitch, the man responds without indignation to the indignity of being urinated on: 'he might have been calling a score, his voice was so devoid of rancour'. That this fact would strike Belacqua is apt given his sharpened sensitivity to any invasion of privacy. It is surprising, however, that he would recognise in the man an 'instinctive nobility', since such a realisation implies awareness of a personal shortcoming. As in 'Ding-Dong', Belacqua is 'embarrassed in the last degree'. But here it is not due to a failure on his part or merely to his dog's actions. Rather, it is because the vagabond's humble acceptance of affront puts to shame Belacqua's quickness to anger. He sees in the man what Iris Murdoch says is one of the rarest sightings: a person liberated from the 'anxious tentacles of the self'.[72] The moment of introspection is even more astounding for Belacqua's recognition that any eventual humility he might wish to attain will be the consequence of applied divestment. Unlike the vagabond, he will have to 'acquire' such an attitude. This does not happen, though Belacqua cons himself into a kind of bedside conversion in 'Yellow' when 'sacrifice[ing] his sense of what was personal and proper to himself to the desirability of making a certain impression on other people' (*MPTK*, 155). Nevertheless, the vagabond episode presents an uncanny encounter between the literary transmutation of Beckett's 'misery & solitude & apathy & the sneers' (*L1*, 258) – in short, his sense of superiority – and the kind of humility that takes embarrassment as an unassuageable existential condition. It is the kind of humility that resists kicking against the pricks.

Notes

1. See James Knowlson, *Damned to Fame: The Life of Samuel Beckett* (New York: Simon & Schuster, 1996), 183. See also *L1*, 121, where Beckett regrets his caricature of Thomas Rudmose-Brown as the Polar Bear.
2. For a detailed account of the book's poor sales, see John Pilling, *Samuel Beckett's 'More Pricks than Kicks': In a Strait of Two Wills* (London: Continuum, 2011), 3.
3. In a letter to MacGreevy, Beckett uses 'embarrassed respirations' to refer to the story 'Walking Out' (*L1*, 83); in a letter to Seamus O'Sullivan (80), it serves as shorthand for some of his poems.
4. Theodor W. Adorno, *Notes to Literature*, Vol. 1, ed. Rolf Tiedemann, trans. Shierry Weber Nicholsen (New York: Columbia University Press, 1991), 257.

5. For an overview of Beckett and Costello's romantic involvement see Knowlson, *Damned to Fame*, 186–7.
6. My agreement with the first of Christopher Ricks's three propositions is implicit: 'embarrassment is very important in life'. Ricks, *Keats and Embarrassment* (London: Oxford University Press, 1974), 3.
7. Cf. *Dream*, 233; *MPTK*, 164.
8. See Beckett, 'Psychology Notes', TCD MS 10971/8/22. For her excellent exposition of formication in D. H. Lawrence, see Rachel Murray, *The Modernist Exoskeleton: Insects, War, Literary Form* (Edinburgh: Edinburgh University Press, 2020), 61–94.
9. Ernest Jones, *Papers on Psycho-Analysis* (London: Baillière, Tindall and Cox, 1913), 159.
10. Jones, *Papers*, 159.
11. See, for instance, *CP*, 28, 45; *Watt*, 192; *Eleutheria*, 118; *Company*, 11.
12. Beckett himself shed light on the joke in a letter of 20 March 1983 (*L4*, 607): 'Formication: "sensation of ants creeping over the skin." (*OED*). Cf. French fourmi – fourmillement. Winnie doesn't know the word, confuses with fornication. Willie amused, Winnie appalled, at thought of ants crawling over her.'
13. For the most comprehensive account of Beckett's 'Psychology Notes', see Matthew Feldman, *Beckett's Books: A Cultural History of the Interwar Notes* (London: Continuum, 2006), 78–115.
14. For the most recent and fullest account of Beckett's engagement with quietism, see Andy Wimbush, *Still: Samuel Beckett's Quietism* (Stuttgart: Ibidem-Verlag, 2020).
15. Not entirely bathetically, he also aligns himself with Belacqua (*MPTK*, 152): 'I am what I am. He had read the phrase somewhere and liked it and made it his own.'
16. 'Pudenda of my psyche' is taken and changed from '*verenda* of the soul' in John Earle, *Micro-Cosmography, Or, A Piece of the World* (London: Salisbury, 1786 [1650]), 164–5. In this section the author comments on the vulnerability implicit in close friendship. As *Proust* shows, Beckett saw in such intimacy a threat to artistic creation (*PTD*, 63).
17. Beckett, 'Psychology Notes', TCD MS 10971/7/4.
18. Karin Stephen, *Psychoanalysis and Medicine: A Study of the Wish to Fall Ill* (Cambridge: Cambridge University Press, 1960), 207.
19. Stephen, *Psychoanalysis*, 194.
20. Beckett, 'Psychology Notes', TCD MS 10971/7/4.
21. Feldman, *Beckett's Books*, 101.
22. This has a biographical spring. See *L1*, 222.
23. Silvan Tomkins, *Affect Imagery Consciousness: The Complete Edition* (New York: Springer Publishing Company, 2008), 438–40.

24. Fyodor Dostoevsky, *Notes from Underground* and *The Double*, trans. Jessie Coulson (London: Penguin Books), 121.
25. Victor Frankl, *Man's Search for Meaning*, Revised Edition (New York: Washington Square Press, 1959), 147.
26. See Peter Paul A. Mersch et al., 'Somatic Symptoms in Social Phobia: A Treatment Method Based on Rational Emotive Therapy and Paradoxical Interventions', *Journal of Behavior Therapy and Experimental Psychology* 23.3 (1992): 200.
27. See W. Ray Crozier, *Blushing and the Social Emotions: The Self Unmasked* (New York: Palgrave Macmillan, 2006), 196.
28. In *Dream* (210), the Polar Bear refers to Christ's 'individualism'. The change to 'solipsism' in *More Pricks* invites closer association between Belacqua and the Polar Bear's anti-social Christ.
29. William Cooper, *Flagellation and the Flagellants: A History of the Rod in All Countries from the Earliest Period to the Present Time* (London: William Reeves, 1877), 207.
30. For Lafcadio's discourse on the 'gratuitous crime', see André Gide, *The Vatican Cellars*, trans. Dorothy Bussy (London: Penguin, 1952), 169–71.
31. Beckett claimed in one of his lectures at Trinity College Dublin that there is a 'Coherence in Gide that ... he can't avoid.' Quoted in John Bolin, *Beckett and the Modern Novel* (New York: Cambridge University Press, 2013), 48.
32. Beckett, 'Psychology Notes', TCD MS 10971/7/4.
33. Beckett, 'Psychology Notes', TCD MS 10971/8/4.
34. These 'local arrangements' also bear comparison with 'divorce law reform' and the 'Drink question' in *Eeldrop and Appleplex*. See Chapter 1.
35. An illuminating study of the relation between guilt, punishment and embarrassment in Kafka is Ben Robinson's 'State of Embarrassment: Kafka's "*In der Strafkolonie*"', *The Germanic Review: Literature, Culture, Theory* 90.2 (2015): 101–22.
36. The *OED* defines *antiphlogistic* as 'counteracting or reducing inflammation'. A secondary definition – and one more germane to the tenor of the letter given the mention of anterotics and blushing – is 'allaying excitement'. Beckett also uses the word, or a variant of it, in *More Pricks* (179) and *Dream* (53).
37. There is here a correlate with Kafka's antiquated torture devices in 'The Penal Colony', since – as Robinson argues – the guilt which justifies the existence of these devices belongs to a bygone, pre-Nietzschean era. See 'State of Embarrassment', 101–6.
38. For classic accounts of this rupture, see André Modigliani, 'Embarrassment and Embarrassability', *Sociometry* 31.3 (1968): 313–26; and Goffman, *Interaction Ritual*, 97–112.

39. E. S. Burt, 'Regard for the Other: Embarrassment in the "Quatrième promenade"', *L'Esprit Créateur* 39.4 (1999): 56.
40. For avowed disavowals of the *mot juste*, see *Dream*, 172, 186.
41. This articulate neologism is Ben Robinson's in 'State of Embarrassment', 117.
42. Ricks, *Keats and Embarrassment*, 3.
43. See Jean-Michel Rabaté, *Think, Pig!: Beckett at the Limit of the Human* (New York: Fordham University Press, 2016), 56. Rabaté points out that the word for 'lobster' in *L'Innommable* is 'langouste' and not 'homard'. In her French translation of Beckett's collection, however, Edith Fournier gives 'homard'. In this translation, Belacqua fails to find the Italian for lobster. Samuel Beckett, *Bande et Sarabande*, trans. Edith Fournier (Paris: Les Éditions de Minuit, 1999), 35–6.
44. Dante Alighieri, *The Divine Comedy of Dante Alighieri: The Italian Text with a Translation in English Blank Verse and Commentary, Volume 1: Inferno*, trans. Courtney Langdon (Cambridge, MA: Harvard University Press, 1918), 20.28–30; hereafter *Inf*.
45. For Beckett's other references to this punishment in *Inferno* 20, see *MC*, 4; *CSP*, 145; *CDW*, 191.
46. See, for instance, Seán Lawlor, 'Making a Noise to Drown an Echo: Allusion and Quotation in the Early Poems of Samuel Beckett: 1929–1935', PhD thesis, University of Reading, 2008, 73; Ruby Cohn, *A Beckett Canon* (Ann Arbor: University of Michigan Press, 2001), 46–7.
47. Daniela Caselli, *Beckett's Dantes: Intertextuality in the Fiction and Criticism* (Manchester: Manchester University Press, 2005), 61.
48. For the sources of these quotations, see John Pilling, *A Companion to Dream of Fair to Middling Women* (Tallahassee, FL: Journal of Beckett Studies Books, 2004), 255–6.
49. Beckett's distaste for Carducci is made clear in his university examination preparation notes on Italian Literature (TCD MS 10965), in Matthijs Engelberts, Everett Frost and Jane Maxwell (eds), *Samuel Beckett Today / Aujourd'hui: Notes diverse holo: Catalogues of Beckett's Reading Notes and Other Manuscripts at Trinity College Dublin, with Supporting Essays* (Amsterdam: Rodopi, 2006), 59. See also *LI*, 32–3 and *Dis*, 68.
50. Cf. Caselli, *Beckett's Dantes*, 59; also Kay Gilliland Stevenson, 'Belacqua in the Moon: Beckett's Revisions of "Dante and the Lobster"', in *Critical Essays on Samuel Beckett*, ed. Patrick A. McCarthy (Boston: G. K. Hall, 1986), 41.
51. Hutchinson, *Lateness & Modern European Literature*, 245.
52. In arriving at this last fine phrase, I am pre-empted by Marjorie Garber. See *Shakespeare's Ghost Writers: Literature as Uncanny Causality* (New York: Routledge, 2010), 70.

53. Jason Harding and John Nash, 'An Introduction to Modernist Non-Translation', in *Modernist Non-Translation*, ed. Jason Harding and John Nash (Oxford: Oxford University Press, 2019), 2.
54. See Beckett, 'Psychology Notes', TCD MS 10971/7/4.
55. Cf. 'Yellow', *MPTK*, 152.
56. For a discussion of the other Christs that emerge in Beckett's work, see Andy Wimbush, 'Hey Prestos and Humilities: Two of Beckett's Christs', *Journal of Beckett Studies* 25.1 (2015): 78–95.
57. With markedly similar effect, the phrase 'Jesus Christ Son of God Saviour' features in 'Serena III', a poem that pivots on the pained self-consciousness of a speaker infatuated with an elusive lover. Lawrence Harvey's Dartmouth College notes suggest that Beckett's feelings for Nuala Costello inspired the poem. See *CP*, 290 and 293. The annotation to line 17 ('girls taken strippin') suggests that there is a merging of identities also between the adulteress and Costello, whose name Beckett punned on as 'nu[e] à la côte à l'eau' ('naked on the seashore').
58. See also *DN*, 96, item 666, for Beckett's entry on 'prenatal coenaesthesis'.
59. Max Nordau, *Degeneration*, trans. Max Simon (London: Heinemann, 1913), 249.
60. The context suggests that Beckett's 'consultant' is meant in the first sense given by the *OED*. That is, one who consults another, rather than a consulting physician.
61. Chris Ackerley, 'Samuel Beckett and Max Nordau: Degeneration, Sausage Poisoning, the Bloodied Rafflesia, Coenaesthesis, and the Not-I', in *Beckett after Beckett*, ed. S. E. Gontarski and Anthony Uhlmann (Gainesville: University Press of Florida, 2006), 171–2.
62. Nordau, *Degeneration*, 252.
63. Anthony Cuda's term 'passion scene' is apposite here; it designates the boundary collapse between 'psyche and soma'. *Passions of Modernism*, 14.
64. Bryden also sees the injection administered by Nurse Miranda in 'Yellow' as a phallic-role reversal (*MPTK*, 161). See Mary Bryden, *Women in Samuel Beckett's Prose and Drama* (Lanham: Barnes & Noble Books, 1993), 45.
65. Cf. Beckett (*CP*, 20) 'Serena III': 'Jesus Christ Son of God Saviour His Finger / girls taken strippin that's the idea'.
66. Cf. *DN*, 83, item 578.
67. Adorno, *Notes to Literature*, 256.
68. C. J. Ackerley and S. E. Gontarski, eds, *The Faber Companion to Samuel Beckett* (London: Faber and Faber, 2006), 204.
69. In Chapter 6, I elaborate on the futility of Winnie's search for comfort in half-remembered quotations.

70. Geulincx's axiom of morals is mentioned in the Introduction and also discussed in Chapter 4.
71. Max Scheler, *Person and Self-Value: Three Essays*, ed. and trans. M. S. Frings (Dordrecht: Martinus Nijhoff Publishers, 1987), 19.
72. Iris Murdoch, *The Sovereignty of Good* (London: Routledge, 2014), 101.

3

Mr Eliot's Sermons and Sermonising: Participation, Good Will and Humility in *Murder in the Cathedral*

Still quietly basking in the success of *Murder in the Cathedral* three months after its premiere at the Canterbury Festival on 15 June 1935, Eliot received a letter that was likely to dampen his spirits. Henry, his ever-supportive sibling whose correspondence was seldom other than affectionate and urbane, had now written a protracted missive of rebuke. It complains of Tom's eager assumption of a disingenuous Bloomsbury persona, his tendency to abstract when evidence is wanted, the faux-modest shtick of professing ignorance but actually denigrating an opponent's intelligence, and a schoolmasterly tone that occasionally inflects his prose:

> Sometimes you remind me of a gentleman in full evening dress and white gloves attempting to put something right with the kitchen plumbing without soiling his attire. You are hampered by the fact that, whatever you may want to say, your public expects it to be a worthy permanent addition to the world's literature ... I fear it is largely this, and a certain manner of speaking, which has drawn the fire of so many antagonists. (*L7*, 749)

At the heart of the letter are graver criticisms. One concern is the incompatibility between Eliot's deep-rooted scepticism and his turn towards the Church of England. Another is the motivation behind certain polemical pronouncements and allegedly opportunistic allegiances. The harshest imputation pertains to dramatic posturing and a consequential danger of literary, political and spiritual presumptuousness. If these criticisms seem prompted by the doubts of Thomas Becket in *Murder in the Cathedral* (which Henry had recently read), they nonetheless comprehend a time before the play's inception, asking whether Eliot's practice of chastity, austerity and humility amount to right deeds done for the wrong reason.

To many onlookers, Eliot's religious seriousness after 1927 marked a rupture in his career and life. Those outside (and probably a few within) the fold of Anglo-Catholicism found it difficult to comprehend his need for 'ascetic' and 'violent' spiritual discipline (*L4*, 129). Geoffrey Faber thought his colleague was 'putting [himself] in some danger by the rigidity of [his] way of life' (in *L3*, 710). Ezra Pound, with crosshairs locked more on the Pope of Russell Square than on Old Possum, sniped that Eliot had begun 'disguising himself as a corpse'.[1] And Stephen Spender objected to the stringent askesis that Eliot espoused: '[it] convey[s] to me (and hundreds of other people like me, I think) the feeling of staying in an old school-room chapel unheated by a metal stove and doing nothing but be as consciously miserable as possible' (in *L6*, 159).[2]

It was not only the extreme observances of faith – a vow of celibacy while married, regular fasting, partaking in the sacrament of penance – that provoked doubts.[3] Not failing to take him at his all-too-quotable word in the preface of *For Lancelot Andrewes* (1928), reviewers lamented that Eliot's literary criticism had become inseparably entwined with moral criticism. He was lambasted as an 'intolerant cleric' and patronised for an apparent rejection of 'Modernism for medievalism'.[4] The aura of incredulity did not abate with time. One reviewer of *After Strange Gods* (1934) could admire its author but could not agree with his arguments; another belittled the lectures as sermonising of an 'Auntie Eliot knows best' variety.[5] Possibly the most incisive assessment of the dichotomy that confronted contemporaneous readers – and that also confronts the primary concerns of this book – is presented by Stephen Spender's 1933 review of *The Use of Poetry and the Use of Criticism*: 'I think that Eliot is a writer of genuine humility, and often a writer of great frankness ... Therefore it seems the more surprisingly inconsistent that he often gives the impression of being snobbish and superior.'[6] The statement, itself offered in frank humility, tacitly admits that an allegation of pride rests on the appearance of incompatible attitudes in Eliot's writing.

Given the struggle of many readers to reconcile apparently contradictory aspects of Eliot's writing between 1927 and 1935, the sermon in *Murder in the Cathedral* presents a nexus of tension. On the one hand, it constitutes a crucial dramatic component of a play that was almost universally lauded and, on the other hand, a subtle retracing of a number of Eliot's religious injunctions that alienated many readers. The language of the sermon is interspersed with theological assimilations that recur in essays and lectures since the time of his confirmation. Lancelot Andrewes's imprint is felt in the exposition of the main scripture reading, while F. H. Bradley's diffident scepticism resonates in a phrase ('a disappointment and a cheat') that spectres Eliot's writing elsewhere. The sermon also rehearses some of the dogmatic pronouncements that Eliot made in public addresses of the early 1930s: it is shadowed by the conviction that human benevolence is futile without divine grace and that love for one's neighbour is validated only by a primary love for God. As such, it appears partly informed by the moral superiority and intolerance that so many critics deprecated.

In circling around recurring phrases and influences, my aim is to trace a conceptual genealogy behind the play's sermon. In so doing, I offer a revaluation of *Murder in the Cathedral* as the creative culmination of Eliot's ongoing engagement with secular humanism. In the first two sections I focus on Lancelot Andrewes's reading of Luke 2: 14 and Eliot's use of the Douay-Rheims English bible in order to situate his understanding of good will theologically. The third and fourth sections extend inquiry into Eliot's personal misgivings about human good will and his belief in the doctrine of grace; Eliot's early philosophical scepticism is here cast in relief with his later religious conviction. The final section explores two further parts of Gospel scripture found in the sermon and in contemporaneous public addresses. Here I tease out Eliot's profound belief in proportional adherence to the Summary of the Law and his rejection of humanitarianism that is separated from the love of God, suggesting that the dogmatism which disenchanted many readers is an integral element in Eliot's Christian humility.

Humble Participation

No discussion of the play's sermon can neglect that sermoniser most esteemed by Eliot, Lancelot Andrewes. Reflecting on certain life-long influences in 1961, the poet rather coyly admits indebtedness to the prose of the seventeenth-century preacher: 'there may be a faint reflection in the sermon in *Murder in the Cathedral*' (*CP8*, 464). Of course, borrowings in 'Gerontion' show the Bishop's influence on Eliot to reach back to 1919, the same year in which he grumpily remarked that 'no one reads Andrewes' (*CP2*, 13).[7] By 1926, approaching his confirmation in the Church of England, Eliot began to conceive the importance of Andrewes for his general outlook on literature, politics and religion. Having accepted a commission for a *Times Literary Supplement* (*TLS*) leader that would appear just after the third centenary of the preacher's death (later the centrepiece of *For Lancelot Andrewes: Essays on Style and Order*), he flagged the personal significance of the essay: 'I shall have to clear up my mind and try to come to conclusions, in connection with Bishop Andrewes, *affecting my whole position*' (*L3*, 209, my emphasis).

One of the conclusions to which Eliot came was Andrewes's equipoise between the 'old authority' of Catholic Europe and the 'new culture' of Protestant England. For Eliot, the Reformation was one of the great tragedies of history because it constituted the 'intellectual break up of Europe' (*L3*, 131). At the same time, he saw post-Reformation Catholicism in England as schismatic due to its wilful divorce from the history and tradition of the nation.[8] Andrewes, however, was a man who represented the middle way between two extremes, a man who possessed the roundedness of a consummate Anglo-Catholic:

> [T]he voice of Andrewes is the voice of a man who has a formed visible Church behind him, who speaks with the old authority and the new culture. It is the difference of negative and positive: Andrewes is the first great preacher of the English Catholic Church. (*CP2*, 819)

This *via media* is pertinent to the sermon of *Murder in the Cathedral*. As both Barry Spurr and Chene Heady have shown, Eliot saturated his Catholic protagonist's words with Anglican liturgy, thus achieving an anachronistic consolidation of Rome and England.[9] But the consolidation is even more tellingly achieved by the intertextual presence of Andrewes, whose influence on the sermon goes beyond a mere question of 'style and order'.

As a champion of *Seventeen Sermons on the Nativity*, Eliot could hardly have failed to remember that two of Andrewes's Christmas sermons minutely unpick the same Gospel verse as that featured in Thomas Becket's sermon: Luke 2: 14 ('Glory to God in the highest, and on earth peace to men of good will).[10] The first – Sermon XII, preached before James I at Whitehall on Christmas Day 1618 – had an abiding impact on Eliot. It is woven into

'Gerontion', and a number of its phrases are strategically highlighted for Eliot's own readers in 'Lancelot Andrewes'. But its two central messages – of Christian humility and of the necessity to recognise the consanguinity of Christ's birth and death – are of particular import for *Murder in the Cathedral*. While the second of these messages has direct correlation in the sermon, the first has implicit significance for Thomas's flirtation with spiritual pride and his eventual martyrdom.

Dissecting Luke 2: 12–14, the 1618 Christmas sermon dwells at length on the signs and significance of the nativity.[11] The lowliness of Christ's birth – both humble sign and sign of humility (*'signum humile, signum humilis'*) – suggests at once the nature of the event and the nature which the event seeks to inspire.[12] What matters more than the facticity of the unassuming setting is its discovery. Andrewes insists that the sign of humility is not only the Christ-child's *being* in such modest surroundings, but our *finding* him there:

> For what is *natus est* without *invenientis*? Such a one there "is born." What shall we be the better, if we "find" Him not? As good not born, as not known – to us all one ... *Christus inventus* is more than *Christus natus*. Set down *invenientis* then first.[13]

On the one hand, then, is the humble sign; on the other, its call to humility. We have the humility of the incarnation, of God become man, of kenosis. At the same time, there is the humility of the shepherds – men drawing near the humble sign with sufficient humility to recognise its glory. Stressing the importance of participation, Andrewes defines the difference between signs and miracles. With reproof he writes that 'Signs are taken for wonders', lambasting the Pharisaic insistence on unambiguous evidence of Christ's divinity.[14] The Pharisees are after a 'wonder' and not a 'sign'. They wish to be overwhelmed by theophany rather than submit to the 'lesson of the cratch': Christ was humbly born for the humble.[15]

The second message of the sermon adumbrates the mutually reflective significance of the Incarnation and the Passion – a hallmark, as Erich Auerbach noted, of the 'low style' of the *sermo humilis*, the humble sermon.[16] If the cratch signals humility, it also foreshadows the suffering of the crucifixion. As Thomas does in the play's 'Interlude', Andrewes reminds his congregation that taking the Eucharist on Christmas Day implies the consummation of

Christ's birth through his death. He argues that the discovery of the Incarnation mystery – the *invenientis* of its meaning – depends on a discovery of Christ's sacrifice upon the cross: 'For finding His flesh and blood, ye cannot miss but find Him too . . . For Christ in the Sacrament is not altogether unlike Christ in the cratch.'[17] When Andrewes turns to the final verse of his scripture reading – the verse in *Murder*'s sermon – he asserts that the praise rendered unto God by men achieves its fullest significance when they have partaken of the sacrament: 'For then sure of all other times are we on earth most near to Angelic perfection, then meetest to give glory unto God, then at peace with the whole earth, then a goodwill and purpose in us if ever.'[18]

Conceived under the rubric of recognition and participation, the telescoping of Christ's birth and death is a familiar Eliotic motif. 'Journey of the Magi', another poem indebted to Andrewes, frames Christ's birth as an event of 'Hard and bitter agony' (*P1*, 102). In 'The Cultivation of Christmas Trees', the meaning of Christmas is 'concentrated into a great joy / Which shall be also a great fear' (*P1*, 109–10). And 'Gerontion' assimilates phrases from this and another sermon in the following minatory lines:

> Signs are taken for wonders. 'We would see a sign!'
> The word within a word, unable to speak a word,
> Swaddled with darkness. In the juvescence of the year
> Came Christ the tiger
> . . .
> The tiger springs in the new year. Us he devours . . . (*P1*, 31, 32)

The change of Andrewes's 'Christ is no wild-cat' to 'Christ the tiger' eliminates apophatic hedging in order to suggest the harsh implications of the advent and the crucifixion. Unlike the Magus in Eliot's later poem, who is surprised to find Christ's birth is 'like Death, our death' (*P1*, 102), Gerontion knows the Incarnation to imply terror.[19] The coinage 'juvescence' creates a temporal ambiguity that compresses the new calendar year and the cruel rebirth of spring, effecting a simultaneity that collapses the time between Epiphany and Easter.

In *Murder*'s sermon, too, Thomas sees Christmas morning and Good Friday as coterminous: 'at this same time of all the year . . . we celebrate at once the Birth of Our Lord and Death upon the Cross' (*CPP*, 260). But he is not the only one aware of this concurrence.

At the outset of the play, the charwomen of Canterbury are the first to intuit a temporal contraction:

> Since golden October declined into sombre November
>   And the brown apples were gathered and stored, and the land became sharp brown points of death in a waste of water and mud,
>   The New Year waits, breathes, waits, whispers in darkness.
> (*CPP*, 239)

The lines recall 'Gerontion', not only in its echoes ('New Year', 'whispers', and even the muddy worlds of Canterbury and Thermopylae correspond) but also by duplicating the early poem's concern with paralysed virtue, fatedness and terrible anticipation. It is telling that both texts open with the word 'Here', with an assertion of spatial fixity that eventually reveals itself as temporal fixity also. Yet between Gerontion's 'Here I am, an old man . . . waiting for rain' (*P1*, 31) and the charwomen's 'Here let us stand, close by the cathedral. Here let us wait' (*CPP*, 239) falls the difference between resignation and readiness. Like the Pharisees who wait upon divine revelation, Gerontion passively waits for the drought-breaking rain. Like them, he does not participate in the active discovery of a spiritual truth. By contrast, the waiting of the chorus is deliberate: let us stand, let us wait.

Of course, their participation is not a straightforward act of volition, and their motives, looking toward Thomas's, are in question. Indeed, they are '*forced* to bear witness' (*CPP*, 239, my emphasis). This involvement is awkwardly forced upon the audience too. Reminding us of the play's first performance in the Charterhouse at Canterbury Cathedral, Ria Banerjee writes that the '*here* of the theatre in 1935 was the same as its historical referent from 1170', which coincidence creates 'an altered, almost spatialized relationship between contemporary and historical time'.[20] For his part, Chene Heady shows how the liturgical elements of *Murder* actively enlist audience participation and void objectivity; by doing so, the play erases 'any line that cordons life off from art, the spectator from the literary work'.[21] Perhaps nowhere is the distance between actor and onlooker as forcefully collapsed as at the play's conclusion. Confronted by the Knights' meta-dramatic confidences and accusations, the audience is also 'forced to bear witness', forced to consider their role in a play which Eliot first considered calling 'The Archbishop Murder Case' (see *L7*, 523). In the film of *Murder in the Cathedral*, the First Knight spells out our complicity as a form of *bovarysme*:

> If you have now arrived at a just subordination of the pretensions of the Church to the welfare of the State, remember that it is we who took the first step. You accept our principles; you benefit by our precedent; you enjoy the fruits of our action. Yet we have been dead for nearly 800 years and you still call us murderers. In a moment you will see the Archbishop laid before the altar and acclaimed as a martyr. Then ask yourselves, who is more representative of the thing you are: the man you call a martyr, or the men you call his murderers?[22]

The only other moment of comparable dramatic directness is Thomas's sermon. His apostrophic address similarly involves the audience, similarly deploys questions to discomfit, similarly challenges us to discover not merely the sign but the significance of the eventual martyrdom (or 'murder case'). Behind the rhetorical manoeuvres and behind the hermeneutic injunction stands Andrewes. In addition to the embodied and enacted theatrical elements such as transhistorical simultaneity and liturgical communion, the Christmas sermon of 1618 reinforces a theology of participation. The sum effect is to achieve one of Eliot's conditions for an authentic theatrical experience: 'the performers and the audience should be in direct contact, and there should be *participation*' (*CP8*, 40, Eliot's emphasis).

Graced Good Will

The other nativity sermon likely to have guided Eliot's hand was delivered by Andrewes in 1619 and focused exclusively on Luke 2: 14. A key point for the sermon in *Murder* concerns the translation of 'good will'. Permitting himself scholarly flourish before a monarch known for his keen interest in theology, Andrewes notes that the Greek and Latin versions apply different cases and thus nuance meaning in different ways: εὐδοχία is in the nominative and extends 'good will' itself to 'men', whereas *bonae voluntatis* is in the genitive and limits 'peace' ambiguously to those who are themselves 'of good will' or to those who receive God's favour.[23] The Authorized Version of 1611, to which Andrewes contributed as translator, follows the Greek nominative ('and towards men good-will'), while the Latin rendering which accompanies the English at the head of the sermon keeps both cases alive: the Vulgate's genitive (*bonae voluntatis*) is parenthetically supplemented by 'good will' in the nominative (*bona voluntas*).[24] For Andrewes, however, the spirit trounces the letter of the verse: '"To men a good-will;" or "to men of good-will" – no great matter, so long as εὐδοχία refers to God and to His "good pleasure," not to men or any will of theirs.'[25]

In several essays of the 1930s, Eliot concurs with the emphasis on divine will over human good will. In 'Catholicism and International Order' (1933), the humanitarian acts of 'non-Catholics of good will' are said to amount only to 'vague benevolence' because they are not grounded in 'moral conversion' (*CP4*, 542). 'The Modern Dilemma' (1933) reiterates this belief and the phrase 'vague benevolence' (*CP4*, 813) once more. And in *The Idea of a Christian Society* (1939), written in the aftermath of the Munich Agreement and published a month after Hitler's invasion of Poland, Eliot affirmed that 'only in humility, charity and purity – and most of all perhaps humility – can we be prepared to receive the grace of God without which human operations are vain' (*CP5*, 735).

Though not an exhaustive catalogue of Eliot's rejection of 'vague' or humanitarian benevolence, the above statements – along with Andrewes's careful treading around 'good will' – throw into relief the final choice of biblical translation in *Murder*'s sermon. As it appears in the *Complete Poems and Plays*, the wording of the Gospel reading from St Luke ('Glory to God in the highest, and on earth peace to men of good will') is not taken from the Authorized Version, as it had been in the first three editions of the play, but from the Douay-Rheims Bible.[26] Robert W. Ayers was the first to point out that Eliot opted for the English Catholic translation in the play's fourth edition, though no guesses for this change have yet been ventured.[27] I propose that the annotations in the Douay-Rheims provide a clue, since these link up with the play's emphasis on participation.

With its New Testament published in 1582, the translators of this English Catholic bible sought to supply a palliative to Protestant translations of Holy Scripture. Their preface states that the work of translation was not inspired by the 'erroneous opinion . . . that the holy Scriptures should always be in our mother tongue'; rather, it was necessitated by 'special consideration of the present time, state, and condition of our country, unto which, diverse things are either necessary, or profitable and medicinable now, that otherwise in the peace of the Church were neither much requisite, nor perchance wholly tolerable'.[28] Counter-Reformation sentiment, however, is not of concern for Eliot's play; as I have already suggested, harmony between the Church of England and the Catholic Church is one of the sermon's subtle achievements. A more likely explanation for the choice of translation – and one which accords with Andrewes's emphasis on God's goodness – is found in the Douay-Rheims's annotation to Luke 2: 14. The gloss on 'men of good will' reads as follows: 'The birth of Christ giveth not peace of mind or salvation but to such as be of good will, because he worketh not our good against our wills, but our wills concurring.'[29] Here is conjunction between the grace of the Incarnation and the necessity of human submission and humility in order to partake of that grace. As Sermon XII makes clear, Andrewes similarly sees in the Lucan nativity account the significance of such 'wills concurring'.[30] Though grace is given, it requires participation.

That said, neither Andrewes nor the Douay-Rheims translators suggest level standing between divine and human operations. For his part, Andrewes stresses that no mortal *finding* of the sign is possible without its heavenly *gratuitousness*. His exegesis moves from the sign's literal manifestation (the star of Bethlehem, the choir of Angels) to its spiritual signification (the humble surroundings indicating Christ's humility to submit to temporal conditions). Finally, he arrives at its 'co-indicant' theological meaning, love:

> Indicant it is of humility; co-indicant of that which in Him and on His part, as pride on ours, was the cause that made Him stoop to this humility, and that was His love. He left *gloriam in excelsis* for εὐδοχία ἐν ἀνθρώποις, 'His glory on high,' for 'His good-will towards men.' It was a sign of love too this.[31]

Between the two Andrewes sermons there is thus perfect consistency in the exposition of good will: whether 'good-will towards men' or 'peace to men of good-will', good will itself is constituted by God's love and grace. This view is also compatible with St Augustine's in his *Miscellany of Questions in Response to Simplician*, which is cited in the Douay-Rheims annotation and specifically dwells on the relation between grace and good works.[32]

While *Murder*'s deployment of the Catholic bible could be constellated within the broader phenomenon of British intellectuals turning to Rome in the 1930s, such a reading would have to contend with the fact that Eliot made only this single scriptural substitution. The next verse quoted by Thomas (John 14: 27) returns us to the Authorized Version, which subsequently resonates in the Introit at the opening of Part II: 'And he kneeled down and cried with a loud voice: / Lord, lay not this sin to their charge' (*CPP*, 264).³³ In an unpublished address of 1933, Eliot pointedly stated his preference for the Authorized Version's translation of these verses from Acts 7: 59–60 over that given in the Roman Missal (via the Douay-Rheims): '"kneeled down" is more to my mind than "falling to his knees"' (*CP4*, 700). The reasons are not explicitly adduced, but given Thomas's conscious sacrifice, the King James offers a clear statement of participatory humility. Another reason for *Murder*'s sustained use of this translation is Eliot's admiration for it. In the same address, he takes it as universally recognised that the 'Bible of the Authorised Version is the greatest masterpiece of English literature', and that it is superior to all other translations (*CP4*, 695, 699). Much later, he would identify 'English prose style' (*CP8*, 530) as a criterion for judging the value of a biblical translation.

However, it is Eliot's other two criteria that explain his eventual use of the Douay-Rheims: doctrine and accuracy of translation. The Catholic bible's scholarly apparatus leads onto Augustine's emphasis on divine good will, which, in its turn, corresponds with Andrewes's position. For Augustine, 'good works ... do not beget grace but are begotten by grace'.³⁴ In both of Andrewes's sermons, 'good will' is clearly a divine property. Following these, Thomas concludes that martyrdom is the 'design of God' and an outflow of 'His love for men' (*CPP*, 261). The Douay-Rheims and the Andrewes sermons also converge in their encouragement of active submission on the part of believers. Augustine, citing the Gospel verse in question, affirms that '[i]t is necessary ... to will and to run, for it was not without purpose that it was said, *Peace on earth to men of good will*'.³⁵ Andrewes declares the necessity of humility in order to understand the Incarnation and the Passion as the kenotic expression of grace. And Thomas – having been tempted by spiritual pride – now recognises that a martyr must become 'the instrument of God' and 'los[e] his will in the will of God' (*CPP*, 261). Both these components – the primacy of grace and the secondary response of man – are balanced in the Lucan verse. While the Authorized Version does nothing to diminish this balance, Eliot likely saw in the Douay-Rheims a correspondence with Andrewes he was happy to emphasise on revising the play for its fourth edition. It is in this light that his choice of translation should be read, and so too his scepticism about human operations removed from the love of God.

Human Benevolence: A Deception and a Cheat

The question of scepticism brings me to F. H. Bradley and the 'colouring' he gives to *Murder in the Cathedral*.[36] Following his palimpsest evocation of Good Friday on Christmas, Thomas asks whether the angels' proclamation of peace amid a time of strife is spurious: 'Does it seem to you that the angelic voices were mistaken, and that the promise was a disappointment and a cheat?' (*CPP*, 260). The answer – if foreign and domestic concord, communal stability and personal security are taken as criteria – is yes. But 'disappointment and a cheat', with the sceptical freight it drags into the play, intimates that human measures of peace and goodness are themselves illusory.

Eliot encountered the phrase in the conclusion to F. H. Bradley's *Principles of Logic* (1883). Here Bradley communicates the hope that the phenomenal realm might ultimately gesture towards a supreme reality that is not entirely incompatible with what we already know:

> That the glory of this world in the end is appearance leaves the world more glorious, if we feel it a show of some fuller splendour; but the sensuous curtain is a *deception and a cheat*, if it hides some colourless movement of atoms, some spectral woof of impalpable abstractions, or unearthly ballet of bloodless categories.[37]

Eliot's esteem of the passage is evinced in his borrowings and recasting. He claims in a graduate essay that Bertrand Russell's *Principia Mathematica* is 'directing with passionate enthusiasm his unearthly ballet of bloodless alphabets' (*CP1*, 90). He also quotes the Bradley passage as an example of masterly prose in 1917 and again a decade later (*CP1*, 540 and *CP3*, 306).

But by severing 'deception and a cheat' from its epistemological spring and inserting it into theological contexts, Eliot made the phrase his own. In one form or another, it occurs six times in his writing, invariably as a kind of shorthand for the hollowness of human good will divorced from the love of God.[38] *Murder in the*

Cathedral twice employs the words, first in the Four Tempters' catalogue of vain earthly pursuits (*CPP*, 256), and then in the sermon itself. In the address where he dismisses the 'vague benevolence' of non-Catholics (see above), Eliot asserts that 'the second half of the Summary of the Law is a *delusion and a cheat* if you erase the first half' (*CP4*, 537, my emphasis).[39] Still earlier, he had declared in his *TLS* review of Bradley's *Ethical Studies* that humanist morality uninformed by 'some doctrine of Grace' constitutes the 'same inoperative benevolence which we have all now and then received – and often resented – from our fellow human beings. In the end it is a *disappointment and a cheat*' (*CP3*, 311, my emphasis). And in a telling letter that documents Eliot's estimation of 'saintliness and heroism' (*L3*, 711), we encounter a profound expression of the vanity he sees in human relations when undirected by divine grace:

> if one makes the relation of man to man (or still more to woman) the highest good, I maintain that it turns out a *delusion and a cheat*. But if two people . . . love God still more than they love each other, then they enjoy greater love of each other than if they did not love God at all . . . [F]or one's relations to one's friends and lovers, apart from the love of God, always, in my experience, turn out a *delusion and a cheat*. Either they let you down, or you let them down, or both; but no human relation is in itself, satisfactory. (*L3*, 712, my emphasis; 18 September 1927)

Circumscribed at either end by Eliot's confirmation and his sundering from Vivien, the bitterness in these reiterations cannot wholly be isolated from biography. When he wrote the above letter to Geoffrey Faber, Eliot had already resigned himself to an 'absolutely hostile' (*L2*, 627) marital situation and would within the next year take a vow of celibacy. By the time he instructed solicitors to draw up a deed of separation in 1933, lovelessness had reached its nadir. Yet to see Eliot's attitude towards interpersonal relations – whether in the form of romantic, friendly or neighbourly love – as defined solely by his tortuous private life is to neglect two contiguous aspects: an entrenched philosophical scepticism about human good will stretching back as far as his graduate years, and an eventual belief that divine grace is the sanctioning element in our love for others.

Philanthropy as an end in itself, particularly in a liberal humanistic cast, is a major point of contention in the writings of the early

1930s. Eliot held grave doubts about the 'myth of human goodness [that] replaces belief in Divine Grace' (*CP3*, 117), a myth he closely associated with his family's Unitarian faith. But as certainly as these doubts were tinged by a definite theological perspective during his Christian life, they were first shaded by the intractable scepticism he evinced as a philosophy graduate. The 'Report on the Ethics of Kant's *Critique of Practical Reason*' is a representative piece of doubting inquiry. It also supplies an uncanny lexical background against which to interpret the eventual animadversion of 'vague' or 'inoperative benevolence'.[40]

In the essay, a twenty-four-year-old Eliot boldly details certain limits of the categorical imperative, targeting Kant's conception of good will and his notion of humanity as an end in itself. At the start of his *Groundwork of the Metaphysics of Morals* (1785), Kant explains that good will is the only pure and unconditional good that exists; its goodness is a priori and thus not contingent on any positive outcomes it might achieve.

> A good will is . . . only [good] because of its volition, that is, it is good in itself and, regarded for itself, is to be valued incomparably higher than all that could merely be brought about by it in favour of some inclination and indeed, if you will, the sum of all inclinations.[41]

Eliot admits the position ('"good will" is the only <u>direct</u> value') but immediately relativises it in a way that cuts across the grain of Kant's deontology. '[I]t is soon seen,' Eliot writes, 'that good will is an indirect value also: a world without contingent goods is not a good world' (*CP1*, 54). The contention is that the good will is not impervious to relations and external objects. Ultimately, it 'must be a particular good will' – that of an individual – and thus the 'categorical imperative has meaning only in relation to . . . arbitrarily chosen goal[s]'. Whether Eliot's qualifications are valid is not of concern; more significant is his scepticism about a goodness that is fundamental to all humanity and from which moral actions are supposed to emanate.

The second point of attack is Kant's postulate of humanity as an end in itself and the famous imperative that issues from it: 'So act that you use humanity, whether in your own person or in the person of any other, always at the same time as an end, never merely as a means.'[42] What upholds this imperative is a belief in human beings' absolute worth, which in turn predicates on the givenness of the good will. Eliot is doubtful about humanity's position within Kant's kingdom of ends. He opines that 'it is not only inexact but dangerous . . . to regard humanity . . . as more than a provisionally postulated end' (*CP1*, 54–5). Further on he puts the case even more strongly: 'If humanity is the end (absolutely), the idea of the *Summum Bonum* [the highest good] is only a means. And unless the *Summum Bonum* is the end, humanity is meaningless' (*CP1*, 55).[43] He claims that the strictures which apply to Kant's deontology also apply to his teleology; means and ends are provisional. So while the preservation of human dignity is a commendable goal, it is nonetheless subject to each individual's acknowledgement and active pursuit of it as such, which is far from given: 'as the same situation <u>never</u> recurs, one may say that the categorical imperative is *always*, or that it is <u>never</u>, *operative*' (*CP1*, 54, my italics, Eliot's underlining). On the one hand, the categorical imperative is always operative in the realm of ideas where the contingencies of time and perspective are void. On the other hand, it is never operative in reality, since no two moral agents can live through the exact same experience. In either case, humanity as an end is subject to 'inoperative benevolence', which is not to say that good will has no value, but only that its value is relative rather than absolute.

Bolstered by a defined theological outlook, this early philosophical scepticism about human good will lingers in *Murder in the Cathedral*. The Four Tempters, speaking together like the self-deceiving Hollow Men, declare man's life to be empty and insignificant as they submit into evidence a catalogue of vanities:

> Man's life is a cheat and a disappointment;
> All things are unreal,
> Unreal or disappointing:
> The Catherine wheel, the pantomime cat,
> The prizes given at a children's party,
> The prize awarded for the English Essay,
> The scholar's degree, the statesman's decoration.
> All things become less real, man passes
> From unreality to unreality.
> This man is obstinate, blind, intent
> On self-destruction. (*CPP*, 256)

There is a poignant escalation in these anachronistic instances of worldly desire. They invite us to recognise Eliot's (as much as

Thomas's) literary, social and even spiritual ambitions. Implicit in all these deceptions, but particularly in the determination for 'self-destruction', is a wariness of well-meaning but inoperative benevolence. This wariness is glimpsed elsewhere in Eliot. 'Choruses from *The Rock*' casts prayerful doubt over the 'man of excellent intention and impure heart', since 'the heart is deceitful above all things, and desperately wicked' (*P1*, 165). The sentiment would resurface as the third 'gift reserved for age' in *Little Gidding*:

> the shame
> Of motives late revealed, and the awareness
> Of things ill done and done to others' harm
> Which once you took for exercise of virtue. (*P1*, 205)

And, again uncannily troubling the margins, 'Gerontion' declares that 'Unnatural vices / Are fathered by our heroism' (*P1*, 32).

What unifies the various types of disappointment in *Murder in the Cathedral* is the satisfaction of human will. But when the phrase recurs moments later in the sermon, an inversion is achieved. Having been primed by the choric Tempters to see temporal accomplishment as 'unreal', the audience is now asked to consider an eternal truth. Thomas rhetorically asks whether the prevalence of strife on earth means that the 'angelic voices were mistaken, and that the promise was a disappointment and a cheat' (*CPP*, 260). And, finally aware that to 'do the right deed for the wrong reason' (258) is tantamount to sin, he urges pursuit of a peace that is beyond human design.

Bradley and the Doctrine of Grace

If the essay on Kant shows Eliot's philosophical misgivings about an unfluctuating human good will to be underpinned by epistemological variance, his later theological misgivings pivot on an unwavering belief in the doctrines of the incarnation, original sin and grace.[44] The first two of these, as Eliot would have known, are directly addressed in the Thirty-Nine Articles of Religion as sanctioned by the Church of England since 1571. Grace, however, is treated more tangentially and presents a complex matter, as ceded in the Church of England's 1922 report on Christian doctrine.[45]

In the Articles it is stated that fallen humanity cannot of its own volition turn to God, nor can it do any good deeds 'pleasant and acceptable to God, *without the grace of God by Christ preventing us,* that we may have a good will, and working with us, when we have that good will'.[46] An exposition on the Articles explains that there are thus two types of grace. The first is prevenient grace, which has its foundation in Christ's freely given sacrifice. It is this type of grace to which the lines in *East Coker* refer: 'if we do well, we shall / Die of the absolute paternal care / That will not leave us, but *prevents* us everywhere' (*P1*, 190, my emphasis).[47] The second type of grace is cooperative grace, which enables the 'renewed man to exert himself in the strength of that grace, and to work under its influence'.[48] Declaring that faith in Christ is the sole criterion for salvation and that good works flow from such faith, the Articles emphatically view the grace of Christ as the sanctioning element for any good deed that is acceptable to God. Without this grace, no moral action has any worth.

Such an understanding of cooperative grace is pointedly reflected in Thomas's sermon: '[A martyrdom] is never the design of man; for the true martyr is he who has become the instrument of God, who has lost his will in the will of God . . .' (*CPP*, 261). Eliot would later amend these words slightly in the film of *Murder in the Cathedral* in order to emphasise cooperative grace:

> A martyrdom is never the design of man; for the true martyr is he who has become the instrument of God, *who has lost his will in the will of God, not lost it but found it, for he has found freedom in submission to God.*[49]

Augustine and Andrewes again come into focus: God's love is inaugural; it foregoes, initiates and ultimately sustains human love.

Surprisingly, F. H. Bradley may also be mentioned in this connection with grace. With the first republication of *Ethical Studies* in 1927, Eliot took the opportunity to bring wider public attention to the British Idealist's thought and 'attitude of extreme diffidence' (*CP3*, 304). As much as the review extolled Bradley's virtues as prose writer and ethicist, it also sought to score a polemical victory for religion against humanism. A line in the sand is drawn between a slightly plumped-up Bradley and a somewhat hollowed-out Matthew Arnold and Irving Babbitt. Bradley is startlingly compared with John Henry Newman, his philosophy labelled as 'catholic, civilized, and universal' (the third adjective cancelling out the suggestion that the first is meant in its general etymological sense) and his avowal of Protestant belief suppressed through selective quotation.[50] In their turn, Arnold and Babbitt are harshly yoked together in their failure to perceive the necessity of conforming one's private will to that of the divine:

> [I]t is a process which neither Arnold nor Professor Babbitt could accept. But [if] there is a 'will of God,' as Arnold, in a hasty moment, admits, then some *doctrine of Grace* must be admitted too; or else the 'will of God' is just the same *inoperative benevolence* which we have all now and then received – and often resented – from our fellow human beings. In the end it is a *disappointment and a cheat*. (CP3, 311, my emphasis)

Ostensibly demonstrating the suitability of Bradley's prose for his subject, Eliot's review rehearses a minor skirmish in the 'Concluding Remarks' of *Ethical Studies*. With lengthy quotations from the book, the essay offers a ventriloquised critique of Arnold's dual emphasis on the salvific function of 'righteousness' and the need for verifiability in religion. Bradley's footnotes point the reader to Arnold's two-part defence of *Literature and Dogma* (1873) in the pages of *The Contemporary Review*, where Arnold explains that his efforts were born out of the conviction of the 'indispensableness of the Bible'.[51] But Bradley is impatient with what he sees as a fundamentally vacillating Christianity. He derides Arnold's religious outlook as 'literary clap-trap' that '[leaves us] with the assertion that "righteousness" is "salvation" or "welfare"', imputing to his contemporary a facile eudemonistic outlook that eliminates the need for the grace of God.[52]

The implicit charge of Pelagianism is Eliot's cue. His own critique of Arnold focuses on the claim that the function of culture is to make 'reason and the will of God prevail' – a mantra repeated several times in *Culture and Anarchy*.[53] Eliot's concern is that the 'will of God' subserves the judgement of an anthropocentric culture that entertains thoughts of perfectibility.[54] As mentioned in the Introduction, for Eliot the belief in human perfectibility is anathema to the doctrine of original sin. Yet the charge brought against Arnold is that he conceives of good will as impelled by humanity's own rational capacity – by 'our best self' or 'right reason' (L3, 310) – rather than by grace. Eliot's critique of Arnold (and Babbitt) is analogous to his critique of Kant: both the categorical imperative and 'our best self' are seen as standards for conduct subject to individual caprice. What Eliot sought instead was something more substantial than 'sweetness and light and culture' (*L5*, 210). Twelve years after the publication of 'Cousin Nancy', Arnold still remained the 'guardian of [a] faith' (*P1*, 24) which Eliot could not accept.

Given that *Culture and Anarchy* defines 'our best self' in relation to the importance of institutional checks and against 'doing as one likes' – and given his own endorsement of the Hulmean belief in the necessity of institutions – Eliot too glibly equates 'our best self' with 'Matthew Arnold slightly disguised' (*CP3*, 310).[55] His reading of the term is qualified by its perceived relation to Irving Babbitt's 'inner check', the implication being that excessive emphasis is placed on the individual's capacity to supply the necessary restraint where the 'curbs of class, or authoritative government, and of religion' are found wanting.[56] Any doctrine of self-control, Eliot explains elsewhere, only has significance within religion (*CP3*, 457). This is the main complaint against both Arnold and Babbitt: the former, a proto-humanist, allows 'Culture ... to usurp the place of Religion' (*CP4*, 178), while the latter attempts to make 'humanism itself into a Religion' (*CP3*, 457).[57]

In 'The Humanism of Irving Babbitt' (1928), Eliot diagnoses the failings of the ethical principles of his old professor as a 'dread of organized religion' (*CP3*, 458), which apparently springs from a belief that religion petrifies the autonomous individual spirit. This fear, Eliot suggests, is due to a misconception of the way in which religion directs morality. It is not the function of the Church to police bad behaviour, but to engender a supreme '*inner* control' which repairs to an absolute moral standard and so differs from the '[precarious] private notions and ... judgement' (*CP3*, 458) by which the humanist sets his moral compass. Implicit in this understanding is the belief in grace, which is 'prior ... to that "supernatural" goodness or sanctification which results from the work of the Holy Spirit *in and through* the Church'.[58] Though Eliot does not mention it directly, his claim about Babbitt's misapprehension is very probably elicited by the negative conception of grace put forth in *Democracy and Leadership* (1924).[59] Here Babbitt hails the 'critical attitude' of the Reformers because it paved the way for independence and 'private judgement' (the language pays subtle homage to the self-reliance of Emerson and Kant's *Aufklarung*). But he also laments the resurgence of the doctrine of grace, since it proved a stumbling block on the way to enlightenment: 'the Pauline and Augustinian form that a Luther or a Calvin sought to revive, was the very negation of self-reliance; it was designed to make man feel his utter and helpless dependence on the divine will'.[60]

Neither Luther nor Calvin, but certainly Paul, Augustine and Andrewes inform Eliot's understanding of the doctrine of grace. And if 'our best self' and the 'inner check' amount to a disappointment and a cheat, if the benevolence of Arnold and Babbitt is inoperative because of a failure to admit the role of grace, Eliot finds a humbler, more doctrinally sound alternative in Bradley's thinking:

> How can the human-divine ideal ever be my will? The answer is, Your will it never can be as the will of your private self, so that your private self should become wholly good. To that self you must die, and by faith be made one with the ideal. You must resolve to give up your will, as the mere will of this or that man, and you must put your whole self, your entire will, into the will of the divine. That must be your one self, as it is your true self; that you must hold to both with thought and will, and all other you must renounce.[61]

Eliot quotes this passage (*CP*3, 310) from *Ethical Studies* and cedes that it might appear compatible with both Arnold's and Babbitt's 'eminent doctrines'. It acknowledges imperfection, endeavours towards its opposite and conveys a message of self-abnegation. It also advocates a kind of surrender which risks dissolving the believer and the object of belief into an undifferentiated monistic whole: pursued to its logical conclusion, Bradley's philosophy 'might diminish the value and dignity of the individual' (310). But the issue is not laboured, and it appears that Eliot chooses not to expand on this danger since there are polemical points to be scored: just like good 'Arnold-baiting', persuasive Bradley-plumbing requires strategic lighting. Helen Thaventhiran has written perceptively about Eliot's forestalling tactics when quoting, but the present case rather gives the impression of an eagerness to pass over objections rather than a readiness to meet them: 'in any event' and 'in all events' (310–11), no matter the metaphysical niceties, Bradley is not like Arnold or Babbitt.[62] And the fundamental difference is that no gradation of selfhood such as the schema of ordinary or best self is admitted. 'The distinction,' Eliot asserts, 'is between the individual as himself and no more, a mere numbered atom, and the individual in communion with God' (310). The highest good, then, is not determined by the beckoning of a better self, but by a spiritual reality that surpasses mere morality.

For Bradley, like Eliot, religion alone facilitates such transcendence while at the same time preserving the practical necessity of morality. In *Appearance and Reality*, religion is characterised by a profound humility through which individuals recognise the object of devotion as infinitely greater than themselves and so feel 'quite powerless and worthless'.[63] In words mirrored by Eliot's letter to Geoffrey Faber (see above), Bradley comments on the existence of 'incomplete forms of religion' such as the adoration of a lover or commitment to a cause, explaining that these are incommensurate with the 'highest sense of religion' in which there is one unchanging object of good.[64] Love or causes may inspire fear, but they are also susceptible to feelings of rebellion. Religion, seen in contrast and understood as an awe-inspired realisation of humility, implies 'moral prostration'.[65] This moral prostration is not some kind of anti-humanist degradation of the will which culminates in aboulia or Calvinist notions of predestination, but rather an acknowledgement that religion fulfils morality.[66]

Logically, morality is an ideal which can never be attained, since to do so implies a negation of its very conditions: 'Where there is no imperfection there is no ought, where there is no ought there is no morality.'[67] In itself, morality predicates on a frustration of its ends, and it is only through religion that this frustration can be overcome. Both *Ethical Studies* and *Appearance and Reality* posit religion as a practical belief system inscribed with moral duty. The difference, again, between 'mere' morality and morality realised within religion is that while the former is ontologically locked in potentiation ('ought to'), the latter is actual: 'The importance for practice of this religious point of view is that what is to be done is approached, not with the knowledge of a doubtful success, but with the forefelt certainty of already accomplished victory.'[68]

This seeming paradox – to strive for the fulfilment of what is already fulfilled – constitutes the crux of Bradley's conception of faith. Its formula is belief working in conjunction with the will; faith has both an intellectual and a volitional component. Dichotomously, the former is the ideal of morality (perfection) which is now realised as a result of its giftedness (or grace), while the latter is the continued practice of morality despite the fulfilment of its end (as prescribed by belief).[69] Belief is thus made up of the intellectual assent that the ideal is real, or that goodness is consummated, and that this consummation is independent of my actions. This, in turn, nuances the moral prostration experienced in religion as an attitude of humility in which I simultaneously acknowledge the grace of an infinitely greater Other, and also that this grace depends on none of my own moral endeavour. What prevents such belief from culminating in quietist despair is the volitional component. The will, for its part, locates faith in a practical sphere and depends for its realisation on operating in spite of the belief that evil is already overruled. Faith's maxim, in Bradley's words, is this: 'Be sure that opposition to good is overcome, and nevertheless act as if it were there.'[70]

Though Eliot recognised the danger of Bradley's monism, he approved its dual emphasis on belief and will – the striving of the Christian sinner on the surety of his salvation – since it approaches '*some* doctrine of Grace' (my emphasis). He knew that the philosopher's quasi-mystical ethics, though shaded by Christian doctrine, was by no means orthodox.[71] But more triumphant in polemic than right in reason, the *TLS* essay sought a means of realigning theories of culture and conduct with Christian religion and, more specifically, with a doctrinal position which regards as inoperative any human endeavour divorced from the love of God. If it is as 'colouring ... that Bradley stayed in [Eliot's] mind', as Hugh Kenner remarked, it is the same colouring that tints Thomas Becket's message: worldly peace and good will are a disappointment and a cheat, and only divine grace promises some fuller show of splendour.[72]

'Not as the world gives': Christian Sacrifice

A second verse of scripture in the sermon of *Murder in the Cathedral* reinforces this theme of divine peace. Having considered the angelic annunciation of good tidings at the Saviour's birth, Thomas reflects on Christ's message to his disciples shortly before His death on the cross: 'Peace I leave with you, my peace I give unto you: not as the world gives, give I unto you' (John 14: 27). The tension between joy and mourning is drawn out by the tension between the two Gospel passages: if the Lucan verse exults, the Johannine verse exhorts. To make sense of this exhortation, I now turn to some of Eliot's contemporaneous public addresses on Christian morality – what might harshly be called his sermonising. My focus is on those pieces that directly cast light on the second verse of scripture in Thomas's sermon and, by extension, Eliot's understanding of Christian engagement.

Prior to *Murder in the Cathedral*, John 14: 27 occurs in two of Eliot's public addresses. The first of these is 'The Search for Moral Sanction' (1932), penultimate in a series of BBC radio broadcasts discussing the relation between politics, science, economics and religion.[73] Responding at the outset to letters received after the first programme ('Christianity and Communism'), Eliot draws sharp division between the 'philosophies' of communism and Christianity. 'It may seem a paradox,' he says,

> but the Christian wants a better social order just [because] he believes that the world is transient and secondary. And in Christianity there must always be a residue of Tragedy in this world and its satisfactions. There are very profound implications, in the terrible words: '*Not as the world gives, give I unto you*' (*CP4*, 446, my emphasis).

The capitalised 'Tragedy' serves as a shorthand recapitulation of moral values Eliot had catalogued in the preceding two talks. During the first he declared that Christianity provided him personally with the only viable scheme within which to maintain his 'belief in holy living and holy dying, in sanctity, chastity, humility, austerity' (*CP4*, 428). The following broadcast supplied a near-verbatim axiology, adding only 'asceticism' and 'the belief in [Christian] Tragedy' (*CP4*, 439).

The second address that alludes to the Gospel scripture and similarly enfolds it in a call for austere religious discipline is 'The Modern Dilemma' (originally 'Two Masters'), delivered in 1933 to the Boston Association of Unitarian Ministers. Hardly enthused about the prospect of addressing Unitarian clergymen although eventually yielding to repeated invitation, Eliot made little effort to hide his espousal of Catholic doctrine and his distaste for Unitarianism. A specious disclaimer that the lecture does not present 'an argument in favor of Catholicism' (*CP4*, 811) is soon undercut by an unflattering comparison between 'conservatives' and Catholics. Conservatives are concerned with mere 'habits and conventions', the vestigial mores of preceding Christian generations. They fail to see pride as a deadlier sin than sexual immorality and do not realise the spiritual danger implicit in feeling virtuous. As a consequence, both their denouncement of what Eliot had once called 'Bad Form' (*L3*, 228) and their over-estimation of ethical and reformist action implicate them in lukewarm humanitarianism. The fundamental distinction between the conservative and the Catholic, as Eliot sees it, is a belief in the supernatural.

Despite Eliot's weariness with the debate over humanism and religion which dominated so much of his thought and writing between 1928 and 1930, 'The Modern Dilemma' reiterates two central concerns from that period: an acknowledgement of human sinfulness, and the need to submit to an authority higher than that of personal conscience.[74] Barely concealing his contempt for the Unitarian soteriology of character and progress, he strikes an unyielding medieval pose, declaring the modern world defective on two counts: 'the decay of the study of Latin and Greek and the dissolution of the monasteries' (*CP4*, 813).[75] If the perceived privation is tinged by nostalgia for a pre-Reformation world, it is shaded by the need for the asceticism which issues from the 'sense of sin' (813). Eliot draws a direct parallel between 'self-abnegation, self-discipline, and the love of God' (813). He also argues that the 'ascetic ideal ... seems to me implied in the Summary of the Law' (813). In barbed language he denounces an ethics pursuant of happiness and pits against it a meshed paraphrase of the Summary of the Law and John 14: 27, the second verse in Thomas's sermon: 'But the real love of our neighbour, in and for God, means transcending the bounds of love and benevolence as we know them, and reaching a plane at which what is given is not as the world gives' (813–14).

Three months later Eliot would again invoke the Summary of the Law. In 'Catholicism and International Order', the emphasis is less on austerity and more on a proportional observance of love for God and love for one's neighbour. Without the former, the latter lapses into mere 'humanitarianism' because of an 'excessive love of created beings' (*CP4*, 537). With its echo of St John of the Cross, the statement harks back to the desolate cannibal-isle imagined in *Sweeney Agonistes*, which takes its second epigraph from *The Ascent of Mount Carmel*.[76] As discussed in Chapter 1, Eliot's unfinished play of 1926 centres on the individual soul's awful encounter with absolute moral law. Sweeney sees the sin of the murderer in its eternal aspect and recognises that no temporal measures (language, law, public reform) can assuage its harrowing implications. The importance of this theological point is undiminished in 1933: 'The conception of individual liberty,' Eliot writes, 'must be based upon the unique importance of every single soul, the knowledge that every man is ultimately responsible for his own salvation or damnation' (*L4*, 537). Where *Sweeney Agonistes*' focus is on eternal consequences of individual import alone, the essay nuances divine union with an eye on this world and considers the responsibility of Christians within their given economic and political contexts. Congruous with the essay's dual concern, the sermon of *Murder in the Cathedral* emphasises that martyrdom – the ultimate sacrifice – is meant to glorify God and serve one's neighbours: 'A martyrdom is always the design of God, for His love of men, to warn them and to lead them, to bring them back to His ways' (*CPP*, 261). Although it takes the charwomen of the Chorus some time to see Thomas's death as more than personal loss, they eventually realise that 'From [the ground of sacrifice] springs that which forever renews the earth' (*CPP*, 282).

In light of his desire for certain inward-facing austerities, Eliot's claim that the 'second half of the Summary of the Law is a delusion and a cheat if you erase the first half' (*CP4*, 537) might appear misanthropic or even heretically unbalanced. But this would be to overlook his appeal for a more deeply humane benevolence that neither predicates on commitment to 'any form of temporal order' (*CP4*, 541) nor enforces one people's idea of the good on others. With poignancy that carries into the context of both democratic imperialism and extremist tyranny in the twenty-first century, Eliot writes that 'it is very difficult for any of us to know in what ways we are superior to other peoples, and in what ways merely different' (*CP4*, 540). So, far from advocating pious indifference to secular matters, the essay acknowledges the necessity of engagement, but engagement which neither sacrifices eternal values to temporal ones, nor loses sight of the theological beliefs that impel it in the first place.

'The Modern Dilemma' also stresses the primacy of proper belief over proper action. And here, too, 'vague benevolence' occurs in conjunction with Eliot's intractable scepticism about the quest for human flourishing untethered from doctrinally sound motives:

> We like to interpret the love of our neighbors as ourselves as a *vague benevolence*, or as practical charity alone. We like to think that as we want to be happy, and have some 'right' to be happy, so we must remember that our neighbors have rights too and that we should try to make them happy: the love of our neighbours becomes fair play, and doing the decent thing. (*CP4*, 813–14, my emphasis)

The anaphoric statement of predilection ('we like'), the pincer-grappled notion of 'right[s]', the coy phrases 'fair play' and 'decent thing' all rhetorically locate 'practical charity' within what Eliot sees as self-satisfied, self-serving ethics.[77] In the unpublished conclusion to the address, he warned that the dilution of spiritual ideals to a human standard entails a descent into 'complacency and self-conceit' (CP4, 816).[78] Eliot opposes not the pursuit of progress but the belief in its possible fulfilment. In the Criterion 'Commentary' of October 1932, he expressed the need to balance aspiration and self-knowledge, to temper the desire for a perfect society with the awareness that humans are always at an 'infinite remove from perfection' (CP4, 502).[79] Christ's words in Matt. 5: 48, *'estote perfecti'* ['be ye perfect'] are interpreted here, in 'Christianity and Communism', and in the Boston address, as an injunction to spiritual progress which aims at but never attains perfection.[80] In one aspect, then, the modern dilemma appears to invite a choice between belief in the achievability of moral equilibrium and belief in unceasing moral striving.

As antidote to the spiritual pride concomitant with human notions of perfectibility, Eliot recommended the ideal of saintliness. In a Pauline inversion of logic, 'The Modern Dilemma' posits saintliness as the lowest possible ideal with the intimation that spiritual progress is inversely proportional to the recognition of one's fallen nature (CP4, 814). It is a notion borne out by Eliot's formula, stated during a lecture to Harvard undergraduates also in 1933, that 'Real Evil is to Bad just as Saintliness and Heroism [are] to Decent Behaviour' (CP4, 773). And it is such recognition which pre-empts the gnomic statement in *East Coker*: 'The only wisdom we can hope to acquire / Is the wisdom of humility: humility is endless' (P1, 188). At home in a work that dwells on the contact between beginnings and ends, the lines recall Eliot's early philosophical insight that any infinite, endless goal implies a contradiction of terms. In the graduate essay on Kant discussed above, Eliot remarked that 'if a goal is never to be reached, it is not a goal at al . . . [T]he "infinite goal" is reduced to a means' (CP1, 55). The goal in that case was holiness, but the formulation applies equally well to humility. Divested of teleology, it becomes a way of being that persists unrelieved by the prospect of attainment. In the context of the prose pieces discussed above and, later, in *Four Quartets*' wrestle after 'objects not in the contract', as Denis Donoghue puts it, unattainability should not be seen in a negative or discouraging light, but rather as an essential element of saintly sacrifice – a giving that is not as the world gives.[81] That *Murder in the Cathedral* dramatises such sacrifice seems obvious. What is less obvious, however, is the way in which Eliot, through Thomas's unassuming homiletic voice, asserts the mutual significance of Christ's birth and death, the primacy of divine grace over human good will, and the balance between love for God and love for one's neighbours.

Notes

1. Quoted in Stefan Collini, *Absent Minds: Intellectuals in Britain* (Oxford: Oxford University Press, 2006), 322.
2. Spender was responding to Eliot's remarks in a BBC broadcast entitled 'Christianity and Communism'. See *CP4*, 428.
3. For Eliot's use of the sacrament of penance, see Barry Spurr, *'Anglo-Catholic in Religion': T. S. Eliot and Christianity* (Cambridge: Lutterworth, 2010), 136.
4. In Jewel Spears Brooker, ed., *T. S. Eliot: The Contemporary Reviews* (Cambridge: Cambridge University Press, 2004), 149, 152.
5. In Brooker, *Contemporary Reviews*, 281.
6. In Brooker, *Contemporary Reviews*, 240.
7. A more intimate interest is suggested by his 'pilgrimage' to Andrewes's tomb in 1930 (*L5*, 318–19) and his love for the Bishop's posthumously published book of prayers and devotions, *Preces Privitae*, which he read when unable to fall asleep.
8. See 'Political Theorists', *CP3*, 137. Eliot rejects as historically ignorant Anthony M. Ludovici's suggestion that Toryism has more in common with the Church of Rome than with the Church of England. In 'Thoughts after Lambeth' (*CP4*, 237), he writes more forcefully still that 'the Roman Church in England is a sect'.
9. Barry Spurr, 'Liturgical Anachronism in *Murder in the Cathedral*', *Yeats-Eliot Review* 15 (1998): 3–7. See also Spurr, *'Anglo-Catholic in Religion'*, 237; Chene Heady, *Worlds of Common Prayer: Liturgical Time and Poetic Re-enchantment, 1827–1935* (Vancouver: Fairleigh Dickenson University Press, 2019), 123–49.
10. As given in *CPP*, 260. Eliot is here following the Douay-Rheims Bible (see discussion below).
11. Luke 2: 12–14: 'And this shall be a sign unto you; ye shall find the Child swaddled, and laid in a cratch. And straightaway there was with the Angel a multitude of Heavenly soldiers, praising God, and saying, Glory be to God on high, and peace upon earth, and towards men good-will.' As given in Lancelot Andrewes, *Seventeen*

Sermons on the Nativity (London: Griffith Farran Okeden and Welsh, 1887), 193.
12. Andrewes, *Seventeen Sermons*, 193.
13. Andrewes, *Seventeen Sermons*, 193.
14. Andrewes, *Seventeen Sermons*, 200.
15. Andrewes, *Seventeen Sermons*, 202.
16. See Erich Auerbach, *Mimesis: The Representation of Reality in Western Literature*, Fiftieth Anniversary Edition, trans. Willard R. Trask (Princeton: Princeton University Press, 2003), 151: 'In antique theory, the sublime and elevated style was called *sermo gravis* or *sublimis*; the low style was *sermo remissus* or *humilis*; the two had to be kept strictly separated. In the world of Christianity, on the other hand, the two merged, especially in Christ's Incarnation and Passion, which realize and combine *sublimitas* and *humilitas* in overwhelming measure.'
17. Andrewes, *Seventeen Sermons*, 210–11.
18. Andrewes, *Seventeen Sermons*, 211.
19. For 'Christ is no wild-cat', see Andrewes, *Seventeen Sermons*, 254.
20. Ria Banerjee, 'From Humiliation to Epiphany: The Role of Onstage Spaces in T. S. Eliot's Middle Plays', *South Atlantic Review* 82.2 (2017): 60, author's italics.
21. Heady, *Worlds of Common Prayer*, 137.
22. T. S. Eliot and George Hoellering, *The Film of* Murder in the Cathedral (London: Faber and Faber, 1952), 117.
23. Andrewes, *Seventeen Sermons*, 215, rather strangely gives εὐδοχίας to suggest the Latin reading; I have substituted his Greek for the Latin of the Vulgate above.
24. Andrewes, *Seventeen Sermons*, 212. Sermon XII, however, gives the verse only as it is found in the Vulgate (193).
25. Andrewes, *Seventeen Sermons*, 215.
26. The Authorized Version reads: 'Glory to God in the highest, and on earth peace, good will toward men.'
27. Robert W. Ayers, '*Murder in the Cathedral*: A Liturgy Less Divine', *Texas Studies in Literature and Language* 20.4 (1978): 597.
28. Douay-Rheims Bible, or *The Holy Bible: Faithfully Translated into English out of the Authentical Latin, diligently conferred with the Hebrew, Greek, & Other Editions in Divers Languages*, (Rouen: John Cousturier, 1636), i. Page numbers refer to those given in the New Testament. I have provided standardised spelling.
29. Douay-Rheims, 142.
30. Andrewes, *Seventeen Sermons*, 195.
31. Andrewes, *Seventeen Sermons*, 204.
32. See Augustine, *Responses to Miscellaneous Questions: Miscellany of Eighty-Three Questions; Miscellany of Questions in Response to Simplician; and Eight Questions of Dulcitius*, Part 1, Vol. 12, intro.

and trans. Boniface Ramsey; ed. Raymond Canning (New York: New City Press, 2008), 159–205.
33. The difference between the two translations comes down to the slightest prepositional difference: 'give I unto you' (Authorised Version) versus 'give I to you' (Douay-Rheims).
34. Augustine, *Responses*, 187.
35. Augustine, *Responses*, 193.
36. See Hugh Kenner, *The Invisible Poet: T. S. Eliot* (London: Methuen, 1965), 39. Kenner remarks that it is as 'coloring, not as a body of doctrine, that [Bradley] stays in [Eliot's] mind'.
37. F. H. Bradley, *The Principles of Logic* (New York: G. E. Stechert and Co., 1912), 533, my emphasis.
38. In addition to the instances discussed here, see *CP1*, 208, 540.
39. Cf. Mark 12: 30–1: 'And thou shalt love the Lord thy God with all thy heart, and with all thy soul, and with all thy mind, and with all thy strength: this is the first commandment. And the second is like, namely this, Thou shalt love thy neighbour as thyself. There is none other commandment greater than these.'
40. M. A. R. Habib gives the most comprehensive account of Eliot's engagement with Kant, though he does not explore Eliot's references to Kant's *Groundwork of the Metaphysics of Morals*. See Habib, 'The Prayers of Childhood: T. S. Eliot's Manuscripts on Kant', *Journal of the History of Ideas* 51.1 (1990): 93–114.
41. Immanuel Kant, *Grounding of the Metaphysics of Morals*, trans. and ed. Mary Gregor (Cambridge: Cambridge University Press, 1997), 8.
42. Kant, *Grounding*, 38; I have removed the original italics.
43. Compare the uncannily similar claim in Max Scheler's *Ressentiment*: 'for the Christian, life – even in its highest form: human life – is never the "greatest good." Life, and therefore human society and history, is only important because it is the stage on which the "kingdom of God" must emerge. Whenever the preservation and advancement of life conflict with the realization of the values which exist in the kingdom of God, life becomes futile and is to be rejected, however valuable it may seem in itself.' Scheler, *Ressentiment*, ed. and intro. Lewis A. Coser; trans. William W. Holdheim (New York: The Free Press of Glencoe, 1975), 106–7. A more recent expression of this tension between Christian sacrifice and the greater good is found in Charles Taylor's *A Secular Age*, 17: 'The call to renounce doesn't negate the value of flourishing; it is rather a call to centre everything on God, even if it be at the cost of forgoing this unsubstitutable good; and the fruit of this forgoing is that it become on one level the source of flourishing to others, and on another level, a collaboration with the restoration of a fuller flourishing by God.'
44. Eliot was 'inexorably committed to the dogma of Incarnation' (*CP4*, 342), assented that the 'classicist point of view . . . is essentially a belief

in Original Sin' (*CP2*, 472) and denounced 'the myth of human goodness which for liberal thought replaces the belief in Divine Grace' (*CP3*, 117).
45. *Doctrine in the Church of England: The Report of the Commission on Christian Doctrine Appointed by the Archbishops of Canterbury and York in 1922* (London: Society for Promoting Christian Knowledge, 1938), 52.
46. *Doctrine in the Church of England*, 52.
47. Ricks and McCue's annotation indicates that the Book of Common Prayer is echoed: 'That thy grace maye always prevente and folowe us' (*P1*, 949).
48. Edward Harold Browne, *An Exposition of the Thirty-Nine Articles, Historical and Doctrinal*, Fourteenth Edition (London: Longmans, Green, and Co., 1894), 271.
49. Eliot, *Film of Murder*, 82, my emphasis.
50. See F. H. Bradley, *Ethical Studies* (London: Henry S. King and Co., 1876), 289.
51. Matthew Arnold, 'Review of Objections to *Literature and Dogma*, I', *The Contemporary Review* XXIV (1874): 796.
52. Bradley, *Ethical Studies*, 283. Lee Oser persuasively argues that Bradley's vitriol is misguided since Arnold did not unequivocally equate virtue with happiness. See Oser, *The Ethics of Modernism: Moral Ideas in Yeats, Eliot, Joyce, Woolf, and Beckett* (Cambridge: Cambridge University Press, 2007), 57.
53. Matthew Arnold, *Culture and Anarchy* (Oxford: Oxford University Press, 2006), 35.
54. Cf. Arnold, *Culture and Anarchy*, 9. 'Culture,' Arnold pronounces in his preface, 'is the study of perfection [which] leads us . . . to conceive of true human perfection as a *harmonious* perfection, developing all sides of our humanity; and as a general perfection, developing all parts of our society.'
55. Arnold writes that 'culture suggests the idea of *the State*. We find no basis for a firm State-power in our ordinary selves; culture suggests one to us in our *best self*.' Arnold, *Culture and Anarchy*, 71.
56. Cf. Irving Babbitt, *Rousseau and Romanticism* (Boston: Houghton Mifflin, 1919), 150: 'The permanent or ethical element in [man] towards which he should strive to move is known to him practically as a power of inhibition or inner check upon expansive desire.'
57. Placed in relation to those categories of humility discussed in my Introduction, both Arnold and Babbitt may be seen as proponents of humanistic humility. See Introduction.
58. *Doctrine in the Church of England*, 52.
59. See *L3*, 491: 'I have had in suspense in my mind an essay pointing out Babbitt's (unconscious) relation to orthodox Christianity:

his doctrine of Grace, in *Democracy and Leadership*, is singularly near to Christianity, and in my opinion cannot be made acceptable without Christianity.'
60. Babbitt, *Democracy and Leadership*, 188.
61. Bradley, *Ethical Studies*, 290.
62. See Helen Thaventhiran, *Radical Empiricists: Five Modernist Close Readers* (Oxford: Oxford University Press, 2015), 48–57.
63. Bradley, *Appearance*, 439.
64. Bradley, *Appearance*, 440.
65. Bradley, *Appearance*, 439–40.
66. Cf. *CP4*, 346: 'The Calvinists emphasized the degradation of man through Original Sin, and considered mankind so corrupt that the will was of no avail; and thus fell into the doctrine of predestination.'
67. Bradley, *Ethical Studies*, 211.
68. Bradley, *Ethical Studies*, 298.
69. Bradley, *Appearance*, 441.
70. Bradley, *Appearance*, 443.
71. See Eliot to P. E. More on 10 August 1930: 'I admit freely that I am a Bradleian; and that my thought and my belief may be more deeply influenced by Bradley than I know. And that between different doctrines, I choose that which seems to me the "less false", inasmuch as there are degrees of untruth' (*L5*, 292).
72. Kenner, *Invisible Poet*, 39.
73. The talk, originally titled 'The Modern Dilemma', was broadcast on 20 March, 1932.
74. For Eliot's progressive disinterestedness with the humanism debates, see *L5*, 290, 358–9, 623.
75. See James Freeman Clarke, *Vexed Questions in Theology: A Series of Essays* (Boston: Geo. H. Ellis, 1886), 14–17. The five doctrines of the 'new theology' of Unitarianism are outlined in the book, the last two of which pertain to its soteriological position. That is, salvation can be achieved through character and the belief in humanity's perpetual progress.
76. See *P1*, 113: 'Hence the soul cannot be possessed of the divine union, until it has divested itself of the love of created beings.'
77. The passage bears comparison with a statement in the graduate essay, 'The Ethics of Green and Sidgwick' (*CP1*, 159): 'An act may be <u>right</u> because it produces happiness, but if we perform the act with one eye on the happiness and not on the rightness, it is not altogether a moral act. And yet if we are totally indifferent to others' happiness, we become worthy of something like moral aversion. The fact is that it is not always moral to be moral.'
78. Cf. *L6*, 291: 'I am not concerned with how people behave, but with what they think of themselves in their behaviour; and I believe that

the man who thinks himself virtuous is in danger of damnation, *whatever* line of conduct he adopts.'
79. Cf. T. E. Hulme, *Speculations: Essays on Humanism and the Philosophy of Art*, ed. Herbert Read (London: Routledge and Kegan Paul, 1924), 47: 'Ethical values are *not* relative to human desires and feelings, but absolute and objective . . . Religion supplements this . . . by its conception of *Perfection* . . . In light of these absolute values, man himself is judged to be essentially limited and imperfect. He is endowed with Original Sin. While he can partake of perfection, he can never himself *be* perfect.'
80. Cf. *CP4*, 428 and 814.
81. Denis Donoghue, *Words Alone: The Poet T. S. Eliot* (New Haven: Yale University Press, 2000), 229.

4

A Defence of Wretchedness: *Molloy* and Humiliation

In July 1946, *Les Temps modernes* published part of Beckett's short story, 'Suite'. Simone de Beauvoir had not understood, nor did she particularly care, that the piece was incomplete or that its author expected the concluding segment to appear in the review's next instalment. Naturally, Beckett was anguished by her refusal to let the story – later to be called 'La Fin' – come to an end.

> You are giving me the chance to speak only to retract it before the words have had time to mean anything. You are immobilising an existence at the very moment at which it is about to take its definitive form. There is something nightmarish about that. I find it hard to believe that matters of presentation can justify, in the eyes of the author of *L'Invitée*, such a mutilation.
>
> Your view is that the fragment which appeared in your last number is a finished piece. That is not my view. I see it as no more than a major premise.
>
> Do not be offended by this plain speaking. It is without rancour. It is simply that there exists a wretchedness which must be defended to the very end, in one's own work and outside it. (*L2*, 42)

The situation was humiliating for reasons beyond the compromise of artistic integrity. Beauvoir believed Beckett's attempt to submit further writing under the same title to be an act of deception, a ploy to secure publication in two consecutive issues and earn a greater fee than had initially been agreed upon. She also thought, as James Knowlson points out, that the abounding scatology in the second part was unsuitable for the review.[1] Careful and deferential, Beckett's letter attests to an awareness of his awkward position: an *inconnu* on the French literary scene ('Suite' was his first work in French) who had now made a potentially damaging professional blunder. And yet he does not seek to redress the miscommunication or to save face but instead pleads for the fictional character who has been 'denied his rest'.

The task of defending the 'wretchedness' in his work was something Beckett had to face throughout his career. He refused, for instance, to capitulate to Houghton Mifflin's demands for major cuts to *Murphy*. He fought against the Lord Chamberlain's insistence that *Endgame*'s infamous line, 'The bastard! He doesn't exist!' (*CDW*, 119), be excised or replaced. And when *New World Writing* published a 'horrible montage' (*L2*, 432) from *Molloy* without indicating that the text was not continuous, he expressed his annoyance in a letter to Barney Rosset: 'The excerpt is always unsatisfactory, but let it at least be continuous. I don't mind how short it is, or with how little beginning or end, but I refuse to be short-circuited like an ulcerous gut' (*L2*, 432).

These examples are not exhaustive, but they serve to reveal the opposing desires of the author and of publishers (and censors). The two principal considerations that appear to compel editorial alterations are narrative cohesion and the moderation of obscenity. For Beckett, however, streamlining and sanitisation were not processes distinct from each other. Given the anxious conclusion to 'The End', the rest that Beckett felt his 'creature' had been denied was not merely a question of narrative resolution. The rest also inhered in those debasing and indecent elements to which Beauvoir had objected. Bodily functions and dysfunctions – what the narrator of *How It Is* calls the 'great categories of being' (*HII*, 9) – are part of what gives Beckett's work its 'definitive form'.

That famous reflection on Joyce's *Work in Progress*, 'Here form *is* content, content *is* form' (*Dis*, 27), has justifiably been applied to Beckett's own work: the words falter because the sense is faltering. Yet there was a time when Beckett was not Beckettian. This was before his realisation that the 'way [of his art] was in impoverishment, in lack of knowledge and in taking away, in subtracting rather than in adding', before the broken epiphany dramatised in *Krapp's Last Tape* (see *CDW*, 220).[2] This was also the time before Beckett's widespread fame, before critical and public opinion marked him as an artist whose concern, both in form and content, was weakness. Beauvoir's decision falls within this period. And leaving aside questions of taste and personal disgruntlement, her failure to appreciate how essential infirmities and humiliations are to 'Suite' may be explained as a failure to appreciate the Beckettian 'agenda'.

Today the opposite complication may be at play: the Beckettian agenda is perhaps too well appreciated. This is to say that critics have identified coherence where previously there was dehiscence or distinction. One example is the collective title often applied when speaking of *Molloy*, *Malone Dies* and *The Unnamable*: the 'Trilogy'. Using this goes against the author's expressed wishes; a sin committed quite often and, for the largest part, unwittingly. The third volume of letters, published in 2014, evinces Beckett's strong opposition to this handle by which to grab three separate bundles. Though he was pleased about John Calder's decision to publish the three works together, he could not propose a general title and was against Calder's suggestion, 'Trinity': 'It seems to me the three titles should be enough' (*L3*, 187). A month later, in a tone of greater desperation, he dismissed his publisher's next proposal: 'Not "Trilogy", I beseech you, just the three titles and nothing else' (*L3*, 191). As the publication date of the 'three in one' was approaching, Beckett expressed the same apprehension to Barbara Bray about Calder's potential editorial choice: 'Please God he doesn't call it a trilogy' (*L3*, 222).

The 1959 publication was titled *Three Novels* and not 'Trilogy' – not, at least, until the Picador reprint of 1975 yoked the works together under the title, *The Beckett Trilogy*.[3] But to lay the blame solely at Calder's feet is to overlook that *Molloy*, *Malone Dies* and *The Unnamable* are generally regarded as having more in common than just a single binding. Use of the term 'trilogy' is pervasive in Beckett studies. V. S. Pritchett – one of *Three Novels*'s earliest reviewers – referred to the book as a 'Trilogy' in the opening sentence of his review.[4] Since then, scholars as eminent as Hugh Kenner, Northrop Frye and Harold Bloom have all applied it to these post-war novels. Even Christopher Ricks, who takes critics to task for curtailing titles, uses this substitutive word.[5] In the 2014 issue of *Samuel Beckett Today / Aujourd'hui* that 'revisits' the three novels, five contributors use 'Trilogy' in the titles of their respective articles.[6]

This terse survey is not intended to point to lapses in critical practice. Rather, it is to indicate how the similarity of philosophical and aesthetic landscapes across Beckett's 'three novels' has shaped its subsequent cartography. Ackerley and Gontarski argue that '"trilogy" or not, the three novels ... form a cohesive and extended exploration of the imaginative consciousness'.[7] This is undeniable. The question is where the cohesion begins and ends, and where the borders are to be drawn. Beckett himself saw *Molloy* as the 'second last of the series begun with Murphy, if it can be said to be a series', and the stories that became *Texts for Nothing* as the 'afterbirth of *L'Innommable*' (L2, 71, 300). This is not to suggest that critics have failed to explore the commonalities that extend from *Murphy* to *Texts for Nothing* or even beyond. But thinking of *Molloy*, *Malone Dies* and *The Unnamable* as a trilogy or even as three works more intimately related than any other series of works in the Beckett canon – forgetting that three separate texts are collected not because of authorial design but because of publishing savvy – creates a problem not too dissimilar from the one identified in Beauvoir's 'mutilation' of 'Suite'.

My concern here is not with an exclusionary effect, with the fact that the 'series' Beckett conceived is amputated at both ends or that other products of the 'siege in the room' (*Quatre Nouvelles, Mercier et Camier, Eleutheria, En Attendant Godot*) are – by dint of the definition of 'trilogy' – not allowed to push this particular triangulation into a larger framework. My concern, rather, is with a surplus of correspondence that is created among these three works, with the possibility that this hyper-connection could lead to the *mobilisation* of an existence beyond its definitive form. As early as 1929, Beckett warned that, for criticism, the 'danger is in the neatness of identification' (*Dis*, 19). But it is a danger that his works court through what appears to be their cohesive though amorphous quality. 'The amoeba's neck,' he remarked in reference to the prospect of cutting *Murphy*, 'is not easily broken' (L1, 383). If omission in Beckett is a violation that deprives characters of a necessary stasis, over-identification beyond the distinct borders of texts might amount to the same thing.

Humiliating Associations and Effacements

An equivalent over-identification emerges in *Molloy*. The two principal characters, Molloy and Moran, share a strange resemblance. So uncanny is their likeness that *The Faber Companion to Samuel Beckett* lists twenty-one similarities between them. The correspondence goes deep enough for the editors to claim not just kinship but a kind of vanishing twin syndrome:

> It is not so much that Moran has become Molloy, or that the second half should precede the first, but that Molloy was always part of

Moran, as were Gaber and Youdi, agents of a superego . . . What the Moran section offers, and why it follows the Molloy section (and why the novel is called *Molloy*, not *Moran*), is a fiction written by Molloy of Molloy as Moran encountering Molloy.[8]

This theory may account for the abrupt change in perspective at the end of the novel where Moran is replaced as the first-person narrator; it may also suggest what Molloy's writing contains. But it perpetrates the same kind of permeability that use of the term 'trilogy' allows, and fails to appreciate the novel's 'definitive form' that realises itself not only in parallels but also in differences.

It is telling that towards the end of the novel – the point at which he most closely shadows Molloy – Moran reflects on the divergence that may be found in ostensible similarities. Studying the dance of his bees, he remarks:

> I first concluded that each figure [of the dance] was reinforced by means of a hum peculiar to it. But I was forced to abandon this agreeable hypothesis. For I saw the same figure (at least what I called the same figure) accompanied by very different hums. So that I said, The purpose of the hum is not to emphasize the dance, but on the contrary to vary it. And the same figure exactly differs in meaning according to the hum that goes with it. . . . But there was to be considered not only the figure and the hum, but also the height at which the figure was executed. And I acquired the conviction that the selfsame figure, accompanied by the selfsame hum, did not mean at all the same thing at twelve feet from the ground as it did at six. (*TN*, 163–4)

Moran admits that he could be wrong, that the dance could be as pointless as the 'dances of the people of the West'. But he is content not to subject the phenomenon to his 'cogitations' and refuses to conceive of the bees as creatures constituted by his understanding. He explains: 'I would never do my bees the wrong I had done my God, to whom I had been taught to ascribe my angers, fears, desires, and even my body.' Where previously Moran is fastidious, authoritarian and partial to the symmetries of accounting, he now resists the temptation to calibrate the world in familiar terms: 'I could no longer be bothered with these wretched trifles which had once been my delight' (155). Although he does not achieve the 'ataraxy' of Molloy, since his mind remains 'avid . . . of the flimsiest analogy', he is ready to concede the unassimilable otherness of his bees and of God. Moran's comment on the latter relationship throws his newfound negative capability and former audacity into relief. Early in the narrative his church-going is established as self-serving and self-centred, a ritual that helps to 'buck [him] up' (90). The above statement declares this in its reversal of Gen. 1: 26 ('Let us make man in our image'), but also undoes it: Moran now recognises the 'wrong' inherent in a subject-defined, Cartesian-inflected ('cogitations') interpretation of external reality.

The passage signals both Moran's metamorphosis and an ethical encouragement to resist planing the edges of difference. The two things cannot be divorced, since it is at this point that Moran – sharing so many of Molloy's traumas and infirmities, 'becoming rapidly unrecognizable' (164) – has the most lucid grasp of himself. As the different heights, hums and figures of the bees remain beyond exact definition, so too does the exact relation between Molloy and Moran. Beckett brings Moran to the precipice of a humiliating effacement, blurring but not merging his being with Molloy's. This does not, however, preclude our *reading* Moran out of existence. In the *Faber Companion* gloss cited above, for instance, the character suffers a dispossession of self not only within the text proper but also from outside: having been stripped of health, possessions and his familial relations, Moran is also stripped of the subjectivity which these losses ultimately constitute. Like *The Double*'s Yakov Petrovich Golyadkin, Moran faces erasure in the presence of his doppelganger. But where this erasure is operational in Dostoevsky's novel, it is only a suspended potentiality in Beckett's. The text offers an interpretive choice: to inscribe Moran within the consciousness of Molloy and thus to unwrite Moran, or to preserve Moran's otherness in following the ethical imperative implicit in the bee passage.

Conflicting responses to alterity are also explored in some of Beckett's other works. In *Company*, for instance, the narrator reflects on his past actions and their consequences (*Com etc.*, 18–19). He remembers taking 'pity on a hedgehog out in the cold', placing it in a hatbox, supplying it with worms, and feeling warmly triumphal about his humane efforts. He further recalls that the 'glow' was replaced by 'uneasiness' when doubts over his intervention started crowding in; a debilitating guilt delays his return to the hatbox by weeks. When he eventually faces the scene of his charity he is met by a 'mush' and 'stench' that will plague his memory thereafter. Laura Salisbury sees the text as an 'articulation of the ethical that refuses an ethics of knowledge or judgement which might turn otherness into an object of understanding for the self'.⁹ The difference between the bee passage in *Molloy* and the hedgehog passage in *Company* comes down to the difference between contemplative and instrumental reason. This is why Salisbury interprets the later text as an oblique and knotted question about post-Holocaust engagement. But *Molloy* is also a post-Holocaust text. And while it does not explore the problematic ethics of acting on behalf of another to the same extent, it does present the danger of absorbing individual narratives into larger ones.

Directly after pondering the otherness of his bees, Moran reflects on himself with uncertain certainty:

> And to tell the truth I not only knew who I was, but I had a sharper and clearer sense of my identity than ever before, in spite of its deep lesions and the wounds with which it was covered. And from this point of view I was less fortunate than my other acquaintances. I am sorry if this last phrase is not so happy as it might be. It deserved, who knows, to be without ambiguity. (*TN*, 164)¹⁰

The passage is complex because it accommodates the anguish of self-knowledge and a tacit anxiety about its opposite. Moran regards his clear sense of identity as a source of misfortune, a painful awareness that does not afflict his 'other acquaintances'. In their turn, these blessed others would seem to be fading from selfhood. Whether this is due to a collective, swallowing identity (the very thing which menaces Moran in his proximity to Molloy) or to other factors is not known. What is of importance and what can be mapped, if only conditionally, is Moran's understanding of the self *as* self.

If the '[un]happy phrase' comprises the whole preceding sentence, its content and possible meanings can only be defined in terms of the first sentence where Moran's 'point of view' finds expression. But taking him at his word for the time being, the last phrase ('my other acquaintances') betrays a peculiar element of his self-conception. No 'acquaintance' is mentioned in this paragraph, so one cannot read the phrase as a differentiation between one particular acquaintance and other unidentified ones. The word 'other' appears to mark Moran himself, or a version of himself, as one among his familiars. In other words, his sense of identity is contingent on an apperceptive process in which subjectivity becomes objectified: a fault line surfaces between 'I' and 'me'. Moran, then, becomes an object of his consciousness to the same extent that his acquaintances are objects of his consciousness. And while it may be that he has a clearer understanding of himself (than 'ever before', but also than of his acquaintances), it results from within a splintered and self-estranged subjectivity.

In the same paragraph we read: 'it seemed to me I was now becoming rapidly unrecognizable'; 'the face my hands felt was not my face anymore'; 'this belly I did not know remained my belly' (*TN*, 164). This might appear fertile ground for reclaiming Beckett as a Cartesian dualist, but that would be to miss the point that Moran himself misses or can only grasp in ambiguous terms: just as his physical features have suffered a sea change, so too has his ego.[11] Moran's subtle transition between reflection on the physical and reflection on the mental does, however, suggest his awareness of a metamorphic continuum. He does not separate his observations on body and mind with a dividing 'but'; rather, he glissades between the two with 'And'.

It should already be clear that part of the 'unhappiness' in the phrase 'my other acquaintances' is its tentacular, uncontained ambiguity. To find possible explanations for Moran's idea that he is 'less fortunate' than his 'other acquaintances' demands that one consider the sentence in which his 'point of view' is articulated and what, from that point of view, would make him less fortunate. Here, two possible meanings are kept in tension, which I will explore in some detail. On the one hand, Moran is less fortunate because he has a clear sense of identity or, to state it inversely, his acquaintances are more fortunate in not having a clear sense of identity. On the other hand, he is less fortunate because he has a clear sense of identity in spite of the injuries that attend his identity: that is, the lesions and wounds have not had the fortunate identity-obscuring effect they may have had on his acquaintances. Moran thus remains fully conscious of himself and – since there is a self-identifying subject to experience them – his sufferings.

The first meaning may seem an odd way of regarding self-knowledge: surely a clear sense of identity is a good thing? Good, perhaps; fortunate, no. Throughout his life, Beckett was drawn to authors who advocated a deprecated sense of self: certain pre-Socratics, numerous mystics, Thomas à Kempis, Jeremy Taylor, Blaise Pascal, Arnold Geulincx, Arthur Schopenhauer, Emil Cioran and many others. In most of these cases, negative self-regard is rooted in an ontology of fallenness: the individual who truly knows himself also knows the true and eternal condition of humanity. For Bernard of Clairvaux, 'Humility is a virtue by which a man has a low opinion of himself because he knows himself well.'[12] Thomas à Kempis claimed that 'He who knoweth himself well is vile in his own sight.'[13] Jeremy Taylor considered humility to consist not in an external display of wretchedness, but 'in hearty and real evil or mean opinion of thyself'.[14] And Pascal believed that 'Man's greatness lies in his capacity to recognise his wretchedness.'[15]

That Beckett himself also regarded human existence as constituted by an ontological humiliation is borne out in many of his writings. In *Proust*, he reflects on the 'sin of having been born' (*PTD*, 67). From Wilhelm Windelband's *History of Philosophy*, he records Anaximander's 'doctrine that things must perish as an expiation for injustice' and that it 'presents the first dim attempt to conceive the cosmic process as <u>ethical necessity</u> and the shadows of transitoriness . . . as retribution for sin'.[16] A comparable idea finds expression in *Murphy* (43), this time through a reference to Bildad the Shuhite's mocking question, 'How can he be clean that is born of a woman?' (Job 24: 4). *Watt*'s 'Addenda' include an enigmatic Latin phrase about being born 'polluted' (233). In *Malone Dies* (*TN*, 233), Macmann feels, without knowing his 'sin', that 'living was not a sufficient atonement for it or that this atonement was in itself a sin, calling for more atonement, and so on, as if there could be anything but life, for the living'. In *The Unnamable*, the moment of existence is seen as coinciding with punishment: 'I was given a pensum, at birth perhaps, as a punishment for having been born perhaps . . .' (*TN*, 304).

Since Geulincx is directly invoked in *Molloy*, his imperatives of self-inspection and self-disregard are most pertinent in the case of Moran's unhappy existence. It is well-known that the *Ethics* of the seventeenth-century philosopher was a major shaping influence on Beckett's creative output. In particular, Geulincx's 'axiom of morals' – '*ubi nihil vales, ibi nihil velis*' ('wherein you have no power, therein neither should you will') – resonates throughout Beckett's work:

> Note that this axiom includes both parts of humility . . . inspection and disregard. *Wherein you have no power*; we read in this the inspection of oneself . . . *Therein you should not will*; we read in this . . . disregard of oneself, or neglect of oneself across the whole human condition, and resigning ourselves into the power of His hand,

in which we are, indeed, whether we like it or not. . . . Therefore, to will nothing concerning our condition, to leave the whole thing to Him in whose power it really is, this truly is to disregard oneself, this is to build virtue on the unshakable foundation of humility.[17]

In this regard, self-knowledge may well be seen as a source of misfortune. Inspection of oneself leads to a realisation of powerlessness; disregard of oneself necessitates a resignation of will because of that powerlessness.

But if there is no potential to begin with, it is difficult to see how the will can come into play. *Molloy*'s single explicit reference to Geulincx suggests that, although there is some room for wilful ignorance, the conditions of existence are not altered by what one chooses to believe or not to believe:

> I who had loved the image of old Geulincx, dead young, who left me free, on the black boat of Ulysses, to crawl towards the East, along the deck. That is a great measure of freedom, for him who has not the pioneering spirit. And from the poop, poring upon the wave, a sadly rejoicing slave, I follow with my eyes the proud and futile wake. Which, as it bears me from no fatherland away, bears me onward to no shipwreck. (*TN*, 46)

The passage implies Geulincx's axiom of morals and, with its nautical metaphor, directly alludes to an image from the *Ethics* that illustrates the futility of our resistance to divine will:

> Just as a ship carrying a passenger with all speed towards the west in no way prevents the passenger from walking towards the east, so the will of God, carrying all things, impelling all things with inexorable force, in no way prevents us from resisting his will.[18]

But in his conjunction of the *Ethics* and *Inferno* 26, Molloy accepts neither Geulingian predestination nor Dantean ordination. And, as his sardonic tone suggests, neither does he glimpse anything more than momentary escape. Beckett's palimpsest of the transcendentally directed vessel and its cosmologically ill-fated counterpart creates a context in which all individual effort is rendered futile: both that of Geulincx's east-facing rebel and of the intrepid Ulysses who is damned by Dante for pride. Molloy sees himself as a slave – a being with no rights, no status and no worth.

Beckett's manipulation of *Inferno* 26 in this final sentence quoted above significantly rewrites the fate of Dante's Ulysses, whose account of his voyage opens with reference to his family and concludes with a divinely ordained tempest. What spurs on the Dantean Ulysses to forsake his familial duties and to tempt fate is a desire for enlightenment. Encouraging his followers, he says:

> Bethink you of the seed
> whence ye have sprung,
> for ye were not created
> to lead the life of stupid animals,
> but manliness and knowledge to pursue.[19]

But Molloy admits to having killed the 'Aegean' (that is, Ulysses) in himself who craved 'heat and light' (*TN*, 25).[20] He is of the same ilk as the Unnamable, who sees no common ground between himself and that figure of humanist striving discussed in the Introduction, Prometheus: 'between me and that miscreant who mocked the gods, invented fire, denatured clay and domesticated the horse, in a word obliged humanity, I trust there is nothing in common' (*TN*, 297). Molloy's odyssey, then, has neither foundation (whether in the guise of privilege, destiny or duty) nor a knowable *telos* (whether in the attainment of Ulysses' aims or in his destruction); his 'calvary . . . [has] no limits to its stations and no hope of crucifixion' (*TN*, 73). Humiliation, to twist Eliot's line, is endless. Molloy's 'sad rejoicing' thus emerges as an awareness of what Beckett called 'ontological indecency'.[21] The sadness emanates from the state of powerless itself; the rejoicing is a payoff for recognising this unchanging truth. The terms, though opposite, are not equal. If Molloy were a rejoicingly sad slave, he would be someone without worth who takes pleasure in his worthlessness, a masochist.[22] But because his rejoicing is located in an epistemic certainty of humiliation, it remains in the shadow of ontological despair.

In this respect Moran's 'less fortunate' position seems to correspond. The ambiguity of his utterance, to consider another possible grey area, colours the very terms 'less fortunate'. If Moran is less fortunate than his acquaintances because knowledge of his being leads to despair, he may at the same time be more fortunate in following the Delphic imperative to know himself, which, in its turn, occasions despair, and so on. A comparable ouroboros of catastrophe and blessing emerges when Malone loses his stick and can consider its essence 'shorn of all accidents' (*TN*, 201). A still more pertinent example of this ambivalence is found in his claim that

> I would willingly attribute part of my shall I say misfortunes to this disordered sense were I not unfortunately rather inclined to look upon it as a blessing. Misfortunes, blessings, I have no time to pick my words, I am in a hurry to be done. (*TN*, 201)

The very last passage Beckett copied from Geulincx's *Ethics* centres on this Janus-faced kind of happiness: 'A truly humble mind, having not only submitted to, but immersed itself in its Obligations ... *beyond concern* ... is capable of Happiness.'[23] Such happiness – such humility – is a sad rejoicing. It is born from 'obligations' that necessitate the recognition of an abased condition as well as the practice of self-abasement; it entails, in Arsene's words to Watt, opening oneself up 'to the long joys of being [oneself], like a basin to vomit' (*W*, 33).[24] The point is that such happiness (sad rejoicing or humility), dragged into the 'eudemonistic slop' (*TN*, 50), cannot result in a sense of superiority. Unlike Socrates who is the wisest man because he appreciates his lack of wisdom, Moran cannot inflect his identity with any superlatives. Rather, he resembles Kierkegaard's Abraham, who is

> great by reason of his power whose strength is impotence, great by reason of his wisdom whose secret is foolishness, great by reason of his hope whose form is madness, great by reason of the love which is hatred of oneself.[25]

There is, of course, a second possible meaning in Moran's point of view, which intimates that his acquaintances are relieved of identity through their suffering:

> I not only knew who I was, but I had a sharper and clearer sense of my identity than ever before, in spite of its deep lesions and the wounds with which it was covered. And from this point of view I was less fortunate than my other acquaintances.

The key words here are 'in spite of'; they suggest that Moran's heightened sense of self comes as a surprise in light of its 'lesions and ... wounds', that he would expect these afflictions to have an

A Defence of Wretchedness 137

erosive rather than solidifying effect. Again, it is pointless to speculate about the unidentified others; one cannot claim that their pains and tortures have carried them mystically beyond themselves. But what Moran does disclose is a temporal marker: his identity is clearer than 'ever before'. The moment of self-realisation coincides with the moment of greatest suffering. It is significant that these injuries are not physical though they are conceived in the language of bodily pain, which suggests that physical suffering may well occasion a deepened self-understanding. It is also significant that the injuries do not manifest only as part of Moran's new and self-estranged appearance; they belong to his identity itself and are part of its make-up. So another possible meaning is kept alive in the ambiguous point of view: Moran is surer of himself not in spite of the lesions and wounds but because of them. It is a causality suggestively glossed in *The Unnamable*: '[M]utilate, mutilate, and perhaps some day, fifteen generations hence, you'll succeed in beginning to look like yourself' (*TN*, 309).

That suffering provides access to a truer identity is a theory Beckett had propounded in *Proust* (*PTD*, 18–21). Habit and boredom are condemned as enemies of reality because they instil a fallacious belief in the subject as self-consistent. The 'suffering of being', on the other hand, 'opens a window on the Real'. Where habit seeks to create the semblance of continuity between splintered selves, suffering allows 'perilous . . . dangerous, precarious, painful, mysterious and fertile [zones]' to come into focus. At such moments, the subject comes face to face with the division and deformity that result from its temporal existence:

> There is no escape from the hours and the days. Neither from to-morrow nor from yesterday. There is no escape from yesterday because yesterday has deformed us, or been deformed by us. The mood is of no importance. Deformation has taken place. Yesterday is not a milestone that has been passed, but a daystone on the beaten track of the years, and irremediably part of us, within us, heavy and dangerous. We are not merely more weary because of yesterday, we are other, no longer what we were before the calamity of yesterday. (*PTD*, 11–12)

The deformations of repetition also occur in *Watt*:

> Yes, these moments together have changed us, your moments and my moments, so that we are not only no longer the same now as when they began – ticktick! ticktick! – to elapse, but we know that we are no

longer the same, and not only know that we are no longer the same, but know in what we are no longer the same, you wiser but not sadder, and I sadder but not wiser, for wiser I could hardly become without grave personal inconvenience, whereas sorrow is a thing you can keep on adding to all your life long, is it not, like a stamp or egg collection, without feeling very much the worse for it, is it not. (W, 41)

The suffering of being or, as Shane Weller calls it, 'the suffering of ever-less-than-being', has both advantages and disadvantages.[26] The ego undergoes a necessary loss of security when confronted with self-estrangement and 'opposed by a phenomenon that it cannot reduce to the condition of a comfortable and familiar concept' (*PTD*, 21). This counts as an advantage since it makes self-knowledge possible. But the moment that the victim of time and habit becomes an 'ex-victim' is also subject to flux. The self-realisation brought about in the suffering of being disappears 'with a wailing and gnashing of teeth. The mortal microcosm cannot forgive the relative immortality of the macrocosm' (21). Understood in terms of our earlier discussion, the 'immortal macrocosm' may be seen as a condition unchanged and unchanging. The 'mortal microcosm' is the individual's world of experience in which knowledge of the macrocosm is enabled by suffering but simultaneously deformed and distorted by time.[27]

Moran shows some awareness of the interminable nature of degradation:

> I forged my way through [the snow], towards what I would have called my ruin if I could have conceived what I had left to be ruined. Perhaps I have conceived it since, perhaps I have not done conceiving it, it takes time, one is bound to in time, I am bound to. But on the way home, a prey to the malignancy of man and nature and my own failing flesh, I could not conceive it. (*TN*, 160)

Ultimately, there is no Archimedean point from which the subject can fully know himself. Knowledge of one's being remains anchored in time and change. In Eliot's words:

> The knowledge imposes a pattern, and falsifies,
> For the pattern is new in every moment
> And every moment is a new and shocking
> Valuation of all we have been. (*P1*, 187)

Here resides the tension between the vicissitudes of a cruel existence and the essential character of that existence. As with the purgatory Beckett identifies in Joyce's work, there is no culmination, no progress and no absolute (*Dis*, 30). There can be a groping 'worstward', a *becoming* humiliated, but never a finally humiliated *being*.

Moran's self-assessment, then, is not wilfully ambivalent but unavoidably so. The ambiguity of his reflection is a product of his powerlessness. He embodies Fernando Pessoa's beautiful formulation of the impossibility of complete self-knowledge: 'We are two abysses – a well staring at the sky.'[28] But that same ambiguity is also testament to a momentary humility in which Moran does not irritably reach after fact or reason even though realising his insight 'deserves' to be unambiguous. The passage represents an instance in which powerlessness is accepted and his own untranslatable hums are left untouched by instrumental reason.

'Tears and laughter': Responding to Humiliation

In *A Short History of Decay*, Emil Cioran writes that misery

> constitutes the texture of all that breathes; but its modalities have changed course; they have composed that series of irreducible appearances which lead each of us to believe he is the first to have suffered so. The pride of such uniqueness incites us to cherish our own pain and to endure it. In a world of sufferings, each of them is a solipsist in relation to all the rest. Misery's originality is due to the verbal quality which isolates it in the sum of words and sensations.[29]

Whether or not Beckett had read these words before writing *Molloy*, his novel nonetheless achieves something of their astuteness.[30]

What differentiates the two central characters in the end is not their suffering, hardly distinguishable in paraphrase, but their respective responses to suffering. If we briefly consider the concluding moments of the first part, it is clear that Molloy resists all stasis and comfort. At the lowest point of his infirmity, he finds it necessary to continue on a quest which is as much a search for his mother as it is an inexhaustible self-examination. Though an opportunity for capitulation presents itself in the forest, Molloy finds an 'access of vigour' (*TN*, 79) in his 'weakness', and this allows him to realise the Beckettian ethos of 'going on' despite insurmountable obstacles. Molloy is aware that no net-gain is to be hoped for, that a change of location will not mean progress. Still he allows his imperatives to wrench him from situations where, 'if all was not well, all was no worse than anywhere else' (80). Still he 'submits' to this ineffable force though it leaves him in ever greater doubt.

By contrast, Moran's self-insight flickers without flaming into that 'burning illogicality' and stoic uncertainty Beckett admired in St John of the Cross and other mystics.[31] Like the self-centred sufferer described by Cioran, Moran's egotism returns to replace the apparent surrender of a moment before. Afflictions, fulfilling an earlier Freudian slip, become affections; asceticism assumes the aspect of perverse delight.[32] This is far off from Simone Weil's understanding of affliction as a 'state of extreme and total humiliation' in which pride and self-reliance are utterly voided.[33] Abandoning himself to the frailties of his body and the cruelty of the weather, he weds fresh destitution to former joys. His passion for enumeration sparks briefly in the ways his threadbare shirt can be worn; the umbrella/walking stick dilemma recalls his delight in linear logic, which trumps the primacy of bodily needs; and he prefers elemental exposure to facing a reminder of his son that would be brought about by building a real shelter (*TN*, 165–6). In short, there is a re-crystallisation of preferences and prerogatives which causes the Geulingian axiom to gradually lose its grip on Moran. He goes too far in the direction of *despicio sui*, overstepping what may be taken as healthy self-disregard. 'Humility,' Geulincx warns, 'does not require anyone positively to despise himself, to defame himself, scourge himself, or treat himself badly in some way or other.'[34]

Even amid his suffering, Moran rediscovers a sense of superiority: 'The thought of turning for help to the villages, to the peasants, would have displeased me, if it had occurred to me' (*TN*, 166). Leaving aside the difficulty that the writing is reflection – an act of 'decomposition' (21) – the sentence reveals Moran's contentedness in abjection at the time. The thought of seeking help does not even occur to him, and, if it did, he would not turn to 'peasants'. Moran has relapsed, more or less fully, into the microcosm where habit and prejudice solidify identity. Because the tensile connection between self-knowledge (a state of humiliation) and acceptance of what it implies (humility) loses its equipoise, Moran's understanding of himself as 'less fortunate' vanishes. In contrast with Molloy, he stands as a rejoicingly sad slave.

Juxtaposed, the respective conclusions of Parts I and II present a tale of two cries: the 'publican's whinge' and the 'pharisee's taratantara' (*Dis*, 68) – terms Beckett uses in his 1934 essay, 'Humanistic Quietism'. The essay's implicit reference to Luke 18: 9–14 establishes oppositional attitudes of desperate humility and haughty certainty, of inner compunction and observable righteousness, of self-abasement and self-aggrandisement. It is telling that Moran, caught trespassing on another's land (*TN*, 167), resorts to an invented religious justification (a pilgrimage to the 'Turdy Madonna') to account for his misdemeanour. The lie at once saves his skin and lets him feel superior to the 'yokel' he has just duped. In his turn, the Pharisee believes himself justified by the law, which is fulfilled in the advent of Christ and therefore no longer the means of redemption. Moran's '[h]umbly ask[ing] a favour' further extends the hypocrisy. He stands guilty of the 'pretence of submissiveness', as La Rochefoucauld calls it – that 'artifice by which pride debases itself in order to exalt itself; and though it can transform itself in a thousand ways, pride is never better disguised and more deceptive than when it is hidden behind the mask of humility'.[35] Just as the Pharisee's prayer is an affirmation of his superiority over others rather than an acknowledgement of his inferiority before God, Moran's manipulation is indicative of intellectual pride.

But the request, while ensuring that his brains are not knocked out, puts Moran in a position of indebtedness that undermines his cunning victory over the farmer. As evidenced in an earlier episode when an unidentified man asks him for a piece of bread, Moran regards dependency as 'humiliating' (140).[36] To tip the scales in his favour, he at once withdraws his request and reverses the dynamic by offering the farmer a florin. True to his retrospective resolve, Moran does not turn to a peasant for help. Moreover, he cements the achievement of his falsehood by keeping up appearances at all costs: 'Above all nothing to eat', he declares, to show that he is not only a pilgrim but, like the Pharisee, one who observes fasting. With satisfaction he reflects on his accomplishment: 'Moran, wily as a serpent, there was never the like of old Moran' (168).

This resistance to acts of kindness recalls the attitude of the magnanimous man discussed in the Introduction. Aristotle describes him in the *Nicomachean Ethics* as

> the sort of person to do good, but is ashamed to be a beneficiary himself, since doing good is characteristic of a superior, receiving it of an inferior. And he will repay benefits with interest, so that his original benefactor, in addition to being paid, will have become a debtor and a beneficiary.[37]

Moran's anxiety to avoid debts of kindness offers a caricature of the above. Conceived in Beckett's own terms, it pays into the 'quantum of wantum' (*Mur*, 36), the closed circuit in which suffering and happiness remain in constant equilibrium. The idea occurs as early as *Murphy* but is more famously formulated in a speech of Pozzo's in *Waiting for Godot* (*CDW*, 33): 'The tears of the world are a constant quantity. For each one who begins to weep, somewhere else another stops. The same is true of the laugh.' In *Rough for Theatre I*, however, an equilibrium of charity is threatened when B tucks A's leg snuggly without immediately asking a favour in return. Fearful to be indebted indefinitely, A demands to return the kindness (*CDW*, 231): 'you're not going to do me a service for nothing? [*Pause*] I mean unconditionally? [*Pause*] Good God!' It is in this vein – and with comparable pettiness or 'smallness of soul' – that Moran wishes to avoid the humiliation of being done a kindness.

But Molloy, in keeping with a consistent awareness of his weakness, seems more disposed to accept help. Towards the end of his narrative he realises that any further venturing will be rendered impossible without the support of 'some kind person' (*TN*, 82). Not without irony or resignation, he remarks: 'Well, I suppose you have to try everything once, succour included, to get a complete picture of the resources of their planet' (85). But there is an obvious instance where Molloy defies the 'charitable gesture', which occurs during his detention for what appears to be indecent resting. Approached by a woman he takes to be a social worker, he is repulsed at the sight of her unappetising alms. Running still deeper than his disgust with the 'tottering pile of disparates' is his abreaction to unsolicited aid:

> Let me tell you this, when social workers offer you, free, gratis and for nothing, something to hinder you from swooning, which with

them is an obsession, it is useless to recoil, they will pursue you to the ends of the earth, the vomitory in their hands. The Salvation Army is no better. Against the charitable gesture there is no defence, that I know of. You sink your head, you put out your hands all trembling and twined together and you say, Thank you, thank you lady, thank you kind lady. To him who has nothing it is forbidden not to relish filth. (19–20)

The passage is significant in light of Beckett's own charitable endeavours following the war. Having volunteered as quartermaster and interpreter for the Irish Red Cross at the small Normandy town of Saint-Lô in 1945, he witnessed scenes of complete devastation. Memories from this time would later be reworked into the fabric of *Endgame*, but Beckett's most immediate reaction to this experience was an enigmatic and vaguely philosophical report written for radio broadcast that never aired. The tone of 'The Capital of Ruins' is sober: details of the destruction, hunger and squalor are presented factually rather than emotively. But there are notable instances in which Beckett moves from the journalistic to the moralistic:

> What was important was not our having penicillin when they had none, nor the unregarding munificence of the French Ministry of Reconstruction (as it was then called), but the occasional glimpse obtained, by us in them and, who knows, by them in us (for they are an imaginative people), of that smile at the human conditions as little to be extinguished by bombs as to be broadened by the elixirs of Borroughes and Welcome, – the smile deriding, among other things, the having and the not having, the giving and the taking, the sickness and health. (*CSP*, 277)

Simon Critchley points out the proximity between this 'smile' and *Watt*'s *risus purus* (W, 39).[38] For Critchley, it may be classed with the laughter in Beckett's work that so often makes unhappiness its object. The smile, Critchley is careful to point out, is not the cause of unhappiness but rather an indication of the human capacity for greatness in spite of wretchedness, of our ability to recognise our own folly. This Pascalian view, insightful as it is, too triumphantly posits the smile as a response to suffering and sickness; for the smile (which may well be a grimace for its skeletal, unfeeling rigidity) cuts across prosperity and good health. It does not only deride the moribund, but falls on all alike: it plagues him that gives and him that takes. Something of this sentiment lies behind the concluding sentences of 'The Capital of Ruins':

> But I think that to the end of its hospital days it will be called the Irish Hospital, and after that the huts, when they have been turned into dwellings, the Irish huts. I mention this possibility, in the hope that it will give general satisfaction. And having done so I may perhaps venture to mention another, more remote but perhaps of greater import in certain quarters, I mean the possibility that some of those who were in Saint-Lô will come home realising that they got at least as good as they gave, that they got indeed they could hardly give, a vision and sense of a time-honoured conception of humanity in ruins, and perhaps even an inkling of the terms in which our condition is to be thought again. These will have been in France. (*CSP*, 278)

Given the pervasive accounts of Beckett's generosity and sensitivity to the needs of others, the passage should not read as an inveiglement against the Irish effort at Saint- Lô. What it does object to are the feelings of self-satisfaction that attend the charitable gesture. This foreshadows something of the dilemma in *Company*'s hedgehog episode, but it also warns against the creation of a hierarchy between the haves and the have-nots. Where *Company* recognises the danger in universally applying a provisional standard of the good, 'The Capital of Ruins' intimates that neither fortune nor misfortune should obscure from view the fact of humanity's humiliated being or the smile that derides each station.

By the light of this short essay, Molloy's violent reaction to the social worker's offering symbolises an effort to resist the stratification of giving and receiving. One should not forget that Molloy is placed within arm's length of the charitable gesture only because he represents a threat to normative conceptions of the good and the beautiful. His arrest and subsequent treatment, as he rightly reflects, are the result of his disconcerting presence in society, of an awful reminder of humanity in ruins:

> What is certain is this, that I never rested in that way again, my feet obscenely resting on the earth, my arms on the handlebars and on my arms my head, rocking and abandoned. It is indeed a deplorable sight, a deplorable example, for the people, who so need to be encouraged, in their bitter toil, and to have before their eyes manifestations of strength only, of courage and of joy, without which they might collapse, at the end of the day, and roll on the ground. (*TN*, 20)

Molloy does not, cannot, like Moran, turn the tables on his benefactors. But the act of shattering the cup and saucer, deliberately and not accidentally, serves as a refusal – however small – to let a vacuous barrier rise up between the needy and the bountiful. To some extent, Molloy realises Beckett's 'dream', not only of an art, but of an existence 'unresentful of its insuperable indigence and too proud for the farce of giving and receiving' (*PTD*, 141).

'The End' – the eventual form taken by that story Beauvoir had so uncharitably rejected – also questions the good of good will. Pointing a finger at the narrator, who has resorted to begging on the street, a soapbox Marxist interrogates the passers-by: 'Do you ever think? . . . It never enters your head . . . that your charity is a crime, an incentive to slavery, stultification and organized murder' (*CSP*, 94). The narrator, however, is unaffected by the display of pious rage. He believes that the orator must either be a religious fanatic or a fugitive madman; in any case, the discourse is 'all Greek to [him]'. Not only do the terms of capitalism and communism mean nothing to him, but also the idea that charity can be the cause of degradation for those who receive it and a means of elevation for those who bestow it. Like Molloy, he refuses to participate in the vicious differentiation that good will might bring about – not obliviously, but because he recognises that the act of giving is seldom unaccompanied by feelings of superiority. In refusing to thank those who 'stoop' to give him money, the narrator resists entering into an economy of moral debt and credit. Likewise, Molloy's shattering of the crockery disrupts a circular logic which fails to recognise that the human condition, no matter the particular material or moral station, is common to all, humiliating to all.

In the end, Molloy's is only one particular kind of reaction. Transforming the language of 'The End' and admitting that 'tears and laughter' – responses to humiliation and suffering – 'are so much Gaelic to me' (32), he assumes a position of uncertainty that is characteristic of Beckett's aporetic art. By counterbalancing Molloy and Moran, the publican whinge and the pharisaic taratantara, Beckett does not suggest that all responses to suffering are equally ethical or valid. Rather, through the unresolved tensions and opposing perspectives of the novel he achieves an acknowledgement of differences and a defence of wretchedness – in his work and outside it.

Notes

1. Knowlson, *Damned to Fame*, 359. For a comprehensive account of the publishing history around 'Suite' and 'The End', see Dirk van Hulle, 'Publishing "The End": Beckett and *Les Temps modernes*', in *Publishing Samuel Beckett*, ed. Mark Nixon (London: The British Library, 2011), 73–82. See also Emilie Morin, whose contextualisation of *Les Temps modernes* contributes a political dimension to Beckett's defence of wretchedness in 'Suite'. *Beckett's Political Imagination* (Cambridge: Cambridge University Press, 2017), 140.
2. Beckett quoted in Knowlson, *Damned to Fame*, 352.
3. See Peter D. McDonald, 'Calder's Beckett', in Nixon, *Publishing Samuel Beckett*, 153–70.
4. In Lawrence Graver and Raymond Federman, eds, *Samuel Beckett: The Critical Heritage* (London: Routledge, 2005), 216–19.
5. Ricks, *T. S. Eliot and Prejudice*, 112, 116.
6. See David Tucker, Mark Nixon and Dirk van Hulle, eds, *Revisiting Molloy, Malone meurt / Malone Dies and L'Innommable / The Unnamable* (Amsterdam: Rodopi, 2014).
7. Ackerley and Gontarski, *The Faber Companion*, 586.
8. Ackerley and Gontarski, *The Faber Companion*, 378.
9. Laura Salisbury, *Samuel Beckett: Laughing Matters, Comic Timing* (Edinburgh: Edinburgh University Press, 2012), 171.
10. Compare Beckett's letter to his cousin, also mentioned in Chapter 2 (*L1*, 204): 'There is after all an almost never-failing joy, namely the thought of those millions who are less fortunate than I, or ought to be. What a feast that is! But as it becomes clear as soon as one reflects a bit on the matter that no relationship between suffering and feeling is to be found, then even that joy begins to look deceptive.'
11. Feldman's *Beckett's Books* debunks the Kenner-inspired interpretations of Beckett as a Cartesian.
12. Bernard of Clairvaux, *The Steps of Humility and Pride*, trans. M. Ambrose Conway (Kalamazoo, MI: Cistercian Publications, 1989), 30.
13. Thomas á Kempis, *The Imitation of Christ*, 214.
14. Taylor, *Holy Living*, 74.
15. Blaise Pascal, *Pensées and Other Writings*, trans. Honor Levi; ed., intro. and annotated by Anthony Levi (Oxford: Oxford University Press, 1995), 136.
16. Samuel Beckett, 'Philosophy Notes', TCD MS 10967/7.1.
17. Geulincx, *Ethics*, 337.
18. Geulincx, *Ethics*, 317.
19. Dante, *Inf*. 26.118–20.

20. In a letter of 17 February 1954, Beckett explained his conjunction of Geulincx and Dante: 'I imagine a member of the crew who does not share the adventurous spirit of Ulysses and is at least at liberty to crawl homewards . . . along the brief deck' (*L2*, 458). For another discussion of Geulincx in *Molloy*, see David Tucker, *Samuel Beckett and Arnold Geulincx: Tracing 'a Literary Fantasia'* (London: Continuum, 2012), 119–22.
21. Charles Juliet, *Conversations with Samuel Beckett and Bram van Velde* (London: Dalkey Archive Press, 1995), 22.
22. Henry Russell's discussion of Dostoevsky's *Crime and Punishment* provides a suggestive analogy: 'The emphasis on true humiliation as true humility is a doctrinal commitment which should not be translated into any psychological category of masochism as a physical or psychic eros.' Russell, 'Beyond the Will: Humiliation as Christian Necessity in *Crime and Punishment*', in *Dostoevsky and the Christian Tradition*, ed. George Pattison and Diane Oenning Thompson (Cambridge: Cambridge University Press, 2001), 226.
23. Geulincx, *Ethics*, 353, my italics. Beckett (*L1*, 319) himself makes a reference to Janus in explaining his reasons for reading Geulincx in 1936: 'the work [is] worth doing, because of its saturation in the conviction that the sub specie aeternitatis vision is the only excuse for remaining alive. He does not put out his eyes on that account, as Heraclitus did & Rimbaud began to, nor like the terrified Berkeley repudiate them. One feels them very patiently turned outward, & without Schwärmerei turned in-ward, Janus or Telephus eyes, like those of Frenhofer in the Chef d'Oeuvre Inconnu, when he shall have forgotten Mabuse & ceased to barbouiller.'
24. Beckett's image and conception of the self bears comparison with that of Jeremy Taylor: 'Our body is weak and impure, sending out more uncleannesses from its several sinks than could be endured, if they were not necessary and natural; and we are forced to pass that through our mouths, which as soon as we see upon the ground, we loathe like rottenness and vomiting.' Taylor, *Holy Living*, 72.
25. Kierkegaard, *Fear and Trembling*, 12.
26. Shane Weller, *A Taste for Nothing: Beckett and Nihilism* (London: Legenda, 2005), 4.
27. Beckett is indebted to Schopenhauer's *principium individuationis* (the principle of individuation). For a comprehensive discussion of Beckett's debt to Schopenhauer, see Ulrich Pothast, *The Metaphysical Vision: Arthur Schopenhauer's Philosophy of Art and Life and Samuel Beckett's Own Way to Make Use of It* (New York: Peter Lang, 2008).
28. Fernando Pessoa, *The Book of Disquiet*, ed. and trans. Richard Zenith (London: Penguin Books, 2011), 20.

29. E. M. Cioran, *A Short History of Decay*, trans. Richard Howard (London: Penguin Books, 1975), 20.
30. In a letter of 1956, Beckett (*L2*, 678) expresses his wish to reread *Précis de decomposition*, first published in 1949.
31. See Juliet, *Conversations*, 41.
32. 'I was succumbing to other *affections*, that is not the word, intestinal for the most part' (*TN*, 160, my emphasis).
33. Simone Weil, *An Anthology*, ed. and intro. Siân Miles (London: Penguin Books, 2005), 91.
34. Geulincx, *Ethics*, 29.
35. Francois de La Rochefoucauld, *Collected Maxims and Other Reflections*, trans., annotated and intro. E. H. Blackmore, A. M. Blackmore and Francine Giguère (Oxford: Oxford University Press, 2007), 73.
36. Cf. *Malone Dies* (*TN*, 263): 'I had things to ask him, to give me my stick for example. He would have refused. Then with clasped hands and tears in my eyes I would have begged it of him as a favour. This humiliation has been denied to me thanks to my aphony.'
37. Aristotle, *Nicomachean Ethics*, 70.
38. Simon Critchley, *On Humour* (London: Routledge, 2002), 109–11.

5

Assuming the Double Part: Irony as Humility in *East Coker*

> The only wisdom we can hope to acquire
> Is the wisdom of humility: humility is endless.
> *(East Coker, P1, 188)*

How is one to respond to these lines? With meek acceptance, or with the scepticism that the poem's earlier rankling has primed in us? Is this wisdom offered from within the dark wood, or from an Olympian height? Is humility still humility if it speaks its own name? The forcefulness of the utterance – the emphatic colon, the surety of predication – might tempt us to catalogue it among Eliot's sometimes-lofty prescriptions on the subject. In the context of *East Coker*'s second part, at least, it seems to stand as a culminating point among certain suggestions of superiority: a parodic imitation belying the boast that 'there is no competition' (*P1*, 191); disenchantment not just with certain poetic modes but with poetry itself; the gripe against old men. Urging us beyond the soundbite, however, Christopher Ricks writes that these lines resist the status of 'proud apothegm' by not having the 'last word'.[1] They cede the ring of finality to the vanished houses and dancers that round off the movement, thus becoming less of an ending and also less than an end.

An endless goal, Eliot knew, implies a contradiction in terms. It is on this basis that he rejected the transcendental aspirations of *la poésie pure*: 'I believe it to be a goal that can never be reached' (*CP7*, 300); 'pure poetry ... is a goal which, if reached, would annihilate poetry' (*CP8*, 393). And, as we saw in Chapter 3, it is on the same grounds that he had much earlier dismissed Kant's notion of holiness as an ultimate aim: 'if a goal is never to be reached, it is not a goal at all ... [and] the "infinite goal" is reduced to a means' (*CP1*, 55). The formulation applies equally well to humility. Stripped of teleological designs, the virtue is a modality, a *becoming* unrelieved by final *being*.

In a broader sense that reinforces the intersection of truth and sacrifice, humility stands in relation to another modality that implies irresolvable conflict between means and ends – asceticism. Asceticism is, after all, a paradoxical performance of subjectivity: an 'ironic' self desires the surrender of its own will, yet must enjoin that will in pursuing surrender.[2] In Beckett's concise formulation: 'All gnawing to be naught. Never to be naught' (*Com etc.*, 102). As a component of humility, this self-cancelling 'going on' marks each of the last three *Quartets*. *East Coker* emphasises process over product; *The Dry Salvages* advances a continual faring forward while discouraging concern for the 'fruit of action' (*P1*, 198); and *Little Gidding* drives towards the *da capo* of unending endeavour:

> We shall not cease from exploration
> And the end of all our exploring
> Will be to arrive where we started
> And know the place for the first time. (*P1*, 208)

Here, conspicuously at the conclusion of the work where destinations become points of departure, Eliot again employs 'end' against any hint of stasis, reinforcing humility's endlessness. Rhetorically, at least. The question central to this chapter is whether the poetry's performance of humility is commensurate with its statement, whether the act of surrender equals its saying.

On this count, two sceptical positions warrant consideration. In *Either/Or*, Kierkegaard doubts the capacity of art to render what might be called virtues of perpetual unfolding. Conjugal love, patience and humility resist representation due to the fact that they must renew themselves ceaselessly. Unlike their counterparts – romantic love, courage, pride – they are not given to instantiation or apotheosis, which is to say that their endlessness precludes mimesis:

> Humility is hard to portray precisely because it is sequence . . . [I]t is essential to humility to come into existence continuously, and if this is shown to [the observer] in its ideal moment, he misses something, for he senses that its true ideality consists not in its being ideal at the moment but in its being continuous.[3]

In his essay, 'The Prince's Dog', W. H. Auden understands these words to imply not the impossibility of humility's representation but rather the impossibility of its direct representation.[4] Taking up the same theme elsewhere, he offers an example of how a writer might go about depicting a humble person. The imagined figure throws himself into an activity for which he has no special gift, experiences inevitable failure and still emerges 'radiant with self-esteem . . . as if he had triumphed'.[5] Through this refraction, humility thus becomes legible as egoless, communal participation untroubled by personal gain or loss. This skirts close to both Kierkegaard and Eliot, for whom in their respective ways 'there is only the trying' (*P1*, 191). But even on its own terms, Kierkegaard's reservations might be seen as sanctioning for a work which, like *Four Quartets*, is shaped by restless repetition.

Harder to answer is Geoffrey Hill's scepticism. Hill's quarrel is not with humility's direct representation but rather with Eliot's directive approach. Homing in on lines from *Little Gidding* that have to do with humility's most recognisable posture ('You are here to kneel . . .' [*P1*, 202]), Hill hears the tone as proprietorial if not peremptory:

> How is the repeated 'you' to be understood? Is it the modern second person singular or the second person plural, or is it the emphatic demotic substitute for what the OED terms a 'quite toneless, proclitic or enclitic, use of "one"'? Is Eliot instructing himself, self-confessor to self-penitent, taking upon himself penitentially the burden of common trespass, or is he haranguing the uninitiated, or some indeterminate other—or others—caught trespassing on his spiritual property?[6]

The rising incredulity here has something in common with Henry Eliot's objections discussed in Chapter 3, particularly as it turns towards spiritual propriety as much as spiritual property. Hill himself trespasses to come away with a partial theft ('indeterminate other – or others' shadows the unidentified old men of *East Coker* who fear 'belonging to another, or to others' [*P1*, 188]) that declares a refusal to be harangued, let alone to bend the knee. By what rights does the poet dictate the terms of prayerful approach? But Hill's actual questions, in spite of themselves, also invite considering by what means the poetry opens onto a poetics of humility.

At least this is how I will misread them here: not as rhetorical foreclosures but as the coordinates for an inquiry into *East*

Coker's 'endless' humility. Bearing in mind the Kierkegaard/Auden caveat about directness, I approach humility through the poem's ascetic, self-undoing irony. Such indirection is a necessary precaution to avoid either bad faith rejection or over-credulous acceptance of the poem's claims about and claims to humility. The focus is therefore on Eliot's *dedoublements*: those poetic re-inscriptions that call into question the accomplishments of the earlier work while casting doubt over late work's authority to do so. The first section offers a brief reflection on the relation between humility and irony before turning to Eliot's tendency to unsettle his own certainties. Here, and in the rest of the chapter, W. B. Yeats is a key interlocutor whose ceaseless exploration is shown as something both idealised and self-critically incorporated into *East Coker*. I then turn to Eliot's Yeatsian parody not merely as 'toneless' but as 'flat'; that is, parody as failed critique.[7] The ironic overlay of 'self-confessor to self-penitent' underpins a section on punitive intertextuality. Finally, the poem's refusal to meekly abdicate its unsettling modes of address comes into view. Giving special attention Eliot's 'haranguing' imperatives and unpleasant pointing, I argue that humility need not be without its edges.

Irony against Himself

In the margin of a student essay submitted by a young Tom Eliot in 1909, the following comment appears in red ink: 'Youthful rashness is not likely to be one of your attributes, at least till you are middle-aged' (*CP1*, 12 fn. 11). The words are Charles Townsend Copeland's, Eliot's instructor for English Composition at Harvard, whose backbiting compliment had been prompted by his student's attack on the 'immaturity' of Rudyard Kipling. The comment, however, appears in Eliot's own hand. Notwithstanding the fact that Copeland dictated these remarks, the juxtaposition between the cocksure claims in blue and the deflating antiphons in red offers a suggestive parallel to the patterns of undoing in Eliot's later writing.

Another name for this is irony. And as asceticism is to humility in religion, so irony is to humility in poetry. By this I do not mean the merely antiphrastic, nor what Cleanth Brooks erects as a 'principle of structure'.[8] Rather, I have in mind a continually destabilising mode that negates finality and keeps ambiguities in tension. Of a piece are Kierkegaard's dialectical irony, Schlegel's permanent parabasis and Paul de Man's endless irony, each in its own way concerned with a perpetual self-cancellation.[9] More to the point of our discussion, it is also the mode Allen Tate identified in his 1931 review of 'Ash-Wednesday', which argued that Eliot's humility might be indexed by his irony.[10] What Tate describes is a self-regarding gesture by which weakness is exposed in the work of art. In its subjective form, humility points to character and conscience; in the context of a poem, it is transformed into something that requires the reader's sensitivity and participation.

> Irony is the particular and objective instance of humility – that is, it is an event or situation which induces humility in the mind of a spectator; it is that arrangement of experience, either premeditated by art or accidentally appearing in the affairs of men, which permits to the spectator an insight superior to that of the actor, and shows him that the practical formula, the special ambition of the actor is bound to fail. Humility is thus the self-respect proceeding from a sense of the folly of men in their desire to dominate a natural force or situation.[11]

The review anticipates the doubled-consciousness that would come to take a more directly self-searching form in Eliot's late poetry. Juxtaposing the seduction scene of *The Waste Land* and the opening of 'Ash-Wednesday', Tate elides the poems' respective critiques of pride and pretension: the young man carbuncular is shown as 'he thinks he is', the poet-speaker is shown 'as he thinks himself for the moment to be'. This insinuates a deliberate *bovarysme* on the poet-speaker's part and thus posits irony as a form of *autocritique* rather than a criticism of the outside world.

Eliot himself prized poetry that goes beyond 'protests against some outside sentimentality or stupidity' (*CP2*, 319). He characterised irony as the 'expression of suffering' (748) and also as a salient feature in the make-up of the 'highly sensitive man' (*CP3*, 304). This was his assessment of Bradley, whose diffident scepticism exuded 'a curious blend of humility and irony'. Another alignment of humility's endless striving alongside irony's ceaseless upheaval occurs in a *Criterion* 'Commentary' of April 1933, where two types of irony are distinguished: irony as a form of tired disillusionment, and irony as means to criticise and question. Echoing his remarks on Bradley, Eliot writes that 'polemic irony ... is a permanent weapon of the sensitive civilized man' (*CP4*, 516); he defends its interrogative function in society and its use to 'express a *dédoublement* of the personality against which the subject struggles'. Unsurprisingly, Eliot's exemplar is Jules Laforgue, whose irony Eliot had written elsewhere is 'always employed against himself' (*CP2*, 744). In contrast to this searching function of polemic irony, Eliot sees the ironic temper as a form of proud complacency:

> What we rebel against ... is the use of irony to give the appearance of a philosophy of life, as something final and not instrumental ...; it seems to us an evasion of the difficulty of living, where it pretends to be a kind of solution of it. (*CP4*, 516).[12]

Such resistance to finality stands behind the moral imperatives of *East Coker* and also much of Eliot's essay writing at the time. Concerned with things said long ago, the prose of the 1940s, 1950s and 1960s is often marked by revision if not correction of Eliot's earlier opinions. Milton comes in for somewhat kindlier treatment; Goethe transitions from idiosyncratic visionary to universal sage; and despite inauspicious beginnings, Kipling is recognised for his maturity.[13] But the most significant reappraisal is of Yeats, whose otherworldliness and craftsmanship had respectively met with bemused nods from a younger, brasher Eliot.[14] It is the older Eliot (more given to qualifications and parentheses) who would acknowledge a deep appreciation for the bare furnishings of Yeats's late poetry as well its ceaseless development.[15]

Eliot's culminating tribute came in 1940 – the year after Yeats's death and the year of *East Coker*'s publication. What is striking about this essay is the degree to which Eliot quietly identifies with Yeats. He singles out, for instance, the prefatory lines to *Responsibilities* which make explicit reference to the poet's age (forty-nine) and remarks that this 'freedom of speech' is a 'triumph' (*CP6*, 81); at the time of the lecture, Eliot was fifty-one – a fact that he highlights (78). Then there is the faint fusion of poetic horizons. Prior to quoting 'The Spur', Eliot writes that 'the old, unless they are stirred to something of the honesty with oneself expressed in [Yeats's] poetry, will be *shocked by such a revelation* of what a man really is and remains' (83, my emphasis). The words are not so much a self-reference to *East Coker*'s 'new and shocking valuation' (*P1*, 187) as an affirmation that Yeats informs that poem's struggle with the unpleasant experiences of age. For Eliot, such fidelity to poetic feeling was inseparable from fidelity to poetic evolution:

> [V]ery few poets have shown this capacity of adaptation to the years. It requires, indeed, an exceptional honesty and courage to face the change. Most men either cling to the experiences of youth, so that their writing becomes an insincere mimicry of their earlier work, or they leave their passion behind, and write only from the head, with a hollow and wasted virtuosity. There is another and even worse temptation: that of becoming dignified, of becoming public figures with only a public existence – coat-racks hung with decorations and distinctions, doing, saying and even thinking and feeling only what they believe the public expects of them. (*CP6*, 82–3)

Something of the Copeland motif is discernible here. The master's lesson seems inscribed in the apprentice's hand, particularly if we are alert to the self-recriminations of a man who had gradually come to represent the establishment rather than the advanced guard.[16] Eliot takes direction from 'Sailing to Byzantium', which likewise rankles against the institutionalised figure cut by the 'aged man'.[17] The poem's 'tattered coat upon a stick' becomes the essay's 'coat-rack'; 'Monuments of its own magnificence' correlates in similar alliterative fashion to 'decorations and distinctions'. Most striking is the mutual rebellion against crediting age with surety and serenity. An old man's singing soul, Yeats intimates, is directly proportional to the 'tatter[s] in its mortal dress', to its humilities and humiliations.

The reappraisal of Yeats's achievement invites comparison with Eliot's denunciations at the time: if Yeats positively exemplified the old man as explorer, John Masefield represented an undesirable opposite. In a carping *New English Weekly* column of September 1935, Eliot took issue with the Poet Laureate's claim that older poets are benevolently disposed towards their juniors. Such a role, Eliot claims, involves pretence, posturing and self-delusion: 'I am sure that all elder poets *believe* that they wish to encourage and help younger ones, they *believe* that they really care for poetry, and not merely for what they write themselves' (*CP5*, 268). Eliot's ironic emphasis frames the established writer's disinterested service as a kind of *bovarysme*, implying that the act of endorsement seldom constitutes more than disguised self-perpetuation. Few older poets are able to admire work other than their own, and they are often blind to the appreciation of imitators:

> [A]n imitation of one's own work, which one enjoys because it reminds one of one's own work, but which one fancies to be highly original, is what gives the maximum of pleasure at the slightest *cost of pain and effort and humility*. (*CP5*, 268, my emphasis).

Eliot's theme is not the relation between young and old but an internal struggle, discerned within the mature poet himself. This struggle disallows sagely self-regard and requires something akin to the sacrifice of personality advocated in 'Tradition and the Individual Talent'. Reformulated as a trenchant mode of self-criticism, the process involves an endless humility that rests upon endless humiliation: in order to focus his attention on the work yet to be done, the mature poet must 'perpetually [reject] his own work, passing through the phase of being embarrassed and ashamed' (269).

The question in turning to the 'endless' humility of *East Coker* is whether the poetry bears any such traces of embarrassment and shame: does it constitute a performance of a self-rejection rather than simply signalling a new point of departure? In a poem whose allusiveness at once bespeaks homage and mastery, such scepticism is valid. On the one hand, the sometimes debt-declaring practice of *Four Quartets* may be seen as part of that 'systematic negation of . . . aesthetic self-sufficiency' which C. D. Blanton identifies in late modernism.[18] Reflecting on the process of ageing, Eliot once noted the peculiar desire to 'shrink into one's family' (*L3*, 649). In literary terms, such desire might involve taking a humble position among your predecessors. On the other hand, Eliot could be seen further to entrench his own canonicity, not so much becoming the bearer of tradition as claiming the position for himself.[19] After all, Harold Bloom hailed him as an exemplary exponent of 'reverse *apophrades*', that paradoxical manoeuvre by which the dead return only to speak in the voices of their descendants.[20] Compelling as this argument is, my interest is in a more modest effect: how the poem's allusions and assimilations may be read as self-correcting rather than self-asserting. Or, to cast the question in terms of the Copeland motif: how do the words of another stand as a critique from within rather than from outside, inscribed within the text itself and in the author's own hand?

A Simulating Style

Given that the opening sequence of *East Coker* II was intended as something less than tributary, something parodic even, such a question seems out of place. Below I quote from the movement's opening lines, followed by Eliot's explanatory letter to Montgomery Belgion:

> What is the late November doing
> With the disturbance of the spring
> . . .
> Late roses filled with early snow?
> Thunder rolled by the rolling stars
> Simulates triumphal cars
> Deployed in constellated wars
> . . .
> Comets weep and Leonids fly
> Hunt the heavens and the plains
> Whirled in a vortex that shall bring
> The world to that destructive fire
> . . . (*P1*, 186–7)

> I don't know whether it strikes a reader . . . that the first passage . . . is meant to be a kind of parody of the earlier Yeats influenced by Blake (some of his poems are very much so); but that at the same time I use the word 'parody' only because I can think of no other: *the effect of a very small pinch of irony is not intended to be comic, and in any case the irony is not directed against Yeats* – is not literary criticism – but a part of something going on within my own mind at that point. (*P1*, 935; 19 July 1940; my emphasis)

It is testament to Eliot's subtlety that readers have been slow to pick up on the imitation. While Ricks and McCue indicate an allusion to Blake's 'To the Jews' in the first line, they venture no echoes of Yeats independent of this letter and another to Geoffrey Curtis.[21] Concealment was perhaps a necessary overcompensation. To have detected the conscious designs would also have required condemning it as in bad taste: how ill-judged to parody the recently deceased. Eliot covered his tracks so well that Gabriel

Hebert, one of the readers to whom a draft was entrusted, registered only echoes of *Burnt Norton* II.[22] The 'rolling stars' and 'constellated wars' bring to mind the 'inveterate scars' and 'forgotten wars' in the first *Quartet*, and there is an obvious return to the earlier sequence of tetrameters. With the 'disturbance of the spring' recalling many other intimations of discomfiting juvescence in his earlier work besides, the fears Eliot harboured about self-imitation were not altogether misplaced.[23]

We might reasonably ask how Yeats is meant to be glimpsed in this 'periphrastic study in a worn-out poetical fashion' (*P1*, 187). An immediate obstacle is diction. A word-scan reveals that 'November', 'disturbance', 'Simulates', 'deployed' and 'triumphal' do not occur in Yeats's poetry. While 'vortex' is a key term in *A Vision*, it might more readily be associated with the whirling bluster of Wyndham Lewis's *Blast*. The flora, too, is alien to Yeats's work. (Roses – of the world, of battle, of peace – are abundant in Yeats, but Eliot's debt here is to Thomas Campion.) Leaving aside the more obvious self-reference to *Coriolan* and its triumphal procession, one plausible correspondence is between 'triumphal cars' and the 'brazen cars' in Yeats's 'Who Goes with Fergus?' Eliot was fond of this lyric and often singled it out among Yeats's early poems for qualified praise: it is an 'anthology piece' (*CP6*, 80), 'exciting' yet 'obscure' (37), 'beautiful but highly artificial' (*CP5*, 35).

Artificiality seems to be the point of *East Coker* II, particularly if the opening glut of symbols stands for a supposedly debased currency. Consider Eliot's pointed evasion of direct comparison: 'Thunder ... *simulates* triumphal cars' (my emphasis). This is a highly artificial way of avoiding usual poetic artifice, of suggesting similitude without resorting to simile. It seems less fanciful to claim that 'thunder is like a triumphal car' than to impute a natural phenomenon's imitation of man-made machinery. 'Like' has the virtue of freeing the associative process from a causality outside the poet's mind; 'simulates' insinuates a clear separation between original and copy.[24] If the comparison's appeal is immediately to our sense of sound (thunder rumbles and rolls like the rushing wheels of a chariot), it is overridden by the silent sight of the stars (Auriga the 'charioteer' is near its zenith in late November). As the triumphal cars themselves emerge as constellations, as things to be seen, what the thunder says is muted. So, too, is the Yeatsian voice we are meant to hear.

Ignoring verbal congruence, a further dislocation is between mode and content. Even if we squintingly glean the silhouette of early Yeats in Eliot's 'apocalyptic visionary mode', as John Xiros Cooper terms it, it is difficult to reconcile this with the ostensible focus: the unpleasant stirrings of youth in age.²⁵ This is a recognisably Yeatsian theme, indeed *the* recognisably Yeatsian theme as singled out in Eliot's memorial lecture.²⁶ But it is synonymous with Yeats's late work and therefore synonymous with what Eliot identified as the late work's 'purging of poetical ornament' (*CP6*, 85). The particular compound ghost that emerges thus has a dual function: it belies the claim that this *was* a way of putting it and, in so doing, casts suspicion on the parabasis that indirectly declares its superiority over a 'worn-out' mode of expression.

Eliot's parody, it would seem, rests on an anachronistic consolidation: it enables the 'recrudescence of an ancient passion in a new emotion, in a new situation' (*CP3*, 722). Though these words refer to Dante and not to Yeats, they have bearing on the emotional reawakening in *East Coker* II, and also on the allusive manoeuvre that pays tribute to a dead master while appropriating his words in a self-punitive fashion. Eliot's memorable phrase occurs in his appraisal of *Purgatory* 30 at the moment when Dante is reunited with Beatrice and deserted by Virgil. Below is his translation of that encounter:

> Olive-crowned over a white veil, a lady appeared to me, clad under a green mantle in colour of living flame. And my spirit, after so many years since trembling in her presence it had been broken with awe, without further knowledge by eyes, felt, through hidden power which went out from her, the great strength of the old love. As soon as that lofty power struck my sense, which already had transfixed me before my adolescence, I turned leftwards with the trust of the little child who runs to his mama when he is frightened or distressed, to say to Virgil: 'Hardly a drop of blood in my body does not shudder: *I know the tokens of the ancient flame.*' (*CP3*, 722, my emphasis)

With youth's love rekindled, Dante wishes to express a renewed and personal appreciation of lines from Book 4 of *The Aeneid* (the italicised lines). But the irony of this allusion is doubled both by Virgil's departure and by the Pilgrim's infelicitous invocation of Dido – infelicitous, because the words here recalled simultaneously point to Dido's own rediscovery of passion and her tragic self-immolation.[27] Comparably, Dante's reunion with Beatrice implies not merely the flame of love but also the flame of purgation since his beloved's first words call him to account for moral fickleness. The passage offers a precursor to the Copeland motif. Given in his Tuscan tongue ('*conosco i segni dell' antica fiamma*') rather than in Virgil's Latin ('*adgnosco veteris vestigia flammae*') and directed at a vanished presence, the allusion fittingly reveals its own vanity – vanity both as emptiness and pride.[28] Though Dante weeps for his literary forebear, he is soon reminded that he should rather weep for his sins.[29] The poetry does not matter, to which the allusion stands as a harsh reminder.

The parallel with the opening of *East Coker* II is far from exact. Dante wishes to pay tribute to his master's language, while Eliot, however tactfully, parodies quaint poetic expression. Yet in both cases the act of imitation becomes an act of assimilation (or simulation) by which the younger poet draws attention to his own failings. This aspect is cast in relief by allusions in both *Purgatory* 30 and *East Coker* II that unambiguously recall and affirm the master's achievement. Dante reproduces a line from Book 6 of *The Aeneid* in Latin and moreover gives it sanctioning rhyme with biblical scripture: 'All of them cried: "*Benedictus qui venis*," / and scattering flowers upward and around, / "*Manibus*, oh, *date lilia plenis*."'[30] Eliot, in his turn, borrows 'frenzy' from 'An Acre of Grass', aligning his own poem's rejection of sage maturity with that of Yeats's. But as in *Purgatory* 30, a contrast emerges in *East Coker* by which the master's achievement remains intact while the apprentice emerges scathed by his misprision.

To read Eliot's parody only as a noble, self-denigrating gesture is to overlook an inherent tension between humility and pride, submission and strength. Alive to this tension also, Geoffrey Hill elsewhere records his doubt whether Eliot 'ever consciously surrenders rhetorical mastery' or that his 'penitential humility . . . inhibit[s] a readiness to accept the status of "maestro" conferred by a supportive yet coercive public'.[31] With pointed reference to *East Coker* II, Harry Blamires has similarly hinted at the potential for false modesty in the opening sequence, arguing that the poet manages 'to have his cake and eat it' by exhibiting great expressive dexterity while denouncing it as inadequate for the ends of modern poetry.[32] Such a view would seem to be borne out by Eliot's remarks in an interview given towards the end of 1940 in which he asserted the necessity of continually bringing poetic expression up to date:

> *the way of putting* words together is always changing. Any style, whether of prose or verse, belongs to its own period: and no writer, however skilful, can say anything that is important for his own time, or for any future time, in a style, however good, which belongs to a past age. (*CP6*, 132–3, my emphasis)

It is tempting to regard the sentiment and the partial echo from *East Coker* as a subconscious admission of the poem's antipathy towards Yeats, or as proof of parody in what Adorno calls its emphatic sense: 'the use of forms in the era of their impossibility'.[33] But if Eliot is to be taken at his word, we should remember that the parody was not intended as 'literary criticism' but as something personal, perhaps even self-reflexive. This is not to discount that he might be embroiled in the anxiety of influence or that he places himself in ambivalently combative relation to Yeats, but to recognise that the critic's mode of speaking is not the poet's.[34] Compare, for instance, Eliot's statement on the subject of emulation in a 1939 *Criterion* 'Commentary' with its humble revision in *East Coker*:

> It is true, I think, that poetry, if it is not to be a lifeless repetition of forms, must constantly be exploring 'the frontiers of the spirit.' But these frontiers are not like the surveys of geographical explorers, conquered once for all and settled. The frontiers of the spirit are more like the jungle which, unless continuously kept under control, is always ready to encroach and eventually obliterate the cultivated area. Our effort is as much to regain, under very different conditions, what was known to men writing at remote times and in alien languages. (*CP5*, 669)

> > And what there is to conquer
> > By strength and submission, has already been discovered
> > Once or twice, or several times, by men whom one cannot hope
> > To emulate – but there is no competition –
> > There is only the fight to recover what has been lost
> > And found and lost again and again: and now, under conditions
> > That seem unpropitious. But perhaps neither gain nor loss.
> > For us, there is only the trying. The rest is not our business.
> > (*P1*, 191)

The poetry is marked by the quiet interplay of those opposites mentioned above. There is a straining modesty in 'men whom one cannot hope / To emulate', not least because of the implicit insistence on male genius (how different is Marianne Moore's idea of emulation as a humble vulnerability, 'the shell which the hermit-crab selects for itself').[35] This modesty simultaneously bespeaks and suppresses the intention to surpass.[36] The strife of desiring another's gift and scope but also of striving against such desire is brought into sharp focus by the interruption, the anacoluthon ('- there is no competition -'), that chastens the double impulse. Similarly, the medial caesura in the penultimate line pulls the speaker up sharply so that he can refocus the poem's understanding of humility: 'But perhaps neither gain nor loss.' These local self-corrections fall within a larger dialogic chastisement in which the poet checks the critic, foreclosing any question of attainment.

The same kind of chastisement is operational in the opening sequence of Part II since it enacts the same fraught emulation. Though the depth of self-criticism in these lines is not immediately apparent without a thorough consideration of the subsequent disparagement of age in which Eliot more openly invokes Yeats, they offer an instance of the master/apprentice tension that assimilates the correcting voice and turns it inward. With the emphasis on an interiority rather than some 'outside stupidity', with 'something going on within my own mind', the subsequent metapoetic discursion invites us to see the parody as self-reflexive: not merely Yeats's Blake-influenced poetry, but Eliot's simulation of it constitutes something 'not very satisfactory' (*P1*, 187). Nor is it, pressing further, merely Eliot's mimicking of himself (*Burnt Norton*, *The Waste Land*, *Coriolan*) that causes dissatisfaction, but rather a poetry that keeps within its stable the parodic, satiric and dismissive. How unpleasant to read Mr Eliot, Mr Eliot seems to say.

Cheated and Cheating: Revisiting 'A Cooking Egg'

Yeats would have concurred. In 1936 he wrote two essays that expressed a distaste for Eliot's negative poetics. The first of these was the introduction to the *Oxford Book of Modern Verse*, which relegated Eliot to the rank of mere satirist and attributed his success to accomplished descriptions of people getting in and out of bed.[37] The second essay, 'Modern Poetry', levelled similar charges, declaring an outright aversion to Eliot's pessimism:

In the third year of the War came the most revolutionary man in poetry during my lifetime, though his revolution was stylistic alone ... No romantic word or sound, nothing reminiscent, nothing in the least like the painting of Ricketts could be permitted henceforth. Poetry must resemble prose, and both must accept the vocabulary of their time; nor must there be any special subject-matter. Tristram and Isoult were not a more suitable theme than Paddington Railway Station. The past had deceived us: let us accept the worthless present.[38]

Yeats here approaches a fleshing out of his satirical poem, 'Three Movements', in which 'those fish that lie gasping on the sand' insinuate something of Modernism's iconoclasm.[39] Though the first sentence in the paragraph situates us among the ironies of *Prufrock and Other Observations* (1917), the chronological sweep of the passage is potentially much broader. The deceiving past brings to mind 'Gerontion', the tragedy of Tristan and Isolde implicates *The Waste Land*, and mention of Paddington Station points, via Blake, to both 'A Cooking Egg' and *Burnt Norton*.[40]

Whether or not this arc was intended, *East Coker* II demonstrates alertness to the essay's possible echoes and criticisms of particular works, not to mention the sly irony in this poetry that very nearly resembles prose. The lines 'Had they deceived us, / Or deceived themselves, the quiet-voiced elders ...?' (*P1*, 187) engage 'Modern Poetry' directly, offering another instance of the Copeland motif. At first glance, they seem to turn Yeats's accusation on its head, implicating not abstract history but an older generation in an act of deceit. Admitting that the disenfranchisement of young men was due to 'the blundering frenzy of old men', the essay invites this line of attack and grants historical grounds for the literature of disillusionment that Yeats deprecates.[41] But the poem's adaptation ('The past had deceived us' becoming 'Had they deceived us') may also be seen to transfer the petulance and fatalism that takes a cheating past as sufficient reason to devalue the present.[42] In this light, the presence of Blake begins to make sense.[43] By recalling in the opening line 'To the Jews' – that wistful quatrain sequence in *Jerusalem* that mourns the loss of paradise – Eliot invites the reader to recall his former allusion to that same poem in 'A Cooking Egg'.[44]

If any of the early works epitomise the fatalistic surrender of youth and hope, it is 'A Cooking Egg'. With 'La Figlia Che Piange' and *Burnt Norton*, it numbers among those poems about a life that might have been. Unlike these poems, however, it stands out in mingling regret with bitter resentment. The speaker's bluster would suggest that Pipit in all her sad domesticity could never live up to his need for honour, capital, society and spiritual enlightenment.[45] But while his daydream permits him handshakes with courtiers and the like, he must eventually ask where the snows of yesteryear have gone. The epigraph, taken from François Villon's *The Testament* (a work that catalogues its author's sins and scandals), obscures only for a moment the glaring fact that the speaker's disgrace stems from inertia rather than misconduct. Similarly, the guest list he imagines suggests his own vitiated earthly existence. He would have us believe that Pipit is past her expiry date (the hint of the title), but it is really his youth that has been squandered and his future that tenders compromise. The typographical break after line 24 is the breaking of the speaker's resolve. Unable to keep up the pretence, he looks wistfully over his shoulder. Gone are the jokes, and gone is the glory. Even the quatrain sequence crumbles, and the poem terminates not on a neat rhyme but on three plodding stresses:

> Where are the eagles and the trumpets?
>
> Buried beneath some snow-deep Alps.
> Over buttered scones and crumpets
> Weeping, weeping multitudes
> Droop in a hundred A. B. C.'s. (*P1*, 39)

As they would be in *Coriolan* (1931), the symbols of victory and dominion are replaced by a base need to sate hunger: the masses seeking distraction in cloned Aerated Bread Company restaurants. It is here that Blake's vision of a long-lost world enters the poem; it is channelled through the overrun London suburbs, pervasive weeping and plaintive *ubi sunt*. While the longing for the intimacy of the shared penny bun is undercut by damning vulgarity (Pipit and the speaker, too, are seen in the shadow of the Dantean hordes eating 'buttered scones and crumpets'), the pining after 'eagles and trumpets' is marred by an implicit sense of entitlement. And while this line – isolated, hyperbolically grandiose – serves as another instance of wry self-awareness, its swagger only highlights that the speaker feels cheated.

This feeling carries into *East Coker* II: 'What was to be the value of the long looked forward to, / Long hoped for calm, the autumnal serenity / And the wisdom of age?' (*P1*, 187). By sleight of hand, the poem casts its gripe as the frustration of a universal hope ('It was not . . . what *one* had expected') before distilling it in more personal terms ('Had *they* deceived *us*').⁴⁶ This modulation of voice demarcates a structural division within the second stanza which more clearly intimates the presence of 'A Cooking Egg'. Since the metapoetic interjection and the impersonal pronoun typify the voice heard in lines 18–22, the actual resumption of the theme is signalled by repeating the interrogative that initiates the movement and also calls Blake to mind. Thus we find verbal and thematic contiguity between 'What are those golden Builders doing' ('To the Jews'), 'Where are the eagles and trumpets?' ('A Cooking Egg'), 'What is the late November doing' and 'What was to be the value' (*East Coker* II).

No less than 'A Cooking Egg', *East Coker* expresses deep disappointment about thwarted expectations. But if the early poem assists us in discerning the plaintive tone of the late poem, it also transfers the theme of complicity. The voice of *East Coker* ostensibly blames the quiet-voiced elders for deceiving the young. But there is an indeterminacy about the position of the speaker that not only tilts the poem's criticisms at the deceptions of the old but also at the complacency and misguided hopes of the young. When pausing to consider what these hopes are, it becomes apparent that a certain self-deception is being exposed. One might reasonably wonder whether the 'long looked forward to, / Long hoped for calm' is a universal concern among the young. A more probable source for the longing is Eliot's own poetry, which so often juxtaposes desire's anxiety and its escape. The tension is central to the experiences of Prufrock, who discounts the possibility that the mermaids will sing to him, while yet hoping for it. The same tension is felt in the undertow of 'La Figlia Che Piange'. The speaker would prefer that his 'afternoon repose' (28) remain undisturbed by the desires of youth, yet he cannot avoid being 'amazed' by what he disingenuously calls 'cogitations' – those thoughts which rekindle an image of lost love. And, as we have seen, 'A Cooking Egg' pits the safe cerebrations about a speculative future against a real life with Pipit.

In *East Coker*, as in each of these cases, the longing for calm is born out of the mixing of memory and desire. And like the earlier poems, it too effects that '*dédoublement* of the personality against which the subject struggles'. Donald Davie remarked that if Eliot parodically inserts himself into his own poems, the reader must know 'when to give almost full credence to what the poetry says, when to make reservations according as he detects the voice of now one persona, now another parodying the first'.[47] This is astute; it prompts us to recognise that while appearing to speak on behalf of those anticipating the 'autumnal serenity' of maturity, the speaker can only be disabused of his misconceptions about age by arriving at the destination himself. In this light, the divide between 'us' and 'them' seems spurious. Just as the parody of Yeats in the opening section implies a parody of Eliot himself, so the complaint against old men functions as a complaint against the speaker himself: neither the early work's resignation nor the late work's recriminations are a satisfying way of putting it.

Lines for Old Men: Complicity, Responsibility, Humility

'You must have humility, and you must have conviction. Humility and conviction should express our attitude towards the past and towards the future. But for humility people are apt to put defeatism, and for conviction cockiness' (*CP5*, 135). These words hardly rebuff Geoffrey Hill's complaints from the opening of this chapter. Not only do they employ an admonishing 'you', but they also concern literal questions of trespass and property. Speaking from the platform of his *Criterion* 'Commentary' in October 1934, Eliot here takes a critical line on the work of the National Trust. The need for preservation, he explains, may index an undesirable state of affairs that goes beyond suburban sprawl or commercial expansionism. Guarding certain sites could mean severing them from the communities they have long served, thus breaking the continuity between past and present ('necessarye coniunction'?). On the other hand, it might project uncertainty about the future. Whether because of pride or timidity, an overreaching conservatism forecloses on a society's capacity for communal ownership. While Eliot's piece has nothing directly to do with *East Coker*, it nevertheless speaks to the poem's general concerns about responsibility – the responsibility to accept past failures penitentially, but not to let penance turn to torpor or timidity. With due deference to Geoffrey Hill, I turn in this final section to the humble conviction behind *East Coker*'s haranguing of old men and old poems.

It is perhaps not surprising to find 'Gerontion' recalled in the later poem's wrangling with the gerontocracy, nor that this recall is effected through Yeats. Beginning as approving reiteration, the third allusion to Yeats transforms into an internalised critique directed at Eliot himself, Yeats and the wisdom of other old men like Gerontion:

> Do not let me hear
> Of the wisdom of old men, but rather of their folly,
> Their fear of fear and frenzy, their fear of possession,
> Of belonging to another, or to others, or to God. (*P1*, 188)

The thread of Yeats's 'An Acre of Grass' is picked up again after the opening of *East Coker*, which admits among its dissipated symbols the 'old house' and a stirring mouse.[48] In the second movement, Eliot recasts that poem's wished-for 'frenzy' and also the urgency of its imperative mood ('Grant me an old man's frenzy'). Side by side, these poems dramatise the disappointments of age and its obscure vantage point. For Yeats, the aged mind cannot 'make the truth known'; for Eliot, there is 'only the knowledge of dead secrets' (*P1*, 187). In the face of such disappointments, the poems pursue a similar antidote through dissimilar means. Yeats affirms the vitalising frenzy in Lear, Timon, Blake (again) and Michelangelo. Eliot, true to form, pursues a *via negativa*, sardonically wishing to be disabused of the virtues of age by exposure to its vices.[49]

Here, too, is a variation on the Copeland motif: the lines absorb and modify both Yeats's poem and the 'blundering frenzy of old men' from 'Modern Poetry'. No reader familiar with Eliot's early and middle poetry can miss the invitation to conjure examples of old or ageing men insulated by overcautious self-possession: the solipsistic Prufrock, the controlling speaker of 'La Figlia Che Piange', the passive Gerontion. The latter offers the most compelling connections. While 'Gerontion' declares that 'History . . . deceives with whispering ambitions' (*P1*, 31–3), *East Coker* II imputes the deceit of 'quiet-voiced elders' (there is thus a triple overlap involving the past, deception and muted communications). Both poems also make reference to an apocalyptic wind. The named creatures of 'Gerontion' are 'whirled . . . in atoms'; so too, in the *Quartet*, stars and comets are 'Whirled in a vortex'. Furthermore, in 'Gerontion', the nightmare of history 'gives' but vainly ('with supple confusion', 'too soon', 'too late'), and in

East Coker II, old men bequeath what is false or no longer useful. Not unlike in 'A Cooking Egg', both speakers feel cheated by an anteriority. But despite these correspondences, the poems stand in antagonistic relationship: in ridiculing the fear and insularity of old men, the late poem asks us to remember Gerontion's inaction and failure of 'closer contact'. Abdicating responsibility, he represents the inverse to Auden's humble figure whose lack of ego allows him to participate and persevere without fear of failure.

Marina MacKay offers a careful reading in which the political recriminations implicit in the early poem are dredged up in the late poem so as to establish continuity between the post-First World War failures and those leading up to the Second World War.[50] This is incisive but can be taken further if we are alive to the tenuous position from which the past is criticised. As *East Coker* II stands inscribed in red next to the enervations of 'Gerontion', so too 'Gerontion' troubles the margins of *East Coker* II. Indeed, the correspondences listed above would suggest something of a self-punitive recollection, an admission of complicity, or what *Little Gidding* calls the 'rending pain of re-enactment' (*P1*, 205). For 'Gerontion' not only triangulates with Yeats's criticism in 'Modern Poetry' and its absorption in *East Coker* II, but it further reinforces the ironic doubling within the late poem that negates hindsight's usual certainty.

In 'Gerontion', the intermediary position of the speaker is consolidated by the poem's epigraph from *Measure for Measure*. While Gerontion's very name identifies him as a little old man, the play's accusatory words locate him in a nebulous zone:

> Thou hast nor youth, nor age,
> But as it were an after-dinner's sleep
> Dreaming on both; for all thy blessed youth
> Becomes as aged, and doth beg the alms
> Of palsied eld: and when thou art old and rich,
> Thou hast neither heat, affection, limb, nor beauty
> To make thy riches pleasant. What's yet in this
> That bears the name of life?[51]

The Duke's speech is meant to fortify the condemned Claudio in a stoic embrace of whatever fate he may meet. He does this by deriding the quintessential weakness of humans: our nobility is a product of our baseness, our selfhood splintered ('thou exist on many a thousand grains'), our life subject to 'skyey influences'.[52]

These sentiments are perpetuated and pushed to an almost quietist extreme in 'Gerontion'. In lamenting the untimely gifts of history and by invalidating the consequences of moral action, Gerontion seems to parody the Duke. Virtue stems from vice (and vice versa), self-consciousness is the sum of 'a thousand small deliberations', and in being 'whirled / Beyond the circuit of the shuddering Bear / In fractured atoms', life is governed by external forces (*P1*, 33). Some of these resignations have residual life in *East Coker* II. Employing a rhetoric of devaluation comparable to Gerontion's and the Duke's, the speaker expresses disenchantment with the 'value' of age. In this depreciation, 'serenity' becomes 'deliberate hebetude', 'wisdom' the 'knowledge of dead secrets', and self-knowledge only an epistemic atomisation: 'every moment is a new and shocking / Valuation of all we have been' (*P1*, 187). There is also a degree of correspondence in the negative pedagogy: to get the most out of what living is left, the Duke instructs, be 'absolute for death'; to gain wisdom, the poem's speaker urges, be edified by folly.[53]

In Chapter 1, I mentioned the difference between sources and allusions: the former stands quietly in background, while the latter is invited into the conversation, asked to trade resonances.[54] The treatment of *Measure for Measure* in *East Coker* II fittingly falls somewhere between these camps: without being directly invoked, it resonates via 'Gerontion'. The effect serves to highlight a dangerous passivity. In its original context, the Duke's wisdom aligns with a Christian disregard for self. Indeed, the phrase 'a breath thou art' draws on James 4: 13–14 and its admonishments against an over-anxious concern for the future (the kind of concern Eliot criticises in his piece on the National Trust):

> Go to now, ye that say, To day or to morrow we will go into such a city and continue there a year, and buy and sell, and get gain: Whereas ye know not what shall be on the morrow. For what is your life? It is even a vapour, that appeareth for a little time, and then vanisheth away.

Likewise, Claudio is instructed in the way of endless, teleologically divested humility: forget yourself and also any question of gain. But in 'Gerontion' this self-surrender is perverted into a fatalistic despair which *East Coker* handles ambivalently. This despair is rejected when calling on 'Old men ... to be explorers' (*P1*, 191) but subsumed in resigning to the notion that quiet-voiced elders have cheated their juniors.

It is worth recalling that 'Gerontion' was written in the aftermath of the First World War and that its personification of moral torpor stands, in Vincent Sherry's estimation, as 'reference and rebuke' to the Treaty of Versailles.[55] As a product of its time, written *'entre les deux guerres'* (*P1*, 191), *East Coker* may similarly be read as a statement of disgust at the Munich Agreement of 1938 and the eventuation of another devastating global conflict. This again is MacKay's view, who persuasively argues that the poem's invocation of 'Gerontion' reinforces its criticism of the 'dissociated passivity' of the gerontocracy leading up to the outbreak of the War.[56] While certainly true as an indictment of contemporary geopolitics, the ironies and ambivalences of the poem make it impossible to see *East Coker* as a condemnation untouched by either self-reflexivity or an admission of complicity. The fact of the speaker's doubleness in *East Coker* II, cumulatively suggested by the presence of the earlier poems, gestures at moral entanglement.[57] And in this regard, the poem stands as a companion piece to the stirring conclusion of *The Idea of a Christian Society*, published just five months before *East Coker* on 26 October, 1939:

> I believe that there must be many persons who, like myself, were deeply shaken by the events of September 1938, in a way from which one does not recover; persons to whom that month brought a profounder realisation of a general plight . . . . *The feeling which was new and unexpected was a feeling of humiliation, which seemed to demand an act of personal contrition, of humility, repentance and amendment; what had happened was something in which one was deeply implicated and responsible*. It was not, I repeat, a criticism of the government, but a doubt of the validity of civilization. We could not match conviction with conviction, we had no ideas with which we could either meet or oppose the ideas opposed to us. (*CP5*, 717, my emphasis)

With this declaration of personal responsibility in mind, it is important to recognise how *East Coker* II disallows too direct a scapegoating of the gerontocracy. During the denunciation of the 'wisdom of old men', one particular line opens onto a syntactical ambiguity that not only extends the disavowal of the quiet-voiced elders but also introduces a critique of the voice that disavows:

'Let me hear of old men's fear of frenzy', as well as 'Let me hear of their frenzy'. Put differently, Eliot's phrasing allows an irreducible doubleness that ironises timidity and brazenness, defeatism and cockiness – hindrances to humility and conviction. Read in this second way ('Let me hear of their frenzy'), the line is representative of the mode within *Four Quartets* that disallows the late poetic voice to find solace and superiority in the fact of its lateness. It is a mode that interrogates those moments that would otherwise declare themselves as interrogative. To use De Man's fine formulation: it is irony that manifests 'specular structures within the self, within which the self looks at itself from a certain distance'.[58] So when the knowing voice of the second movement declares the first to be 'not very satisfactory', there is yet another voice calling it into question. Likewise, as the speaker notes his disappointment at having been cheated out of autumnal serenity, a question arises about the basis of his hope and the extent to which he is responsible for its frustration. So, too, from within the indignant demands to see old men's fear of frenzy exposed, does the poem generate awareness of itself as transgressing to the other extreme. In other words, the syntactical ambiguity facilitates reading the indignation as another form of deception to be guarded against, what *Little Gidding* calls 'the conscious impotence of rage / At human folly' (*P1*, 205).

The latter word, of course, first occurs in *East Coker*. In keeping with the poem's ironic operations, 'folly' is made to bear both negative and positive connotations. The first is the common-sense understanding of folly as foolishness – the 'blundering frenzy of old men'. But steeped in Pascal as he was, Eliot knew that folly could also be a wisdom unlike that of the world:

> Original sin is folly in the eyes of men, but it is put forward as such . . . But this folly is wiser than all men's wisdom, it is wiser than men. For without it, what are we to say man is? His whole state depends on this imperceptible point. How could he have become aware of it through his reason, seeing that it is something contrary to reason and that his reason, far from discovering it by its own methods, draws away when presented with it?[59]

Such folly stands in contrast to 'enchantment', which in *East Coker* II and elsewhere signals the deception of sin.[60] Folly instead speaks to an awareness of sin, of being personally implicated and responsible. And from this awareness there is a decisive movement towards self-forgetfulness and grace: 'belonging to another, to others, or to God' (*P1*, 188). In this aspect *East Coker* differs from 'Gerontion'. The early poem, similarly weighed down by an awareness of sin and guilt, resorts to resignation: 'After such knowledge, what forgiveness?' (*P1*, 32). By contrast, *East Coker* supplements its 'imperfect humility' with 'perfect humility' by stating the necessity of belonging to God.[61]

If the speaker here seems to shed his doubleness, to speak directly and under no threat of self-cancellation, we should recall Eliot to More on the subject of belonging to God. It is the 'feeling of being stripped, as of frippery, of the qualifications that ordinarily most identify one: one's heredity, one's abilities, one's *name*' (*L8*, 442, Eliot's emphasis). Such a stripping seems to take place in the last two lines of the section: 'The houses are all gone under the sea / The dancers are all gone under the hill' (*P1*, 188). I started by alluding to Ricks's observation that these lines, by having the final word, humble the statement about endless humility. In light of the letter to More, we may add to this and say that the stridency with which the speaker asserts himself before this point now gives way to dispossession. Where previously 'Houses rise and fall, crumble, are extended' (*P1*, 185) or may even be identified by a 'silent motto' (a nod to the Eliot family's *Tace et fac*), they now disappear entirely. Where earlier the dancers are given, via Eliot's use of Thomas Elyot and the site of East Coker, ancestral specificity, they are here relieved of identity. The effacement looks ahead to the poem's conclusion: 'Here or there does not matter' (192). A self-cancellation is still taking place, only now it is not driven by the poet's relation to himself or his master but by his relation to God. In this movement of assent, he avoids falling prey to an interminable irony that issues in defeatism or cockiness. By recalling the petulance, insularity and fear of belonging in his early work via Yeats, Eliot meets his criterion for maturity by 'rejecting his own work, [and] passing through the phase of being embarrassed and ashamed'. But by disallowing the late poetry itself to become a form of 'deliberate hebetude' or the complacent wisdom of an older man, he makes *East Coker* itself vulnerable to a degree of embarrassment and shame, disallowing it the complacency of the ironic temper.

Notes

1. Ricks, *T. S. Eliot and Prejudice*, 240–1.
2. See Geoffrey Galt Harpham, *The Ascetic Imperative in Culture and Criticism* (Chicago: The University of Chicago Press, 1987), 18. Also: Gavin Flood, *The Ascetic Self: Subjectivity, Memory and Traditions* (Cambridge: Cambridge University Press, 2004), 13.
3. Søren Kierkegaard, *Either/Or, Part II*, ed. and trans. Howard V. Hong and Edna H. Hong (Princeton: Princeton University Press, 1987), 135.
4. W. H. Auden, 'The Prince's Dog', in *The Dyer's Hand and Other Essays* (New York: Random House, 1962), 199–200.
5. W. H. Auden, 'Dingley Dell & The Fleet', in *Dyer's Hand*, 415.
6. Geoffrey Hill, 'Dividing Legacies', in *Collected Critical Writings*, ed. Kenneth Haynes (Oxford: Oxford University Press, 2008), 377–8.
7. Eliot explained in 1947 that there are 'passages in the poems which are deliberately intended to give an effect of flatness for purposes of contrast' (*P1*, 882).
8. See Wayne C. Booth, *A Rhetoric of Irony* (Chicago: The University of Chicago Press, 1974), 3–8; Cleanth Brooks, 'Irony as a Principle of Structure', *The Critical Tradition: Classic Texts and Contemporary Trends*, ed. David H. Richter (Boston: Bedford / St. Martin's, 2007), 799–806.
9. See Søren Kierkegaard, *The Concept of Irony: With Continual Reference to Socrates*, ed., trans. and intro. Howard V. Hong and Edna H. Hong (Princeton: Princeton University Press, 1989), 131; Schlegel in Paul De Man, *Aesthetic Ideology*, ed. and intro. Andrzej Warminski (Minneapolis: University of Minnesota Press, 1996), 178–9; 169.
10. Allen Tate, 'Irony and Humility', in Brooker, *Contemporary Reviews*, 188–92.
11. Tate, 'Irony and Humility', 190. Cf. Eugene Goodheart, *The Failure of Criticism* (Cambridge, MA: Harvard University Press, 1978), 53: '[Eliot's] severely moralizing habit ... would make for solemnity if it were not for a superb self-irony akin to Christian humility ...'
12. This is put succinctly in *The Cocktail Party* (*CPP*, 417): 'Disillusion can become itself an illusion / If we rest in it.'
13. Most of these reassessments are contained in *On Poetry and Poets*. For the most compelling overview of Eliot's revised opinions, see Ricks, *Decisions and Revisions*.
14. See, for instance, *CP2*, 72–6; *CP1*, 724–5.
15. See Eliot in 'To Criticise the Critic' (*CP8*, 460): 'as we age we tend to make more reservations, to qualify our positive assertions, to introduce more parentheses'.

16. See, for instance, Jeffrey M. Perl, *Skepticism and Modern Enmity: Before and After Eliot* (Baltimore: Johns Hopkins University Press, 1989), 134. It is a delicious fact that Eliot scribbled on the back of his lecture notes a first draft of *Little Gidding* – that penitential poem in which Yeats's voice, among others, would be raised in rebuke.
17. W. B. Yeats, *The Poems*, ed. and intro. Daniel Albright (London: Everyman's Library, 1992), 239.
18. C. D. Blanton, *Epic Negation: The Dialectical Poetics of Late Modernism* (Oxford: Oxford University Press, 2015), 20–1.
19. Consider Eliot's characterisation of borrowing as a type of anointment (*CP2*, 67): 'We do not imitate, we are changed; and our work is the work of the changed man; we have not borrowed, we have been quickened, and we become bearers of a tradition.'
20. Harold Bloom, *The Anxiety of Influence: A Theory of Poetry* (New York: Oxford University Press, 1973), 141–2.
21. Eliot to Geoffrey Curtis, 31 December 1940: 'The first movement of part II is a *serious* kind of parody of early Yeats under the influence of Blake. Otherwise I should have thought that Yeats was chiefly apparent in the references to old age (with a difference)' (*P1*, 935).
22. See *P2*, 496.
23. See Helen Gardner, *The Composition of* Four Quartets (London: Faber and Faber, 1978), 16–17.
24. Cf. *CP2*, 184, my emphasis: '[The poetry of Swinburne] would only be [sham poetry] if you could produce or suggest something that it pretends to be and is not. The world of Swinburne does not depend upon some other world which it *simulates* . . .' On Eliot's 'simulation', see also Ronald Bush, whose chapter remains one of the finest assessments of *Four Quartets*. Bush remarks that Eliot's 'simulated voices fail to convince', though he has in mind Eliot's programmatic or orchestral arrangement across *Four Quartets*, not the simulation of Yeats. Bush, *T. S. Eliot: A Study in Character and Style* (Oxford: Oxford University Press, 1983), 222.
25. John Xiros Cooper, *T. S. Eliot and the Ideology of* Four Quartets (Cambridge: Cambridge University Press, 1995), 176.
26. See Eliot's discussion of Yeats's 'The Spur' and *Purgatory* (*CP6*, 83).
27. See Peter S. Hawkins, *Dante's Testaments: Essays in Scriptural Imagination* (Stanford: Stanford University Press, 1999), 130.
28. Eliot discusses this borrowing in a letter of 1929, comparing the Latin and Italian (*L4*, 706–7).
29. Dante, *Pur.* 30.50–1.
30. Dante, *Pur.* 30.19–21. Here I use Mandelbaum's translation, who preserves the Latin. *The Divine Comedy*, trans. Allen Mandelbaum (New York: Knopf, 1995). The biblical verse is Matt. 23: 39 in

which Christ actually quotes the prophetic words of Ps. 118: 26; the line from *The Aeneid* occurs in Book 6.883.
31. Hill, 'Poetry as "Menace" and "Atonement"', in *Collected Critical Writings*, 5, 12.
32. Harry Blamires, *Word Unheard: A Guide through Eliot's Four Quartets* (London: Methuen and Co., 1969), 53.
33. Adorno, *Notes to Literature*, 259.
34. William V. Spanos, for instance, observes a disjunction between the stridency of Eliot's prose and the 'patent humility of Eliot's poetic voice'. *On the Ethical Imperatives of the Interregnum: Essay in Loving Strife from Soren Kierkegaard to Cornel West* (Cham: Palgrave Macmillan, 2016), 32.
35. Moore, 'Humility, Concentration, and Gusto', 428.
36. Dedicating his *Criterion* 'Commentary' to Yeats on the occasion of his seventieth birthday, Eliot wrote that the older poet's development 'sets a standard which his juniors should seek to emulate, without hoping to equal' (*CP5*, 260).
37. W. B. Yeats, 'Introduction', in *The Oxford Book of Modern Verse: 1892–1935* (Oxford: Oxford University Press, 1936), xxi–xxiii.
38. W. B. Yeats, 'Modern Poetry', in *Essays and Introductions* (London: Macmillan, 1961), 499.
39. Yeats, *The Poems*, 290. Beckett refers to this poem in 'Recent Irish Poetry' (*Dis*, 70); he derides Yeats's derision of those poets who break with convention.
40. Later in the essay (503–4), Yeats quotes from *Burnt Norton*, which had recently been published. The place naming in the third movement calls to mind Blake's *Jerusalem*.
41. Yeats, 'Modern Poetry', 500.
42. Ricks and McCue (*P1*, 937) provide one of Hugh Latimer's sermons as a possible source for lines 25–6. While there is an obvious verbal parallel with the Latimer, its meaning does not transfer since the speaker in the latter work is Christ.
43. Eliot remarked that Blake 'ke[pt] on getting into' *East Coker*. See Gardner, *Composition*, 17.
44. 'What are those golden builders doing / Near mournful ever-weeping Paddington . . .' For the full poem, see William Blake, *Poetical Works*, intro. W. B. Yeats (London: George Routledge & Sons, 1910), 221–4.
45. This much is also suggested by Eliot's scathing declaration on the unveiling of his letters to Emily Hale: his life would have been dull and predictable; see https://tseliot.com/foundation/statement-by-t-s-eliot-on-the-opening-of-the-emily-hale-letters-at-princeton/?fbclid=IwAR1qjObn4ZvMeJIgKcUhlWsxysw-oOAkaivpaJqd4lXKZ1_AOfC9HhHAwTI. Eeldrop projects similar disappointments for Edith in *Eeldrop and Appleplex* (*CP1*, 529).

46. My emphasis.
47. Donald Davie, 'T. S. Eliot: The End of an Era', in *T. S. Eliot: A Collection of Critical Views*, ed. Hugh Kenner (Englewood Cliffs: Prentice Hall, 1962), 204.
48. Yeats, *The Poems*, 348–9. See also 'Ancestral Houses' (246–7) which has in common with *East Coker* a picture of passing legacies: the inheritor of the stately home is 'but a mouse'. See Sabine Roth, 'Eliot Comforted: The Yeatsian Presence in "Four Quartets"', *Journal of Modern Literature* 18.4 (1993): 411–20.
49. In *Timon of Athens*, Eliot identified a 'positive fury' (*CP5*, 549) that would not seem to be far from Yeats's 'frenzy'. And *King Lear*, that 'poor, infirm, weak, and despised old man' (III, ii, 20), seems a figure apposite to Eliot's argument. But whether a similar commodiousness is transferred by the historical figures is less sure. Michelangelo drags in a humanist triumphalism that cuts against the grain of a poem that sees humans and animals levelled in 'Dung and death'. And given that Eliot once described him as a man 'excessive in pride' (*CP2*, 242), Blake seems a presence anathema to a discourse on endless humility. But of course, Blake already spectres *East Coker* without any assistance from 'An Acre of Grass'. He is there in the parodic style of the opening section and, more obviously, in an echo that echoes elsewhere in Eliot too.
50. See Marina MacKay, *Modernism and World War II* (Cambridge: Cambridge University Press, 2007), 74.
51. William Shakespeare, *Measure for Measure*, Updated Edition, ed. Brian Gibbons (Cambridge: Cambridge University Press, 2006), III, i, 32–9.
52. Shakespeare, *Measure*, III, i, 20; III, i, 9.
53. Shakespeare, *Measure*, III, i, 5.
54. See the discussion of Dante and Charles Péguy in Chapter 1.
55. Vincent Sherry, *The Great War and the Language of Modernism* (Oxford: Oxford University Press, 2003), 3.
56. MacKay, *Modernism and World War II*, 74
57. Steve Ellis writes that the 'post-Munich journey is for Eliot not one of collective uplift, enthusiasm and worldwide triumph in the war against selfishness rather than against fascism, but an intensification of a state of penance and alienation, a renewed sense of limitation both personal and collective'. Ellis, *British Writers and the Approach of World War II* (New York: Cambridge University Press, 2015), 28.
58. De Man, *Aesthetic Ideology*, 169.
59. Pascal, *Pensées and Other Writings*, 132.
60. 'Enchantment' features variously in Eliot's essays and poetry. Its clearest link with sin and deception is in *The Family Reunion*, where

it occurs twice. It prominently figures in a speech of Agatha's, which is representative of the play's central concern: atonement (*CPP*, 333, 348): 'You may learn hereafter,' she says to Harry, 'Moving alone through flames of ice, chosen / To resolve the enchantment under which we suffer.'

61. For my earlier discussion of imperfect and perfect humility, see the Introduction.

6

How It Is and the Syntax of Penury

Beckett's aim for *How It Is* was clear to him even during its stuttering incipience: 'to find the rhythm and syntax of extreme weakness, penury perhaps I should say' (*L3*, 211). With the weight he attached to the word 'perhaps', the qualification seems crucial.[1] Stripped of narrative convention, relayed by a shadowy figure and set in a lightless mudscape, the tale is indeed one of penury. Deprivation is ubiquitous: the narrator has suffered the loss of his learning, the loss of his wife and even the loss of his dog. He encounters a fellow-creature, Pim, only to be abandoned. Readers, too, are forced to do without: the text's gasped fragments are bereft of punctuation and narrative footholds. What kindly markers there appear to be soon betray their status as 'ill-said' (*HII*, 3): the three-part schema offers only a mirage of temporal linearity, while the narrator's authority as one describing 'how it is' is undermined by repeated confessions that he catches only every few words uttered by a voice within and without.

Much has been made of the phrase 'syntax of weakness'. This shibboleth of Beckett's failing art has enjoyed critical currency ever since Lawrence Harvey relayed it in 1970, and has been read in relation to Beckett's language, ethics and aesthetic non-conformity.[2] My interest, however, lies with the suggestiveness of the afterthought quoted above – 'the rhythm and syntax of . . . penury'. It aligns with Beckett's declared desire for a formal poverty to match his supposed 'mental poverty' (*L4*, 593). It anticipates the realisation that his was the way of lessness – lessness of form, of content, of the interconnectedness between the new work and the old. But apart from chiming with Beckett's statements about impoverishment, the phrase 'syntax of penury' telescopes a slippage between discrete aspects of the writing. Empirically, we might say that 'syntax of penury' is neglected because it occurs just twice in recently published letters describing the composition of *How It Is*, and that in both cases it is preceded by the better known 'syntax of weakness'. Conceptually, I want to hazard, it is neglected because 'weakness' and 'penury' invite consolidated understanding, as does Beckett's perhaps too-famous concern with 'impotence, ignorance'.[3] What is lost in such an elision is the separation of means and ends. Weakness (weaker cousin of impotence) is a teleological concern for Beckett, the apotheosis of creativity: 'to be an artist is to fail' (*PTD*, 144). But what facilitates this drive is a practice of divestment whose very performance attests to some measure of power (this is the paradox of asceticism discussed in Chapter 5). So the question, then, is this: how does penury propel Beckett's art towards an impotence that is never finally attained? Or, more cynically, can penury be used without turning loss into gain?[4]

Beckett himself seemed uncertain. In a letter of 6 April 1950, he says to Georges Duthuit that there is a clear separation between penury and impotence despite a 'tendency to think of them as standing together' (*L2*, 195). He continues: 'The poor are able to, rather. Not even poor, that is what we have to bear, not even poor and yet not able to . . . Treasures of poverty, maybe; but of impotence, no, we shall do without treasures.' These words speak presciently to the rhythm and syntax of penury in *How It Is* – a novel obsessively concerned with the riches and deprivations of knowledge, with the waning of relations. 'Treasures of poverty' belongs to Beckett's storehouse of poor allusions, evoking the parable in the Gospel of Matthew (13: 44–6) of the man who sells all his possessions in order to buy a hidden treasure, the kingdom of heaven. The oxymoron condenses the problem implicit in a syntax of penury: knowledge that demonstrates an awareness of its own vanity is still knowledge. The incorporation of ascetic or apophatic writings is not a sufficient measure for a poetics of ignorance or a syntax of penury, since it still results in some form of enrichment: the text accrues semiotic significance, while the author courts literary pedigree by association.[5] The same may be said of intratextual relations within the same *oeuvre*, what Beckett called the 'velleities of self-diffusion' (*L1*, 188). Bersani and Dutoit's term is 'narcissistic concentration': a mode of 'self-dispersal, as the simultaneous confirmation *and* loss of identity in a potentially endless process of inaccurate self-replications'.[6] Just as allusion may be a way of affirming traditional belonging ('tradition' here in Eliot's sense), so self-referentiality may entrench an author's canonicity.

John Updike's 1964 *New Yorker* review of *How It Is* was alive to this possibility. Parodying the novel's style, the young American claimed that *How It Is* piggybacked on the achievement of Beckett's earlier work: 'something undergraduate inert a neo-classicism in which one's early works are taken as the classics a laziness in which young urgencies become old rhetoric hermetic avant-gardism unviolated by the outer world the world beyond the skin'.[7] The indictment is ambiguous. On the one hand, Updike seems to suggest that a cynical complacency had crept into Beckett's art. On the other hand, his gripe appears to be with the institution that had sprung up around the writer. The impersonal and passive construction – 'one's early works are taken as classics' – hints at critical canonisation rather than self-appraisal, though it unfurls in an accusation of complacent rehashing that hardly exculpates the author. Oedipal strife aside, Updike's review perspicaciously responds to the pitfalls of Beckett becoming Beckettian.

Beckett himself was not insensitive to the danger. In 1960, shortly after receiving a preview of Martin Esslin's *The Theatre of the Absurd*, he vented his misgivings about 'crritical' interpretations of his work. Wryly he notes the 'usual liminal reference to my right hand bowling, left hand batting and scrum halfing – the popular oaf. This I know makes all clear and Pim mud = Portora playing fields' (*L3*, 358). The word 'usual' is telling. By the time of 'Pim's mud' – that is, the publication of *Comment C'est* in 1961 – the number of scholarly works had started racking up. Federman and Fletcher's meta-critical survey, *Samuel Beckett: His Works and His Critics*, documents the following statistics for publications by 1961: four monographs dedicated solely to Beckett; thirty-one books with partial focus; two doctoral theses and two master's dissertations; one special journal issue; dozens of academic articles and high-profile reviews.[8] The catalogue is not meant to suggest that *How It Is* constitutes a response to the enterprise of Beckett studies, only that the novel was written against the backdrop of an exploding body of scholarship.[9] And though impossible to quantify, Beckett's awareness of this boom must nonetheless be assumed to colour the composition of a text which so obsessively echoes his earlier works.

How It Is is dogged by a certain anxiety of influence. Self-consciously, it stands in the shadow not of Joyce or Proust, but of Beckett's own earlier writing and employs something akin to the kenotic procedures Harold Bloom identifies in *The Anxiety of*

Influence. As I explained in the Introduction, kenosis is of theological provenance and pertains to Christ's self-emptying of his divine nature upon becoming human. In a literary context, it constitutes a 'movement towards discontinuity with the precursor' – in this case, Beckett's younger self.[10] By pursuing kenosis, the writer submits to a form of self-abnegation leading to humility. He empties himself of 'his own afflatus, his imaginative godhood'. Understood in less grandiloquent terms, the writer questions and confronts the poetics or preoccupations that have conferred literary authority. For Beckett, this might mean challenging 'impotence' and 'ignorance' as the basis of his art, no less his fame.

Another suggestive if uneven theoretical analogue to the dynamics of penury is 'late style', coined in Theodor Adorno's influential essay, 'Beethoven's Late Style' (1937). For Adorno, lateness is defined in contradistinction to the harmony and reconciliation one might normally associate with maturity. 'As a rule, [late works] are not well rounded, but wrinkled, even fissured.'[11] The mature phase of important artists is typified by a mode of self-interrogation in which the conventions, expectations and accomplishments of earlier work come under pressure. Developing Adorno's line of thought, Edward Said argued that lateness constitutes 'a moment when the artist who is fully in command of his medium nevertheless abandons communications with the established social order of which he is a part and achieves a contradictory, alienated relationship with it'.[12]

How It Is is neither plainly '*kenotic*' nor typically 'late'. While its self-reflexivity has a revisionist quality, it partakes like Eliot's *East Coker* (see Chapter 5) in an irreducible ironic doubleness that disallows interpreting the work as either allied with or opposed to the author's earlier writing. There is no simple antagonism, nor straightforward extension. On the one hand, Beckett saw the novel as an 'attempt to go from where [*Texts for Nothing*] left me off' (*L3*, 229), which work in turn was seen as the 'afterbirth' of *The Unnamable* (*L2*, 300).[13] On the other hand, critics have quite reasonably read it as the start of a new phase. Maurice Blanchot, one of the text's first and keenest readers, recognised that *How It Is* subjects the operation of reading itself to a divestment of its usual apparatus:

> we find justified in Beckett's case the disappearance of every sign that would merely be a sign for the eye. Here the force of seeing is no

longer what is required; one must renounce the domain of the visible and of the invisible, renounce what is represented, albeit in negative fashion. Hear, simply hear.[14]

The concern of this chapter is not to argue for or against continuity with Beckett's earlier work. Rather, it is to explore a scepticism in *How It Is* which looks askance both at old foundations and new turnings. Having suggested in the foregoing remarks Beckett's awareness of his own literary fame and the *obiter dicta* that had already been reified in scholarly discourse, I now want to show how the novel adopts an interrogative relation to Beckett's earlier work while it nevertheless maintains a self-reflexive suspicion of its own operations. In what follows, I consider three aspects of *How It Is*: its impoverished style, its denuded intertextuality and its self-critical rehearsal of earlier works. In the first section, I examine the 'rhythm' of penury as a function of the text's bereft punctuation. The middle sections offer an accounting of 'syntactical' penury where syntax is understood as intertextual relation: specifically, Beckett's former use of Thomas à Kempis and Charles Darwin is cast in relief with their revenant appearance in *How It Is*. Finally, I ask what the ethical import (if any) of the text's cruel depravations might be. Tying these different considerations of penury together is a broader argument that suggests a softening of the sometimes-dogmatic aesthetic views Beckett espoused about the relation (or non-relation) between the artist and the object of art. Such a softening sees the absolute terms 'impotence' and 'insuperable indigence' relativised as weakness and penury; relativised, because the two latter terms enter into a 'syntax' that is denied by the former. This is not to say that Beckett abandons his project, only that the project itself is interrogated. And on this view, weakness and penury facilitate humility in their resistance to a writing that has the potential to become what it opposes: a totalising poetics.

Rhythm of Penury: Beckett's Caesurae

In matters of linguistic style, Watt and the narrator of *How It Is* appear to be cut from the same cloth. Watt speaks 'with scant regard for grammar, for syntax, for pronunciation, for enunciation, and very likely, if the truth were known, for spelling too' (*W*, 133). Bom – one name given to the narrator for the sake of 'commodity' (*HII*, 52) – murmurs into the mud with little regard for punctuation, at least as far as the reader's eye can tell. In both cases we are asked to acknowledge the artificial relationship between the written and the spoken word. Incorrect spelling cannot be heard, nor can the absence of punctuation. Yet attentiveness to lacunae seems vital for any appreciation of the 'rhythm of penury' in *How It Is*.

Blanchot's injunction to 'simply hear' was serendipitously pre-empted by the text's issue into the world. More than a year before the publication of *Comment C'est*, a snippet in English was performed by Pat Magee, the actor who rendered Beckett's 'moans & groans like [none]' (*L4*, 392). Prior to the event, Beckett tried to prepare Magee for the idiosyncrasy of the work: 'What will meet your disgusted eye is a series of short paragraphs ... separated by pauses during which panting cordially invited and without as much punctuation as a comma to break the monotony or promote understanding' (*L3*, 306). The letter further adumbrates the oral character of Bom's words: they are 'gasps from my pen' suitably thought of as a 'microphone text'.

Though Beckett sent Magee a script containing 'marks to facilitate understanding' (*L3*, 315), the published versions make no such concessions. Apart from typographical breaks, spaces between words, and the strategic use of capitals, *How It Is* is devoid of punctuation.[15] This sparseness, Édouard Magessa O'Reilly remarks in his preface to the Faber edition (*HII*, ix), was not intended from the beginning. Early drafts mimicked the style of *The Unnamable* in its use of lengthy sentences interspersed with commas. It was only after the fourth draft that a deliberate paring back of punctuation took place and that the isolated fragments emerged as units of breath. The eventual work, as Beckett knew from the beginning, was heavily indebted to a 'demolishing process' (*L3*, 230).

While a systematic lessening was already part of Beckett's creative process, Adorno may have exerted an ambient influence on the ascetic use of punctuation in *How It Is*. In November 1958 – a month prior to the first etchings of *Comment C'est* – he gave Beckett a signed copy of his most recent publication, *Noten zur Literatur*. It bore a formal but friendly inscription and contained what would become a celebrated essay on *Endgame*.[16] It also featured a lesser-known piece called 'Punctuation Marks' ('*Satzzeichen*'), which presents aphoristic reflections on its titular subject. Adorno opens by declaring that punctuation marks have an autonomy that extends beyond the syntax in which they are anchored. He goes on to say punctuation marks have undergone an unmooring from both the written and the spoken word, which, in consequence, has exposed their artificiality. Language must therefore become 'distrusting [of] them':

> For through their logical-semantic autonomy, punctuation marks, which articulate language and thereby bring writing closer to the voice, have become separate from both voice and writing, and they come into conflict with their own mimetic nature. An ascetic use of punctuation marks attempts to compensate for some of that. In every punctuation mark thoughtfully avoided, writing pays homage to the sound it suppresses.[17]

Adorno's quiet urging to interrogate the ornamental function of punctuation might have reminded Beckett of his own scepticism about language in 1937. 'Grammar and style,' he exclaims in his well-known 'German letter' to Axel Kaun, had 'become as irrelevant as a Biedermeier bathing suit or the imperturbability of a gentleman' (*L1*, 518). So, too, had the mimetic compulsions of writing. While the visual arts and music had respectively been liberated from representation and tonality, there seemed to be something 'paralysingly sacred contained within the unnature of the word' (*L1*, 518). Finding no good reason that the 'terrifyingly arbitrary materiality' of language should not undergo a similar dissociation, Beckett proffers the 'big black pauses' of Beethoven's Seventh Symphony as an ideal, since they make sound and signification subservient to silence.

Adorno was also an admirer of Beethoven's symphonic silences. In the same year as Beckett's letter, he published the seminal essay, '*Spätstil Beethovens*' ['Beethoven's Late Style'], whose broad thesis I have outlined above. When Adorno turns to Beethoven's case specifically, he makes the following claim:

> The caesurae, ... the abrupt stops which characterize the latest Beethoven more than any other feature, are those moments of breaking free; the work falls silent as it is deserted, turning its hollowness outwards. Only then is the next fragment added, ordered to its place by escaping subjectivity and colluding for better or worse with what has gone before; for a secret is shared between them, and can be exorcized only by the figure they form together ... He does not bring about their harmonious synthesis. As a dissociative force he tears

them apart in time, perhaps in order to preserve them for the eternal. In the history of art, late works are the catastrophes.[18]

Beckett's letter similarly prizes violent sunderings and silences. He wishes to 'drill one hole after another' into language, while Adorno is intent on examining the 'fissures' of late style; both arguments are spectred by Pascal's awe before the 'eternal silence of these infinite spaces'; and both writers perceive a 'nothingness' or 'hollowness' that might be drawn out through caesurae.[19]

Beckett's preoccupation with the caesura was persistent. In *Dream of Fair to Middling Women*, Belacqua asserts his 'strong weakness ... for the epic caesura' (144). He admires St Paul's desire for existential interruption, Horace's praise of the hiatus between seasons, and Beethoven's 'punctuation of dehiscence' (139). As we saw in Chapter 2, *More Pricks than Kicks* relays Belacqua's belief that he 'lived a Beethoven pause' (32), and later showcases his death as something similar: '[Belacqua's] body was between them on the bed like the keys between nations in Velasquez's *Lances*, like the water between Buda and Pest, and so on, hyphen of reality' (171).[20] Though not exhaustive, these examples suggest the expansive nature of Beckett's 'nervous treatment' (*Dream*, 144) of the caesura. It includes a prosodic understanding ('the heart of the metre missing a beat' [*Dream*, 144]) but also a more abstract notion in which death or even the human body may serve as disruptive silence.

How It Is unites this duality. The text's panting rhythm necessitates awareness of Bom's shortness of breath. Similarly, in order to 'hear' his words, the reader must also 'hear' the paradoxical silence which is a condition of their being heard: we only learn 'how it was how it is when the panting stops' (18). The text is thus pervasively caesural: while the white spaces allow a more traditional relenting (the reader's eye rests, Bom regains his breath), the running text implies a suspension of respiratory function. This, perhaps, is no different from conventional uses of the device. Take, for example, the standstill at the heart of Milton's *Paradise Lost*:

> So saying, her rash hand in evil hour
> Forth reaching to the fruit, she plucked, she ate:
> Earth felt the wound, and nature from her seat
> Sighing through all her works gave signs of woe,
> That all was lost.[21]

Eve's bite into the fruit is followed by a terminal caesura which separates a moment's voluptuous surrender and the surrender of eternity, the cleft deepened by delaying the main verb. In the next line, the natural order is already out of joint, and the comma exposes earth's 'wound' more glaringly. But while the two caesurae are rhythmically apposite to the loss of paradise, they do not themselves bring about any loss. In fact, they assist in rendering the poetry's force. *How It Is*, by contrast, implicates caesurae in an actual loss of content. It should be remembered that the 'quaqua' Bom hears within and without is a steady stream; what we see is only what he manages to catch when the panting stops, which might be 'a third two fifths or every word' (79). To deepen the loss, this minimum of content is 'murmur[ed] . . . in the mud' to no audible effect.

Text and white space thus assume different caesural functions that bring about an irresolvable tension between legibility and audibility. In Steven Connor's synaesthetic turn of phrase: 'The unpunctuated text enjoins from the hard-of-hearing eye a constant process of auditory sieving, or decanting of utterance.'[22] *How It Is* thus sustains warring phenomenological experiences of itself. As a work to be read, its typography visually determines textual interruptions or 'silences'. But as a work to be heard, the white spaces become audible as panting while the textual articulations constitute breathless silence. Neither of these is compatible with Magee's performance, which unavoidably transgressed the logic of reading and hearing: in panting between fragments he 'read' what was not there, and in reading the fragments he voiced what, within the restrictions of the narrative, cannot be heard. Ultimately, there is no ideal rendering of the novel because, as Blanchot remarked, traditional reading 'risks betraying the still unaccomplished movement to which one should respond'.[23] In its perspectival indeterminacy, the aporetic caesura compares to the scientific phenomenon of complementarity in which either waves or particles are observed though never simultaneously.[24] Both as white space and as text, the caesura becomes a cipher that declares a conditional loss, the condition being the preference given to either the written or the spoken word.

Despite the absence of traditional punctuation, Beckett also employs the caesura in a very concrete way by using words themselves as punctuation.[25] Consider the following example: 'one can't go on one goes on as before can one ever stop put a stop that's more like it one can't go on one can't stop put a stop' (*HII*, 78). The words are doubly self-conscious: first, as an echo of perhaps the most famous phrase in Beckett's fiction ('I can't go on, I'll go on' [*TN*, 407]); second, as unpunctuated writing. What is striking about this reiteration of *The Unnamable*'s final words is that the conclusion of that novel is opened to the aporia which it professes to pursue from the outset. Bom's unpunctuated flow of words moves from statement ('one can't go on') to question ('can one ever stop[?]'). The despairing note sounded by this question is cut short by an imperative to enforce some kind of end ('put a stop'), while the self-congratulatory 'that's more like it' hints at pride taken in the resolve behind the imperative rather than in any actual achievement. Neither aim is fulfilled: no stop can be put to Bom's interminable existence, nor can a telegrammatic 'stop' – that is, a full stop – be put into place that might suggest both momentary rest and some kind of authorial control.[26] Both the locutionary and illocutionary acts are at odds with the perlocutionary act. In other words, the intended meaning (self-imperative to make a visible full stop) coincides with the implied meaning (punctuation that effects a pause is necessary here), but both are thwarted by the effect of the speech act itself (in wording the punctuation mark, the punctuation mark is nullified, and so too is the silence it must bring about). Where *The Unnamable* does punctuate its final irreducibility, *How It Is* does not allow the respite of even a knife-edge.

A more extreme example of word–punctuation is found in Bom's vicious inscriptions. Deforming Pim's back into a bloodied *tabula*, the tormentor explains his method: 'from left to right and top to bottom as in our civilisation I carve my Roman capitals'; 'unbroken no paragraphs no commas not a second for reflection with the nail of the index until it falls' (*HII*, 60, 61). If the absence of punctuation in *How It Is* constitutes a perverse heterodoxy in writing, the absence of punctuation in Bom's bloody writing is a perverse orthodoxy. As a matter of pragmatism, Bom adheres to early Western writing conventions not only in his use of the Roman alphabet but also in neglecting all forms of punctuation – even the spacing between words. But because his language, whether French or English, is not case-determined like Latin, he has to rely on alternative methods in making himself understood. His first efforts to extract an account from Pim about his previous existence are marked by an unsettling childlikeness: 'only say this that your life above YOUR LIFE pause my life ABOVE long pause above IN THE in the LIGHT pause light his life above in the light almost an octosyllable come to think of it a coincidence' (*HII*, 62). Bom mouths the words as he writes them. And as if playing a guessing game, he pauses so that Pim has time to decipher the haptic code. With the caesural writing having failed, Bom tries again using different words ('YOUR LIFE HERE BEFORE ME'); the result, however, is 'utter confusion' (63). He next aims at clarity through concision: 'YOUR LIFE ABOVE . . . two lines only' (65), to which Pim responds by turning around with 'tears in the eyes'. Out of patience, Bom resorts to means of greater severity: 'YOUR LIFE CUNT ABOVE CUNT HERE CUNT'.

Unlike 'stop', the function of 'CUNT' is not as readily caught in signification. But like this other punctuation–word, it serves a twofold caesural function. At the prosodic level, both words signify a halt in the rhythm; surprisingly, 'CUNT' perhaps achieves this no less literally than 'stop' since it comes to take the place of the actual pauses in Bom's writing. On the plane of conflict between audibility and legibility, these words force the reader to violate the momentary silence they enjoin. 'CUNT' is obviously the more transgressive word–punctuation. Be that as it may, it is important to not reduce the multivalence of 'CUNT' for reasons of decency by substituting it for euphemisms like expletive, vocative, noun, punctuation mark or even word (these last two ensuring mutual cancellation). It comprises all of these and none of them. By signalling an absence, but also by situating itself within a misogynistic tradition which equates female genitalia with absence, the word signals a nullity at the very point where Pim's extorted 'midget grammar' recalls the 'shaved mound' of Pam Prim, Bom's wife 'above'. Here, then, is Beckett's version of the Elizabethan 'nothing' and also a proof of the Democritean mantra he so admired: 'naught more real than nothing' (*L2*, 427).

Treasures of Poverty I: Precious Pearls

At this moment of coerced speech, we find an imbrication of the rhythm of penury and the syntax of penury, allusively understood; that is, an impoverished intertextual relationality. For the story of Pam Prim is marked not only by a double-caesura (interruption of Bom's narrative and a disruption of Pim's silence) but also by the recurrence of an image which here and elsewhere signals lack: the pearl.

Aside from its iteration in *How It Is*, which I explore in the next section, the image of the pearl has notable significance within Beckett's reading and writing before 1935. In Thomas à Kempis's *Imitation of Christ*, Beckett discovered the *pretiosa margarita* (precious pearl), which he used in *Dream* as a symbol of prized deficiency in art, will and knowledge, and which would ultimately be made to subserve in a 'programme of self-sufficiency' (*L1*, 257). Canto 3 of the *Paradiso* supplied Beckett with a pearl that would feature in his prose and poetry in connection with planetary crepuscule, lunar light and – most importantly for my purposes – feelings of self-love. A third distinct pearl features in *Proust*, where it ostensibly symbolises desirable vulnerability and the forfeit of the ego's safeguards.[27] As such a terse summary suggests, Beckett's use for the pearl image was diffuse though not without continuity. Limiting myself to detailed consideration of the first two pearls, what emerges is less than a consolidated pattern of meaning but more than a coincidental configuration in which a syntax of plenitude, even pride, may be glimpsed, and against which the pearls of *How It Is* can be read.

One of Beckett's most enduring 'treasures of poverty' in this relation is the *Imitation of Christ* by Thomas à Kempis. The fifteenth-century devotional text had the dual merit of appealing to Beckett's interest in quietism while also adding to the 'butin verbal' [verbal booty] (*L1*, 93) for his first novel. The *Dream* notebook includes thirty-five snatchings from the *Imitation*, most of which are given either in English or Latin. Entry 595 is one of a handful to be given in both languages: 'a precious margaret [pearl] & hid from many / *pretiosa margarita, a multis abscondita*' (DN, 86). Taken from the third book of the *Imitation*, the phrase occurs in a section called 'Of self-denial and the casting away of all selfishness' in which Thomas, assuming the voice of Christ, urges an extreme and abject humility:

> I tell thee that thou must buy vile things with those which are costly and great in the esteem of men. For wonderfully vile and small, almost given up to forgetfulness, doth true heavenly wisdom appear, which thinketh not high things of itself, nor seeketh to be magnified upon the earth; many honour it with their lips, but in heart are far from it; it is indeed the *precious pearl*, which is hidden from many.[28]

The passage sources two parables in the Gospel of Matthew (13: 44–6): that of the hidden treasure and that of the costly pearl. Both of these are used by Christ to illustrate the worth of heaven over the worth of the world; they are also coloured by the attendant joy of such a spiritual quest. Thomas's gloomy rendering suppresses this hopeful note and inverts the parables' terms of valuation. While the Gospel highlights the desirability of the kingdom of heaven, Thomas's imagining stresses heaven's undesirability from a worldly perspective. In a Pauline toppling of values, the precious pearl becomes something 'wonderfully small and vile' as Thomas substitutes the promise of attainment for a project of divestment.[29] Another key difference in the *Imitation* is that the precious pearl no longer relates to the kingdom of heaven but rather to heavenly wisdom. This wisdom, according to Thomas, 'thinketh not high things of itself, nor seeketh to be magnified upon the earth'.[30] The nuance implies a shift from eschatology to epistemology that Beckett is likely to have appreciated, particularly for its emphasis on the limits of human reason.

It is not surprising, then, that *Dream of Fair to Middling Women* invariably situates the 'precious pearl' motif in a context where deficiency of some kind is sought. The first and fullest development is seen in Belacqua's defence of clichés, conversational tags and phrases aforethought as they occur in speech and writing. Admiring a friend's prefabricated saying, 'Black diamond of pessimism', Belacqua likens it to the 'precious margaret' and the 'sparkle hid in the ashes'. He then extrapolates from the virtues of the 'tag and the ready-made' to the vices of authors whose craft is overcalculated. Later, Belacqua draws a direct parallel between the precious pearl and the utter abandonment of will ('aboulia of the first water' [184]). He finally goes on to value the Alba's *'savoir ne pas faire'* as a 'jewel of great price' (192), forging a link between ideal ignorance and the parable of the hidden treasure. Taken separately, the three instances signify distinct but related shortcomings: a deficit of style, of will and of knowledge.

Despite *Dream*'s pronounced pilfering from Thomas à Kempis, the practice in Beckett's early writing was mostly driven by opportunism rather than conviction. Chris Ackerley argues persuasively that although a budding quietist impulse may be glimpsed in these borrowings, 'the prose reflects a delight in language more recondite than reverent'.[31] This literary lop-sidedness is confirmed in

How It Is and the Syntax of Penury 191

Beckett's 1935 letter to Thomas MacGreevy, already mentioned in Chapter 2, where he cedes his inability to see how the *Imitation*'s holy aversions could achieve anything but intensify an unhealthy inwardness. Demonstrating something of his own '*savoir ne pas faire*', he asks:

> Am I to set my teeth & be disinterested? When I cannot answer for myself, and do not dispose of myself, how can I serve? Will the demon – *pretiosa margarita*! – disable me any less with sweats & shudders & panics & rages & rigors & heart burstings because my motives are unselfish & the welfare of others my concern? Macché! Or is there some way of devoting pain & monstrosity & incapacitation to the service of a deserving cause? (*L1*, 258, my italics)

The context suggests that 'demon' is shorthand for Beckett's struggles with anxiety, melancholy and bad health. Not oblivious to this self-portrait of the artist as a tortured soul, he equates his hauntings with the '*pretiosa margarita*'. The ironic gesture sums up his earlier confession that the *Imitation* had been meretriciously used: 'I know that now I would be no more capable of approaching its hypostatics & analogies "meekly, simply & truly", than I was when I first twisted them into a programme of self-sufficiency' (*L1*, 257). As a symbol of privation transformed into plenitude, the *pretiosa margarita* may reasonably be assumed to figure within this programme.

A similar categorisation may be made of one of *Dream*'s other stolen pearls. The second canto of *Paradiso* supplied Beckett with the 'eternal pearl' (Dante's metaphor for the moon) which he transferred in a comparatively straightforward manner to Belacqua's footsore night-wandering (*Dream*, 129–30). But it is the dimly visible pearl of *Paradiso* 3 around which Belacqua's self-love accretes. In this canto, Dante likens the faces of the First Heaven's denizens to the faint reflections one might see in a limpid stream or glass. The Pilgrim falls into a reverse Narcissus error, supposing the mesmerising images to be behind rather than in front of him:

> Even as from polished or transparent glasses,
> or waters clear and still, but not so deep,
> that wholly lost to vision is their bed,
> the features of our faces returned

> so faintly, that upon a pallid brow
> a pearl comes no less faintly to our eyes;
> thus saw I many a face that longed to speak;
> I therefore ran into the fault opposed
> to that which kindled love 'tween man and fount.[32]

The passage made a deep impression on Beckett and is alluded to in several places, with *Dream* giving it in fullest form.[33] The reworking there is preceded by a mystical description of the Alba's appearance in the evening light. Comparing her dilated pupils to the monochromatic eyes of the small boy in El Greco's *Burial of the Count Orgaz*, Belacqua becomes entranced by the halo of whiteness that radiates behind the supposed object of his affections. Absorbed, he loses himself in her dark eyes:

> So that as from transparent polished glass or, if you prefer, from tranquil shining waters, the details of his face return so feeble that a pearl on a white brow comes not less promptly to his pupils, so now he sees her vigilant face and in him is reversed the error that lit love between the man (if you can call such spineless creature a man) and the pool. For she had closed her eyes. (*Dream*, 175)

Despite being a close translation of lines from *Paradiso* 3, the final sentence introduces a significant deviation. While Dante's reverse Narcissus error is his mistaken belief that there are beings behind him, Belacqua can only be said to succumb to this reversal after first experiencing the Narcissus error proper. It is only once the Alba has closed her eyes and is seen against the 'albescent evening' that she becomes like the faintly outlined inhabitants of the First Heaven. The implication is that, prior to this moment, Belacqua had gazed so deeply in the pools of her dark eyes that he had fallen in love with the likeness contained in them. Belacqua's navel-gazing, after all, goes undisguised throughout the novel. It is summed up in two tenets: 'Love condones ... narcissism' and 'Love demands narcissism' (38, 39). Upon his departure, Belacqua muses that the encounter (with himself, through the Alba) has possibly supplied him with 'copy for his wombtomb' (175) – that is, further means for a deepened insularity. Just as the *Imitation*'s misappropriated pearl signals self-sufficiency, so the jewel theft from *Paradiso* points to a perverse self-love.

Treasures of Poverty II: Forlorn Solace

Turning now to the pearls in *How It Is*, it may be remarked that they betoken quiet sorrow, hollow words of comfort and a scrap of learning unexpectedly recalled. Collectively they stand in impoverished relation to Beckett's early pearls. The question is how one should read the return of the expressed after an absence of three decades. Can the motif simply be taken as the persistent echo of the *Imitation*'s lovely sayings, for instance?[34] Or is it implicated in a more searching revisionist process, an ironised rehearsal of earlier rehearsals?

The latter seems implied towards the end of Part I, where mention of a pearl is made during a moment of self-dramatisation. With eyes closed, the narrator imagines himself struggling up from his ever-prone position. Not quite erect, he nonetheless manages to raise his head from the mud and mutter something to himself:

> what can one say to oneself possibly at such a time a little pearl of forlorn solace so much the better so much the worse that style only not so cold cheers alas that style only not so warm joy and sorrow those two their sum divided by two and luke like in outer hell. (*HII*, 35)

The humour is typically Beckettian. Able to break the silence that is a condition of his damnation, Bom is in two minds about what to say. When the moment of indecision passes, a 'pearl of forlorn solace' issues. The phrase is neatly ambiguous. On one level it suggests a failing of memory; Bom is at a loss in recalling a formerly reassuring saying. Another possible interpretation, nuanced by the French original, is that solace of the sort on offer is solace alone to one with a resigned predisposition. *Comment C'est* gives 'soulas désolé' (*CC*, 52), which suggests the words provide a sorry or hollow comfort, not unlike the 'abject self-referring quietism' Beckett felt drawn to in the *Imitation* (*L1*, 257). In yet a third reading, the 'pearl of forlorn solace' may be reproduced though its content is nothing but a vanished hope. This accords with what Anthony Cordingley describes as the 'functional value' of the novel's referentiality: that is, a 'residue of past learning' that persists without conferring any benefit.[35] Apposite to a place where 'mute screams [to] abandon hope' (39) are heard (or not heard), solace itself is forlorn even if the words are recalled.

Negated reassurance marks the plays on either side of *How It Is*. *Krapp's Last Tape*, written in 1958, contains the famously voided 'vision' that has often been taken to correlate with Beckett's realisation that his art was impelled by impotence and ignorance: 'Spiritually a year of profound gloom and indigence until that memorable night in March, at the end of the jetty, in the howling wind, never to be forgotten, when suddenly I saw the whole thing. The vision at last' (*CDW*, 220). The epiphany clearly represents some kind of encouragement during a troubling time, yet its substance is withheld. Just as Krapp the younger is about to reveal the 'belief' that had misled him all his life, Krapp the elder impatiently brings the recording to a halt. He winds forward to a point that again brings the voice to the precipice of a revelation (Krapp's insight into his 'dark'), only to interrupt it with curses and another silencing of the machine. This 'mechanized ... aposiopesis', as Dirk van Hulle conceives of it, means that the vision remains hidden from the audience; the substance of the solace is lost.[36] *Happy Days* also unsettles soothing recollections. 'What are those wonderful [/] unforgettable [/] exquisite [/] immortal lines?' Winnie asks variously (*CDW*, 140, 141, 150, 160, 164, 166). Her effort to remember creates the expectation of a moment's reassurance in a situation absurdly dire. But this expectation is soon undercut both by the poetry's subject matter and its fragmented recollection. Lines from Shakespeare, Milton and other 'classics' are brokenly recited, while sufficient content emerges to signal despairing want. There is Ophelia's lament for Hamlet's sanity, Adam's realisation of paradise lost, Thomas Gray's pining for the innocence of childhood.

The solacing pearls of Bom, Krapp and Winnie stand in contradistinction to the wombtombing recitations of Belacqua. In Chapter 2, I mentioned Belacqua's tendency to quote literary works when perceiving a threat to his ego, to recite comforting scraps of verse that insulate him against the outside world. But in Beckett's late writing an ascetic stringency is imposed on his creatures' search for solace. *Krapp's Last Tape* demonstrates that while the younger Krapp might have been seduced by epiphany, his older self is wary and impatient of it. *Happy Days* does not deny Winnie the pursuit of comfort, but it does deny her its attainment. And *How It Is* shows Bom incapable of dreaming up or remembering any words of comfort, even during a flight of fancy.

If the 'pearl of forlorn solace' represents an inability to recall words of comfort, the pearl in Part 2 signals an inability to repress painful memories. Mention of this pearl occurs during a faint flicker of almost-forgotten learning. In the wake of his anguished interrogation of Pim, Bom is briefly reminded of his 'life above' with his wife, Pam Prim. Though vague, the details of this period are sufficient to suggest that Bom lives with a sense of shame. The first thing we learn about Pam Prim is an intimate detail: she at one point shaved her pubic hair. We also discover that the couple's love-life was on the wane and that they attempted to rekindle it through greater daring in the bedroom ('tried to revive it through the arse' [*HII*, 66]). These amorous efforts are cut short by Pam Prim's fall from a window (possibly attempted suicide). She is admitted to hospital with a spinal injury and during her convalescence forgives Bom for an undisclosed transgression. His recollection of this scene is marked by motifs of shame: Pam Prim's pudenda ('blue mound strange idea . . . she must have been dark on the deathbed' [66]), his avoidance of her gaze and his failure to find the 'holly she begged for' (67). He only manages to gather flowers that prompt his etymological recollection: 'marguerites from the latin pearl' (66).

It is important to remember that the Pam Prim episode is the result of the violent extortion discussed earlier in this chapter: Bom tortures Pim in order to hear him tell of 'the good moments I'll have had up there' (67). Throughout the novel, memory seems to be co-opted into the mudscape's punitive design. In Part 1, seven 'images' are visited upon Bom. These have the appearance of memories or dreams since they involve something of a life above, sometimes point to a younger self and are often marked by an awareness of different colours. The images are not unpleasant in themselves (excepting that of a stern mother's gaze), though the forlorn situation in which Bom experiences them aggravates his sense of loss. They therefore constitute what Vladimir in *Waiting for Godot* calls '*Memoria praeteritorum bonorum*' (*CDW*, 80): the unpleasant experience of recalling former happiness in the midst of misery. Given the connection between memory and pain in *How It Is*, it is apt to find a modified allusion to the *Divine Comedy*'s most famous love story, that of Paolo and Francesca: 'in the rectum a redhot spike that day we prayed no further' (30). The latter phrase is a corruption of 'read no further' and occurs in what Beckett once referred to as Dante's 'imperishable reference to the incompatibility of [reading and loving]' (*Dis*, 81) where Francesca reminds the Pilgrim that there is 'no greater pain / than to remember happy days in days of misery'.³⁷

With torments to rival those in the *Inferno*, *How It Is* seems to suggest that there is greater suffering than this. The detail that the couple tried to 'revive it through the arse' recalls the context of sexual deviance in Canto 5 through the earlier explicit mention of 'in the rectum a redhot spike that day we prayed no further'. This earlier phrase is itself revived by the immediate context in which Pim suffers something like a sodomisation with the can-opener. And when we take into account that the acts of recall and story-telling are at once sustaining and mortifying (discussed in more detail below), suffering is experienced even at a biological level. Against such afflictions – shameful memory, physical violation, existential torment – the precious pearl offers no defence, not even a forlorn solace. The banality of the etymological connection between the flowers and the pearl stands in sharp contrast to the fullness offered by Beckett's earlier references, which have the luxury of declaring want as an ideal. In *How It Is*, it speaks to the horror of not having. With this distinction in mind, the last two sections trace other 'treasures of poverty' with the aim of opening onto questions about an impoverished ethics.

Begin Again: Darwin's Caterpillar

The homophonic potential in the title *Comment C'est* has been well noted.³⁸ The most obvious meaning is captured in its English counterpart, then there are various echoes of the verb *commencer* – infinitive, past participle (*commencé*), imperative (*commencez*). What I want to examine in this section, however, is a corresponding motif built around the notions of beginning, beginning again and a lingering awkwardness about origins: Darwin's caterpillar.

When Beckett first read Charles Darwin's *On the Origin of Species* in 1932 he was left unimpressed. Writing to Thomas MacGreevy, he dismissed the book as 'badly written catlap' and claimed to retain the single fact that 'blue-eyed cats are always deaf' (*L1*, 111).³⁹ The dismissal is clearly exaggerated, given that another of the book's scientific observations would be variously reworked before its faint limning in *How It Is*. In a chapter on 'Instinct', Darwin relays Pierre Huber's account of the caterpillar's behaviour during the construction of its cocoon or 'hammock'. Huber noted that if a caterpillar is transplanted from a hammock at an advanced stage of construction to one at an intermediary stage, the insect would proceed from the given product and complete the remaining stages. However, if the caterpillar is taken from a hammock at the middle stage and placed in one at a more advanced stage, it would be at a loss:

> far from feeling the benefit of this, [the caterpillar] was much embarrassed, and, in order to complete its hammock seemed forced to start from the third stage, where it had left off, and thus tried to complete the already finished work.[40]

Beckett first spun Darwin's caterpillar into the short story, 'Echo's Bones', where Doyle prompts Belacqua to finish the contradiction he had started with 'but'. The conjunction offers little help: 'My memory has gone to hell altogether ... If you can't give me a better cue than that I'll have to be like the embarrassed caterpillar and go back to my origins' (*EB*, 42). Nodding to the title of Darwin's *magnum opus*, Belacqua also demonstrates his understanding of Darwinian recall. Habit and instinct, in Darwin's view, are closely aligned, since both are characterised by recurring patterns:

> As in repeating a well-known song, so in instincts, one action follows another by a sort of rhythm; if a person be interrupted in a song, or in repeating anything by rote, he is generally forced to go back to recover the habitual train of thought ... .'[41]

In *Murphy*, Miss Counihan also loses her train of thought and is forced to retrace her way to the original point: 'She quite forgets how it goes on ... she will have to go right back to the beginning, like Darwin's caterpillar' (*Mur*, 130). And in *Watt*, Mr O'Meldon returns to his premise after interruption but is impatiently urged to 'Go on from where you left off ... not from where you began. Or are you like Darwin's caterpillar?' (*W*, 167).

Darwin's caterpillar returns more deeply cocooned in *How It Is*. There is no outright reference as in the earlier instances, only the suggestion of disorienting dislocation and the confused effort to resume:

> I know not what insect wound round its treasure I come back with empty hands to me to my place what to begin with ask myself that last a moment with that
>   what to begin my long day my life present formulation last a moment with that coiled round my treasure listening my God to have to murmur that (*HII*, 19)

Bom shows affinity with the larval members of the lepidopteran order. His existence is marked by a regenerative cycle and, like the caterpillar transplanted to a different hammock, faces with embarrassed uncertainty the question 'what to begin with'. This self-reflexivity parallels his indecision in recalling the 'pearl of forlorn solace', for in both instances there is a groping after something irrevocable or useless. Bom's 'treasure' is his sack, which supplies him with means of sustenance (tins of sardines), a tool for torture (can-opener) and a form of creature comfort (as pillow and an object to kiss). But when listing these virtues, he admits that the sack has lost all value: 'we don't profit by it in any way any more and we cling to it' (56). It has become a treasure of poverty.

What distinguishes Beckett's use of Darwin's caterpillar in *How It Is* from its occurrences in the earlier works is the absence of any analogue between the operations of reason and the behaviour of the insect. The earlier instances all build upon Darwin's rationalistic argument: instinct is never purely instinctual but always informed by habit, which in turn is informed by reason. But in *How It Is*, it is Huber's caterpillar that comes more directly into view. That is to say the thought-inflected appropriation of the caterpillar is jettisoned while its naturalistic aspect is retained. Understood in terms of the metaphor itself, *How It Is* refuses to build upon Darwin's advanced construction, upon his extrapolation from the biological to the rational. Unlike Belacqua and the others, Bom undergoes a phenomenological displacement during which what is lost is not any train of thought but the foundations of instrumental reason itself.

This deprivation inheres in the absence of any epistemic certainty. The mudscape where Bom finds himself is characterised as 'the place without knowledge' (107). Such negation almost renders superfluous his frequent professions of past erudition and precludes attainment of any but the lowest tier in Maslow's hierarchy of needs. Loss of knowledge, in turn, is closely allied to notions of a 'loss of species'. The latter is a phrase that occurs almost exclusively in contexts suggestive of a connection between humanity and higher-order cognitive functions such as the use of memory or mathematical calculations. Here, for instance, is the ontological affirmation offered by arithmetic:

> dear figures when all fails a few figures to wind up with part one before Pim the golden age the good moments the *losses of species* I was young I clung on to the species we're talking of the species the human saying to myself brief movements no sound two and two twice two and so on (*HII*, 39, my emphasis)

The safety of numbers is a familiar Beckettian trope. Molloy deepens his self-knowledge by calculating his farts per day; the Unnamable finds 'nothing more restful than arithmetic' (*TN*, 26, 381); and the speakers of 'Enough' regard mental calculations as a form of escape (*CSP*, 188). In like manner, Bom attempts to resist the hopelessness of his situation by doing small sums. But 'dear figures' is implicated in the same logic of penury as the pearl of forlorn solace, and 'clung' belongs to a distant past. What restores him to the species in this realm is not arithmetic or even its memory but the act of slaking his thirst: 'what to begin with drink to begin with I turn over on my face . . . the tongue comes out lolls in the mud . . . the face in the mud the mouth open the mud in the mouth thirst abating humanity regained' (*HII*, 21). Far from the rationalistic assurances of the *cogito*, Bom's 'great categories of being' (9) are reduced to mere bodily functions: I drink therefore I am.[42]

How It Is puts a chilling gloss on Beckett's avowed preoccupation with the 'eternally larval' (*L2*, 103). Suspended between animal life (*zoē*) and human being (*bios*), between vital needs and a vestige of rationality, Bom inhabits a state of indeterminacy. He parallels Agamben's werewolves, bandits and *muselmänner* in being outside the parameters of the *polis* yet still under its dictates.[43] Bom suffers a reduction of *bios* (the politics, culture and learning which make him human) while still standing under the laws that govern biopolitics. So the paradox may be maintained, as Jean-Michel Rabaté has remarked, that the creatures have their 'being in justice' while being ontologically lessened to the 'piss of being' (*HII*, 108, 115).[44] And if we consider that the thirst-quenching mud is 'nothing more than all our shit' (44), then 'hanging on to the species' equals nothing less than a humiliating dehumanisation.

Revictualling Narrations: Love, Cruelty and Authorship

Like the more explicit references to the pearl, the implied image of the caterpillar has both intertextual and generative significance in *How It Is*. It prompts us to ask how the text's internal operations mirror those of an insect forced to rework its foundations. What kind of residual embarrassment may be discovered in the undisguised echoes of earlier Beckett? What revision is implied? What tension can be traced between the old aporetics and the new? In this final section, I will discuss one instance by which *How It Is* opens itself dialogically both to the single work most readily associated with Beckett's fame, *Waiting for Godot*, and also to a source text that has paramount importance for his entire *oeuvre*, *The Divine Comedy*. In doing so, I want to shed light on the question of authorial cruelty.

Encountering the phrase 'quaqua' in the second fragment, the reader is presented with a familiar echo even before the strangeness of the text has fully taken hold. We are reminded of Lucky's speech in *Waiting for Godot*, whose opening theological hypothesis includes the twice-repeated 'quaquaquaqua' (*CDW*, 42). The uncanniness is not only produced by the verbal repetition but also by a comparable performativity. Where the play's stage directions call Lucky's utterings a 'text' and so implies some kind of recitation, the narrator of *How It Is* likewise reproduces words from a source of uncertain origin: 'how it was I quote . . . voice once without quaqua on all sides then in me when the panting stops tell me again finish telling me invocation' (*HII*, 3).[45] A third overlap is scatology. Lucky's 'quaquaquaqua' issues from the halls and textbooks of the 'Acacacacademy'; Bom's 'quaqua' sounds within a sea of excrement.[46]

The most significant parallel, however, is the texts' respective critique of providential order and justice. In *Waiting for Godot*, Lucky's speech serves to ridicule the idea of a 'personal God quaquaquaqua with white beard . . . who loves us dearly'. During the play's Berlin rehearsals in 1975, Beckett explained that Lucky is trying to say 'quaversalis' – a term that 'concerns a god who turns himself in all directions at the same time' (*TNSB1*, 133).

Lucky's failure to pronounce this word for divine ubiquity correlates thematically with the characters' failure to experience it. As for justice, the choric repetition of 'nothing to be done' (*CDD*, 13; the phrase expressly repeated in *How It Is* in a reflection on justice [108]) dogs any momentary effort to alter the conditions of existence.

The 'quaqua' of *How It Is* also signals an unrealised 'quaversalis'. But where *Waiting for Godot* derides naïve belief in a beneficent Other, *How It Is* attacks the notion of a beneficent author. This distinction is not always easy to make, particularly because Bom often draws on religious language in his existential hypotheses. In Part 3, where his efforts to understand the conditions of his damnation are most trenchant, he posits the 'need of one not one of us an intelligence somewhere a love who all along the track at the right places according as we need them deposits our sacks' (*HII*, 120). This speculative imagining of a grand deviser also intersects with Lucky's speech. First, there is the suggestion of a disembodied presence. Lucky's god is 'without extension' while Bom's god has gone from being an overseeing eye, to an overhearing ear, to an abstract intelligence; in both cases there is thus intimation of a godlike entity paring his nails above the chaos. Second, the 'quaversality' of Bom's god is borne out by his pervasive distribution of sacks among the damned. This, in turn, speaks to a third similarity: the notion that such a distribution is the expression of a divine love.

Love seems intertwined with suffering and cruelty throughout the novel. We encounter the image of a mother's 'eyes burn[ing] with severe love' (10); Bom's mutilation of Pim somehow constitutes an act of 'stoic love' (53); and there is a vague causality between Bom's and Pam Prim's efforts to revive their love-making and the latter's defenestration. Yet the most complex instance of the paradoxical conjunction between love and torment is offered by an embedded allusion to the inscription on Hell's Gate in *Inferno* 3, which declares the woes of the damned to be devised by Godly justice, wisdom and love:

> Justice inspired my high exalted Maker;
>   I was created by the Might Divine, The highest Wisdom and the primal Love.
>   . . .
>   All hope abandon, ye that enter here!'[47]

For Beckett, I contend, these lines were fraught because of their ethical rather than theological implications. The question implicit in *How It Is* (but also in the earliest works) concerns both Dante's lack of humility in creating a cosmological scheme of judgement and his cruelty in inventing attendant tortures. Beckett's awareness of and possible complicity in such perverse pride is neatly captured in 'A Wet Night', where the Alba perceives an unflattering likeness between Belacqua and Dante:

> Surveying him as he stood bedraggled under the lintel, clutching his enormous glasses . . ., bothered seriously in his mind by a neat little point that had arisen out of nowhere in the *vestibule* . . . the Alba thought she had never seen anybody, man or woman, look quite such a sovereign booby. Seeking to be God, she thought, in the slavish arrogance of a piffling evil. (*MPTK*, 69–70, my emphasis)[48]

In *How It Is*, the milieu of *Inferno* 3 is more obliquely evoked. Bom's 'pearl of forlorn solace' comes to him in a place resembling 'outer hell' or '*vestibule*', as the French more pointedly renders it (*CC*, 52).[49] Like Dante's damned, he indulges in 'mute imprecations' against God, and also waves a 'vast banner' resembling that blank flag pursued by the shades in this canto (*HII*, 34, 29).[50] Furthermore, Pim's 'vile tears' (64) appear to have some affinity with the lachrymose worm-fodder of Ante-Inferno.[51] However, the evidence most pertinent to a question of cruel love are those broken echoes of the most famous words in all of *The Divine Comedy*: 'mute screams abandon hope'; 'abandoned here effect of hope'; 'the abandoned arrow effect of hope' (39, 40).

If Bom retains only the last verse of the inscription on Hell's Gate, he nevertheless abides under the full weight of its authority. Divine love and divine retribution are consolidated in a justice that simultaneously sustains and deprives life. The mud epitomises this duality: it quenches thirst and restores species belonging only to perpetuate a dehumanising process of excrement consumption.[52] The same may be said for the sack. As Bom remarks, it is 'thanks to my sack that I keep dying in a dying age' (12).[53] This would explain his strange claim that he 'clutches it at arm's length as he the window-sill who falls out of the window' (56). Throughout the novel, humanity seems dependent on a deliberate 'hanging on'; or, conversely, falling implies a loss of species. But the distance Bom maintains to the sack – arm's length – also betrays its more menacing function.

Consider the pharmakon-like ambivalence in the following statement: 'our unfailing rations . . . enable us to advance without pause or rest' (122). Being unable yet carrying on is transformed from ethos to punitive decree; it is stripped of even the faintest hint of heroism and endowed instead with futility that sinisterly reflects on the creator of its conditions.[54] The recycled phrase from *The Unnamable*, discussed above and also discernible in the last quotation, may be read less as an axiom of Beckett's art than an indictment against it.[55] Here is no triumph against the odds but rather a coercion of the impossible that stands surprisingly yet starkly against the coercion enacted within the novel.[56] Unable to go on and yet impelled to do so – mobilised at the price of all respite – Bom has even less freedom than the Geulincxian subject who can at least pace easterly along the deck of a west-bound ship.[57] He numbers in a procession of bodies moving not westward ('death in the west as a rule') but eastward, towards perpetual rebirth in suffering: 'all advance from west to east year in year out in the dark the mud in torment and solitude' (107, 109).

Given these conditions, it is difficult to share Alain Badiou's optimism about the novel's universality and his belief that 'reduced to a few functions, humanity is only more admirable, more energetic, more immortal'.[58] Badiou is justifiably reluctant to read the text plainly as a piece of political commentary.[59] But in place of one allegory he posits another that draws a parallel between the novel's debasements and the human condition at large. Apart from the note of triumphalism, this sentiment is problematic in its readiness to self-identify with the text's sufferers. Such a neatness of identification not only courts the danger of nullifying humiliation as an individuating experience (addressed in Chapter 4) but also brushes aside the text's tacit corrosion of the ideas about evenhanded justice. One might argue that the novel's cycle of suffering or the 'quantum of wantum' is constant since all tormentors are eventually also victims. But this is to take in good faith that Bom gets his comeuppance in the apocryphal Part 4, and also to regard such circuitous vengeance as balanced.[60] More significantly, it is to neglect questions raised about notions of authorial cruelty.

These questions cluster most visibly around the third example of the providence/punishment dichotomy: narrative itself.

> and this anonymous voice self-styled quaqua the voice of us all that was without on all sides then in us when the panting stops . . . it is at

> last the voice of him who before listening to us murmur what we are tells us what we are as best he can
>
> ...
>
> of him who God knows who could blame him must sometimes wonder if to these perpetual revictuallings narrations and auditions he might not put an end without ceasing to maintain us in some kind of being without end and some kind of justice without flaw who could blame him (*HII*, 122)

The revivifying properties of story-telling are hardly without precedent in Beckett. The narrator of 'The Calmative', for instance, tries to assuage his angst by telling a story and then wonders if it is 'possible that in this story I have come back to life, after my death?' (*CSP*, 61). Similarly, Malone's tales about Sapo and others serve to delay his dying. And in *Endgame*, Nagg is promised a sugar-plum on condition that he submit to an 'audition' of Hamm's 'chronicle' (*CDW*, 116). But stories can also be mortifying – a pensum or labour, as both Molloy and the Unnamable know, that cruelly defers a final rest (*TN*, 27, 308). *How It Is* consolidates these extremes. It also nuances the motif of narrative 'revictuallings' by framing the story of 'how it is' as externally sourced rather than internally generated. The effect, on the one hand, is to deprive the sufferers' agency; on the other, it draws attention to the 'love' or 'intelligence' that conceives such deprivation.

A categorical difference thus arises between the novel's hellish conditions and the creation of its hellish conditions. In other words, where both the elemental mud (*caca*) and the sack represent means to reduce and restore humanity, the constitutive voice ('self-styled quaqua') represents the arbiter of such infernal contingencies. It is this voice that tells 'how it is'. It is this voice which, like the Hell-devising Love in Dante, renders torment and existence interchangeable. I discussed Beckett's almost dogmatic belief in life-as-expiation in Chapter 4, so it suffices to say here that *How It Is* varies the theme by considering the author's role in creating yet another world where this dogma inheres. Bom's rhetorical question – 'who could blame him' – is not nearly as exculpatory as it seems. In conjunction with his poignant, almost Christ-like, hope that this cup of suffering might pass from him, the question insinuates the arbitrariness of 'justice'. It registers a reflexive poignancy similar to the speaker of the eighth 'Text for Nothing', who desperately asks: 'But whom can I have offended so grievously, to be punished in this inexplicable way, all is inexplicable, space and time, false and inexplicable, suffering and tears, and even the old convulsive cry, It's not me, it can't be me' (*CSP*, 133).

How It Is takes up the same question but goes further in exposing the hand behind the benighted kindnesses in Beckett's work. The zero-sum games between Hamm and Clov, Molloy and his mother, the narrator of 'The End' and an anonymous charitable soul all partake of a blessing-as-curse logic but are nonetheless endemic to the fictional realm presented.[61] Taken together they might be read as symptomatic of the human condition, or as a critique of belief in transcendental benevolence (Lucky's speech, for instance). But *How It Is* seems to shift the coordinates. In doing so, it asks not how we can claim goodness for God in the face of all suffering, but whether authors are responsible for the cruelties of their invention:

> and if it may seem strange that without food to sustain us we can drag ourselves thus by mere grace of our united net sufferings from west to east towards an inexistent peace we are invited kindly to consider
>   that for the likes of us and no matter how we are recounted there is more nourishment in a cry nay a sigh torn from one whose only good is silence or in speech extorted from one at last delivered from its use than sardines can ever offer (125–6)

Given what we know about the mud and sacks, about their double-bindedness, it is perhaps not so strange that the creatures of this realm are vitalised by a cruelty which, in due course, will also mortify them. What is strange, however, is that these two fragments form part of a grouping that reads as the single most eloquent section of the entire novel. Apart from the consistently absent punctuation, it bears no trace of the interruptive scraps that unsettle reading elsewhere. Instead, we are presented with a passage of astounding cogency that is comparable in its unexpectedness to Lucky's thinking. So if we are kindly invited to consider that anguish sustains the denizens of this mudscape, we are also invited by this abrupt change of style to consider the party responsible for the rules of this realm. In essence, Beckett tempts us with a kind of reverse formalist reading: having become familiar with a language that declares its literariness through defamiliarisation, we are suddenly confronted with a flow of words that, in their relatively straightforward communicativeness, achieve 'de-automizing perception'.[62]

Considered a different way, this brief fluency draws attention not only to the novel's impoverished syntax but also to its impoverished ethics. And in tandem with the metafictional manoeuvres that declare the arbitrary nature of the novel's 'realism' – the mud, the sack, the apparent temporal linearity – this fluency calls out to the reader to see the author in his guise as ethically dubious creator, an author 'seeking to be God . . . in the slavish arrogance of a piffling evil'. Like Bom, we have only the text, the quaqua, to rely on. And so, like him and like the damned in Dante's Hell, we do not encounter any explicit contradiction of the notion that the creatures of the mudscape 'have their being in justice' (108). But the novel's deliberate declarations of arbitrariness, its revision of old foundations, its naked presentation of cruelty without apparent cause, constitute those ironising gestures that make up the late or kenotic work.

In his acerbic review, John Updike had cast Beckett as a 'proud priest perfecting his forlorn ritual'.[63] As with his claim that *How It Is* offers little more than a variation on a well-worn theme, the implicit charge is not easily dismissed. It is hard to disagree that there is something proud, even arrogant, in the writing of a novel that not only demands impossible patience from readers but also great familiarity with the prior body of work. No less may one find something alienating in the remoteness of this author who, perhaps more like a martyr than a priest, took delight in the novel's unreadability.[64] Yet to level these criticisms is to overlook the unflinching effort of self-emptying behind *How It Is*. It is to take in bad faith the novel's ascetic winnowing of style and intertextuality as proof of the author's pride. A humbler reading, perhaps, means recognising Beckett's sincere effort to achieve level or – perhaps better – levelled standing between his language and his will: 'I hammer and hammer. Hard as iron, the words. I'd like them in dust. Like the spirit' (*L3*, 335).

Notes

1. 'The key word in my plays is "perhaps".' 'Tom Driver in "Columbia University Forum"', in Graver and Federman, *The Critical Heritage*, 241–7.
2. Lawrence E. Harvey, *Samuel Beckett: Poet and Critic* (Princeton: Princeton University Press, 1970), 249. See also: Christopher Ricks,

Beckett's *Dying Words* (Oxford: Oxford University Press, 1993), 82–3; Simon Critchley, *Very Little . . . Almost Nothing: Death, Philosophy, Literature* (London: Routledge, 1997), 207–11; Pascale Casanova, *Samuel Beckett: The Anatomy of a Literary Revolution*, trans. Gregory Elliott (London: Verso, 2006), 90.
3. Quoted in Knowlson, *Damned to Fame*, 772.
4. For an exploration of Beckett's literary cynicism, see Rose, *Literary Cynics*.
5. As Matthew Feldman argues, a similar paradox inheres in Beckett's drive to return to ignorance: '[I]gnorance assumes "ignorance of something"; that is, *some* knowledge of the very thing having "unknown" as a property. Both the word and idea "ignorance" simply cannot be self-contained: how such ignorance? ignorance *of what*? Seeking knowledge implies ignorance, just as seeking ignorance implies knowledge.' Feldman, *Beckett's Books*, 5.
6. Leo Bersani and Ulysse Dutoit, *Arts of Impoverishment: Beckett, Rothko, Resnais* (Cambridge, MA: Harvard University Press, 1993), 6–7.
7. 'John Updike in "New Yorker"', in Graver and Federman, *The Critical Heritage*, 285.
8. Raymond Federman and John Fletcher, *Samuel Beckett: His Works and His Critics: An Essay in Bibliography* (London: University of California Press, 1970), 113–237.
9. This awareness is borne out in letter of 1958 (*L3*, 177): 'I feel I'm getting more and more entangled in professionalism and self-exploitation and that it would be really better to stop altogether than to go on with that . . .'
10. Bloom, *Anxiety of Influence*, 14–15.
11. Theodor W. Adorno, *Beethoven: The Philosophy of Music*, ed. Rolf Tiedeman; trans. Edmund Jephcott (Stanford: Stanford University Press, 1998), 123.
12. Edward Said, *On Late Style: Music and Literature against the Grain*, fwd. Mariam C. Said; intro. Michael Wood (London: Bloomsbury, 2006), 8. Rose posits the dialogue between late and middle Beckett as a form of cynicism produced under the sign of advanced capitalism; it is a dialogue which secures the continued commodification of an already-established artist's work. Rose, *Literary Cynics*, 3–4.
13. In the margin of a late draft of *How It Is*, Beckett even established explicit connections with Molloy and Malone. See Édouard Magessa O'Reilly, 'Preface', in *How It Is*, vii.
14. Maurice Blanchot, *The Infinite Conversation*, trans. Susan Hanson (Minneapolis: University of Minnesota Press, 2003), 329.
15. For a discussion of the novel's spaces as punctuation, see James Williams, 'Beckett between the Words: Punctuation and the Body

in the English Prose', *Samuel Beckett Today / Aujourd'hui* 24 (2012): 250.
16. See the title page in Beckett's copy of *Noten zur Literatur*, BDL, www.beckettarchive.org.ezphost.dur.ac.uk/library/ADO-NOT.html.
17. Adorno, *Notes to Literature*, 97.
18. Adorno, *Beethoven*, 126.
19. Pascal, *Pensées and Other Writings*, 73. Pascal's words are quoted in *Eleutheria*, 137: 'Monsieur! I entreat you! Have pity, have pity on those who dwell in the thick darkness. (*He listens ostentatiously.*) Silence! It's like the eternal silence of Pascal's infinite spaces . . .'
20. Cf. *Eleutheria*, 137.
21. John Milton, *Paradise Lost*, ed. and intro. Stephen Orgel and Jonathan Goldberg (Oxford: Oxford University Press, 2004), 228, ll. 780–4.
22. Steven Connor, '"Was that a Point?": Beckett's Punctuation', in *The Edinburgh Companion to Samuel Beckett and the Arts*, ed. S. E. Gontarski (Edinburgh: Edinburgh University Press, 2014), 277.
23. Blanchot, *Infinite Conversation*, 328.
24. Molloy is scientifically up to date (*TN*, 27): 'Yes, even then, when already all was fading, waves and particles, there could be no things but nameless things, no names but thingless names.'
25. Christopher Ricks has also briefly remarked on this phenomenon, *Dying Words*, 86–7.
26. Compare Beckett's telegram to *The Times* upon being asked to submit his resolutions and hopes for the approaching new year of 1984: 'RESOLUTIONS COLON ZERO STOP PERIOD HOPES COLON ZERO STOP BECKETT' (*L4*, 626).
27. See *PTD*, 31–2
28. Thomas à Kempis, *The Imitation of Christ*, 309.
29. This pessimistic slant might explain Beckett's attraction to the phrase and, by the same token, his seeming indifference to Augustine's use of the reference. The *Dream* notebook's many cullings from *The Confessions* do not include Augustine's own reference to the 'goodly pearl', which occurs in Book 8, from which Beckett took sixteen quotations.
30. Thomas à Kempis, *The Imitation of Christ*, 309.
31. C. J. Ackerley, 'Samuel Beckett and Thomas à Kempis: The Roots of Quietism', *Samuel Beckett Today / Aujourd'hui* 9 (2000): 82.
32. Dante Alighieri, *The Divine Comedy of Dante Alighieri: The Italian Text with a Translation in English Blank Verse and Commentary, Volume 3: Paradiso*, trans. Courtney Langdon (Cambridge, MA: Harvard University Press, 1921), 3.10–16.
33. See *DN*, 155–6; *CP*, 31, 235.
34. See Ackerley, 'Samuel Beckett and Thomas à Kempis', 83.

35. Anthony Cordingley, *Samuel Beckett's* How It Is: *Philosophy in Translation* (Edinburgh: Edinburgh University Press, 2018), 45.
36. Dirk van Hulle, *The Making of Samuel Beckett's* Krapp's Last Tape / La Dernière Bande (Antwerp: University Press Antwerp, 2015), 173.
37. Dante, *Inf.* 5.121–3.
38. See Ackerley and Gontarski, *The Faber Companion*, 105.
39. Dirk van Hulle and Mark Nixon remark that Beckett's initially 'hasty conclusion' about *On the Origin of Species* is balanced by attentive rereadings over subsequent years. Dirk van Hulle and Mark Nixon, *Samuel Beckett's Library* (Cambridge: Cambridge University Press, 2013), 202–4.
40. Charles Darwin, *On the Origin of Species*, ed. Gillian Beer (Oxford: Oxford University Press, 2008), 156.
41. Darwin, *Origin*, 156.
42. The French version renders 'great categories of being' as 'grandes categories d'existence' (*CC*, 12) which more clearly foregrounds the ontological reduction Bom undergoes: existence not only precedes essence but also remains when essence is stripped back.
43. Giorgio Agamben, *Homo Sacer: Sovereign Power and Bare Life*, trans. Daniel Heller-Roazen (Stanford: Stanford University Press, 1998), 105.
44. Rabaté, *Think, Pig!*, 53.
45. For a discussion of Bom's quotation, see Peter Fifield, *Late Modernist Style in Samuel Beckett and Emmanuel Levinas* (New York: Palgrave Macmillan, 2013), 125–6.
46. The conflation of existential and verbal excrement is also present in *Texts for Nothing* and *The Unnamable*. For a discussion, see Yoshiki Tajiri, *Samuel Beckett and the Prosthetic Body: The Organs and Senses in Modernism* (New York: Palgrave Macmillan, 2007), 51.
47. Dante, *Inf.* 3.4–9.
48. Compare the corresponding passage in *Dream*, 233. 'A Wet Night' renders the allusion to Dante more clearly.
49. The vestibule is the zone populated by the *ignavi* and cowards such as Pope Celestine V, with whose 'grand refusal' Beckett was taken (*L2*, 240). In the early poem, 'Malacoda', Beckett also imagines a scene in the 'vestibule' (*CP*, 21).
50. For Dante's reference to this banner, see *Inf.* 3.52–7.
51. This image is reworked in the poem 'Text 3': 'Worms breed in the red tears' (*CP*, 39).
52. Beckett gives a bitter twist to the words of Yeats's Crazy Jane: 'Love has pitched his mansion in / The place of excrement'. Yeats, *The Poems*, 310.
53. Compare Molloy's predicament (*TN*, 18); also relevant is Malone's cynicism (*TN*, 245–6).

54. Compare Paul Sheehan's reading of *The Unnamable*'s concluding lines as simultaneous and not sequential (the latter being the optimistic, humanist reading). Sheehan, *Modernism, Narrative and Humanism* (Cambridge: Cambridge University Press, 2002), 175.
55. As such it accords with Adorno's reflections on lateness and self-repetition: 'the empty phrase is set in place as a monument to what has been – a monument in which subjectivity petrified'. Adorno, *Beethoven*, 126.
56. Bom, we should remember, says that he will not ask Pim to 'do the impossible' (*HII*, 55).
57. See Chapter 4 for my earlier discussion of this image in Geulincx. Geulincx's intertextual presence is explicitly suggested in *How It Is* by the phrase 'all self to be abandoned say nothing when nothing' (72), which rehearses the *ubi nihil vales* imperative as well as the Third Obligation of the *Ethics*: '*to abandon myself, and deliver myself entirely into God's hands*'. Geulincx, *Ethics*, 72, 45.
58. Alain Badiou, *On Beckett*, ed. and trans. Alberto Toscano and Nina Power (Manchester: Clinamen Press, 2003), 46.
59. For readings on *How It Is* as a response to the Algerian War, see Adam Piette, 'Torture, Text, Human Rights: *Comment C'est / How It Is* and the Algerian War', in *Around 1945: Literature, Citizenship, Rights*, ed. Allan Hepburn (Montreal and Kingston: McGill-Queen's University Press, 2016), 151–74; and Morin's excellent *Beckett's Political Imagination*, 184–237.
60. It is also hard to sympathise with David Kleinberg-Levin's optimistic reading that the novel offers 'a strong protest against the ancient conception of justice as revenge'. Kleinberg-Levin, *Beckett's Words: The Promise of Happiness in a Time of Mourning* (London: Bloomsbury, 2015), 243. By contrast, Paul Sheehan convincingly argues that it is impossible to absorb the novel's cruelties into a valorising narrative. See Sheehan, 'A World without Monsters: Beckett and the Ethics of Cruelty', in *Beckett and Ethics*, ed. Russell Smith (London: Continuum, 2008), 99–100.
61. Also relevant is the cruel generosity of Hamm who threatens to give Clov just enough food to keep him from starving utterly (*CDW*, 95), or the 'charity' of Molloy's mother which – like Bom's sack – 'kept [him] dying' (*TN*, 18).
62. Victor Shklovsky, *Victor Shklovsky: A Reader*, ed. and trans. Alexandra Berlina (New York: Bloomsbury, 2017), 93.
63. In Graver and Federman, *The Critical Heritage*, 285.
64. See *L3*, 525: 'Improved C.C. a bit I think and caught up on some bad slips, but it remains unreadable which is a great beauty.'

Conclusion: Humility's Edges

I opened my Introduction by asking whether Monty Python's blessed meek refer to the humble or the humiliated. If this book has succeeded in at least one of its aims, it will have demonstrated that the distinction between humility and humiliation is not always clear, nor is the causal relation between them a straightforward matter. On the one hand, humility may be an attitude that encourages patient submission to different kinds of humiliation – a 'grace formed by suffering', in E. B. Pusey's lovely phrase.[1] On the other hand, humiliation may be a condition or experience that cultivates the meekness extolled in the beatitudes.

In turning to the works of Eliot and Beckett, the conceptual and semantic variance is made no simpler. For Eliot, humility is fundamentally a matter of right belief, of acknowledging one's place in the eternal scheme. This is true in 1917 when Eeldrop voices the inescapability of the individual soul before absolute laws. It is similarly true, after 1927, when the value of good will is determined in relation to the correctness of conviction. In his turn, Beckett could 'understand . . . humility in terms of "there but for the grace of G." or "there but for the disgrace of this old bastard", humility before the doomed & the assumed' (*L1*, 228). But in his writing, humility is most often a product of humiliation. This is glimpsed in the vagabond of 'Walking Out', in Estragon's quiet acceptance of his existential embarrassment, and in the speaker of *Worstward Ho* who registers the agony of his bones but is determined to go on kneeling (*Com etc.*, 86–7). For Beckett himself, there was no great distance between humiliation and humility:

> I can see nothing for us but the old earth turning onward and time feasting on our suffering along with the rest. Somewhere at the heart of the gales of grief (and of love too, I've been told) already they have blown themselves out. I was always grateful for that *humiliating*

consciousness and it was always there I huddled, in the innermost place of *human frailty and lowliness*. To fly there for me was not to fly far . . . (*L3*, 119, my emphasis)

I concluded the Introduction by suggesting that we might get some idea of the differences between Eliot's and Beckett's handling of humility and humiliation in their respective use of Julian of Norwich. But a more arresting if imperfect likeness is between two of their suffering heroines who perform the degradation of Isa. 29: 4 to a disturbingly literal degree: 'And thou shalt be brought down, and shalt speak out of the ground, and thy speech shall be low out of the dust . . .' At the 1949 premier of *The Cocktail Party*, audiences at the Edinburgh Festival overheard what would become apocryphal details. Instead of being obliquely reported as it is in the published version, gruesome touches were added to the account of Celia's already grizzly end.

> It is difficult to say [what remained of the body]
> At such a late stage of decomposition:
> Bodies disintegrate quickly in that climate.
> But from what we know of local practices
> It would seem that she must have been crucified
> Very near an anthill. They smear the victims
> With a juice that is attractive to the ants.[2]

Twelve years later, in 1961, Beckett would similarly bring one of his moribunds low with the ground. Fixed up to her waist in sand, *Happy Days*'s Winnie spots an emmet which causes her some mirth. Reflecting on this piffling sign of life, she asks: 'How can one better magnify the Almighty than by sniggering with him at his little jokes . . .?' (*CDW*, 150). Of course, the joke is on Winnie herself. Beckett explained that '[t]he eggs contain the promise of swarming (devouring) ants to come. This shd. be remembered in Act II when she no longer has arms to defend herself with.'[3] Daniel Albright, who first noticed this indirect correspondence, writes that 'Winnie suffers Eliotesque, or Dantesque, torture' and that the play contains traces of the morality play.[4] I think Albright is right in pointing to Dantesque vestiges, though it is important to remember the play's mockery of transcendental meaning, whether beyond life or beyond the text:

What's the idea? he says – stuck up to her diddies in the bleeding ground – course fellow – What does it mean? he says – What's it meant to mean? – and so on – lot more stuff like that – usual drivel . . . And you, she says, what's the idea of you, she says, what are you meant to mean? (*CDW*, 156)

The answer to the last question ultimately separates Celia and Winnie. Horrific though it may be, Celia's death has a clear meaning: atonement for sin and submission before God. Her martyrdom is in keeping with the voluntary suffering of Dante's penitents. As Eliot remarked, '[t]he souls in purgatory suffer because they *wish to suffer*, for purgation' (*CP3*, 716). By contrast, Winnie's purgatory is like the purgatory Beckett described in Joyce's writing: a place where there is no culmination or consummation.⁵ The difference between the two plays and between the humiliation of their sufferers may effectively be distilled as chosen suffering and given suffering. For Eliot, humiliation is sometimes a necessary component in Christian humility; for Beckett, humiliation is a fact of being to which one can respond in humility. Yet, while these positions imply very different outlooks, there is between the two authors an inclination to trouble the making of our modern mind. Beyond the correspondence of flesh-eating ants, Eliot and Beckett scandalise our valuations of suffering and sacrifice. As in *Happy Days*, we find in *The Cocktail Party* an expression of bafflement and confusion about the point of humiliation: Celia's friends consider her death to be a 'waste' (*CPP*, 438), something beyond explanation and in excess of any measurable value. This pentimento – this nearcoming together between Celia and Winnie – throws into relief Eliot's and Beckett's performances of humility. While their ways up and ways down might not be the same, there is a comparable insistence that lowliness does not imply going gently. An endless humility is not without its edges.

Notes

1. Pusey, *Blessed Are the Meek*, 5.
2. Original script of *The Cocktail Party*, quoted in Browne, *The Making*, 226.
3. Beckett to Alan Schneider on 3 September 1961. In Maurice Harmon, ed., *No Author Better Served: The Correspondence of Samuel*

Beckett and Alan Schneider (Cambridge, MA: Harvard University Press, 1998), 103.
4. Daniel Albright, *Beckett and Aesthetics* (Cambridge: Cambridge University Press, 2003), 72.
5. See *Dis*, 33: 'Mr Joyce's [purgatory] is spherical and excludes culmination ... [There,] movement is non-directional – or multi-directional, and a step forward is, by definition, a step back.'

Bibliography

Works by Samuel Beckett

Beckett, Samuel. *Bande et Sarabande*. Trans. Edith Fournier. Paris: Les Éditions de Minuit, 1999.
—. *Beckett's Dream Notebook*. Ed. John Pilling. Reading: Beckett International Foundation, 1999.
—. *The Collected Poems of Samuel Beckett: A Critical Edition*. Ed. Seán Lawlor and John Pilling. London: Faber and Faber, 2012.
—. *Comment c'est, How It Is and / et L'Image: A Critical-Genetic Edition / Une edition critic-genetique*. Ed. Édouard Magessa O'Reilly. London: Routledge, 2001.
—. *Company; Ill Seen Ill Said; Worstward Ho; Stirrings Still*. Ed. Dirk van Hulle. London: Faber and Faber, 2009.
—. *The Complete Dramatic Works*. London: Faber and Faber, 2006.
—. *The Complete Short Prose, 1929–1989*. Ed. S. E. Gontarski. New York: Grove Press, 1995.
—. *Disjecta: Miscellaneous Writings and a Dramatic Fragment*. London: John Calder, 1983.
—. *Dream of Fair to Middling Women*. Ed. Eoin O'Brien and Edith Fournier. Fwd. Eoin O'Brien. New York: Arcade Publishing, 1992.
—. *Echo's Bones*. Ed. Mark Nixon. New York: Grove Press, 2014.
—. *Eleutheria*. Trans. Barbara Wright. London: Faber and Faber, 1996.
—. *How It Is*. Ed. Édouard Magessa O'Reilly. London: Faber and Faber, 2009.
—. '"Le Concentrisme" and "Jean d Chas": Two Extracts'. Trans. John Pilling. *Modernism / Modernity*, 18.4 (2011): 883–6.
—. *The Letters of Samuel Beckett, Volume 1: 1929–1940*. Ed. Martha Dow Fehsenfeld, Lois More Overbeck, Georg Craig and Dan Gunn. Cambridge: Cambridge University Press, 2009.

—. *The Letters of Samuel Beckett, Volume 2: 1941–1956*. Ed. George Craig, Martha Dow Fehsenfeld, Dan Gunn and Lois More Overbeck. Cambridge: Cambridge University Press, 2011.
—. *The Letters of Samuel Beckett, Volume 3: 1957–1965*. Ed. George Craig, Martha Dow Fehsenfeld, Dan Gunn and Lois More Overbeck. Cambridge: Cambridge University Press, 2014.
—. *The Letters of Samuel Beckett, Volume 4: 1966–1989*. Ed. George Craig, Martha Dow Fehsenfeld, Dan Gunn and Lois More Overbeck. Cambridge: Cambridge University Press, 2016.
—. *Mercier and Camier*. New York: Grove Press, 1975.
—. *More Pricks than Kicks*. Ed. Cassandra Nelson. London: Faber and Faber, 2010.
—. *Murphy*. New York: Grove Press, 1957.
—. 'Philosophy Notes'. TCD MS 10967. Trinity College Dublin.
—. *Proust and 'Three Dialogues with Georges Duthuit'*. London: John Calder, 1965.
—. 'Psychology Notes'. TCD MS 10971/8/22. Trinity College Dublin.
—. *The Theatrical Notebooks of Samuel Beckett, Volume 1*: Waiting for Godot. Ed. Dougald McMillan and James Knowlson. London: Faber and Faber, 1994.
—. *Three Novels: Molloy, Malone Dies, The Unnamable*. New York: Grove Press, 1994.
—. *Watt*. Ed. C. J. Ackerley. London: Faber and Faber, 2009.

Works by T. S. Eliot

Eliot, T. S. *After Strange Gods: A Primer of Modern Heresy*. London: Faber and Faber, 1934.
—. *The Complete Poems and Plays*. London: Faber and Faber, 1969.
—. *The Complete Prose of T. S. Eliot: The Critical Edition, Volume 1: Apprentice Years, 1905–1918*. Ed. Jewel Spears Brooker and Ronald Schuchard. Baltimore: Johns Hopkins Press; London: Faber and Faber, 2014.
—. *The Complete Prose of T. S. Eliot: The Critical Edition, Volume 2: The Perfect Critic, 1919–1926*. Ed. Anthony Cuda and Ronald Schuchard. Baltimore: Johns Hopkins Press; London: Faber and Faber, 2014.
—. *The Complete Prose of T. S. Eliot: The Critical Edition, Volume 3: Literature, Politics, Belief, 1927–1929*. Ed. Frances Dickey, Jennifer Formichelli and Ronald Schuchard. Baltimore: Johns Hopkins Press; London: Faber and Faber, 2015.

—. *The Complete Prose of T. S. Eliot: The Critical Edition, Volume 4: English Lion, 1930–1933*. Ed. Jason Harding and Ronald Schuchard. Baltimore: Johns Hopkins Press; London: Faber and Faber, 2015.
—. *The Complete Prose of T. S. Eliot: The Critical Edition, Volume 5: Tradition and Orthodoxy, 1934–1939*. Ed. Iman Javadi, Ronald Schuchard and Jayme Stayer. Baltimore: Johns Hopkins Press; London: Faber and Faber, 2017.
—. *The Complete Prose of T. S. Eliot: The Critical Edition, Volume 6: The War Years, 1940–1946*. Ed. David E. Chinitz and Ronald Schuchard. Baltimore: Johns Hopkins Press; London: Faber and Faber, 2017.
—. *The Complete Prose of T. S. Eliot: The Critical Edition, Volume 7: A European Society, 1947–1953*. Ed. Iman Javadi and Ronald Shuchard. Baltimore: Johns Hopkins Press; London: Faber and Faber, 2019.
—. *The Complete Prose of T. S. Eliot: The Critical Edition, Volume 8: Still and Still Moving, 1954–1965*. Ed. Jewel Spears Brooker and Ronald Schuchard. Baltimore: Johns Hopkins Press; London: Faber and Faber, 2019.
—. *The Film of* Murder in the Cathedral. With George Hoellering. London: Faber and Faber, 1952.
—. *For Lancelot Andrewes: Essays on Style and Order*. London: Faber and Faber, 1928.
—. *Inventions of the March Hare: Poems 1909–1917*. Ed. Christopher Ricks. London: Harcourt Brace & Company, 1996.
—. *The Letters of T. S. Eliot, Volume 1: 1898–1922*, Revised edn. Ed. Valerie Eliot and Hugh Haughton. London: Faber and Faber, 2009.
—. *The Letters of T. S. Eliot, Volume 2: 1923–1925*. Ed. Valerie Eliot and Hugh Haughton. London: Faber and Faber, 2009.
—. *The Letters of T. S. Eliot, Volume 3: 1926–1927*. Ed. Valerie Eliot and John Haffenden. London: Faber and Faber, 2012.
—. *The Letters of T. S. Eliot, Volume 4: 1928–1929*. Ed. Valerie Eliot and John Haffenden. London: Faber and Faber, 2013.
—. *The Letters of T. S. Eliot, Volume 5: 1930–1931*. Ed. Valerie Eliot and John Haffenden. London: Faber and Faber, 2014.
—. *The Letters of T. S. Eliot, Volume 6: 1932–1933*. Ed. Valerie Eliot and John Haffenden. London: Faber and Faber, 2016.
—. *The Letters of T. S. Eliot, Volume 7: 1934–1935*. Ed. Valerie Eliot and John Haffenden. London: Faber and Faber, 2017.
—. *The Letters of T. S. Eliot, Volume 8: 1936–1938*. Ed. Valerie Eliot and John Haffenden. London: Faber and Faber, 2019.

—. *Notes towards the Definition of Culture*. London: Faber and Faber, 1948.
—. *On Poetry and Poets*. London: Faber and Faber, 1957.
—. *The Poems of T. S. Eliot, Volume 1: Collected and Uncollected Poems*. Ed. Christopher Ricks and Jim McCue. London: Faber and Faber, 2015.
—. *The Poems of T. S. Eliot, Volume 2: Practical Cats and Further Verses*. Ed. Christopher Ricks and Jim McCue. London: Faber and Faber, 2015.
—. *Selected Essays*. London: Faber and Faber, 1951.
—. *The Waste Land: A Facsimile and Transcript of the Original Drafts Including the Annotations of Ezra Pound*. Ed. Valerie Eliot. London: Faber and Faber, 1971.
—. *To Criticize the Critic and Other Writings*. London: Faber and Faber, 1965.

General

Ackerley, C. J. *Demented Particulars: The Annotated* Murphy. Edinburgh: Edinburgh University Press, 2010.
—. 'Inorganic Form: Samuel Beckett's Nature.' *Journal of the Australasian Universities Language and Literature Association* 104 (2005): 70–89.
—. 'Samuel Beckett and Anthropomorphic Insolence.' *Samuel Beckett Today / Aujourd'hui* 18 (2007): 77–90.
—. 'Samuel Beckett and Max Nordau: Degeneration, Sausage Poisoning, the Bloodied Rafflesia, Coenaesthesis, and the Not-I.' *Beckett after Beckett*. Ed. S. E. Gontarski and Anthony Uhlmann. Gainesville: University Press of Florida, 2006, 167–76.
—. 'Samuel Beckett and Thomas à Kempis: The Roots of Quietism.' *Samuel Beckett Today / Aujourd'hui* 9 (2000): 81–92.
Ackerley, C. J. and S. E. Gontarski (eds). *The Faber Companion to Samuel Beckett*. London: Faber and Faber, 2006.
Ackroyd, Peter. *T. S. Eliot*. London: Abacus, 1984.
Adams, Hazard. *Blake and Yeats: The Contrary Vision*. New York: Russell & Russell, 1986.
Adams, John F. 'The Fourth Temptation in *Murder in the Cathedral*.' *Modern Drama* 5 (1962): 381–8.
Adorno, Theodor W. *Beethoven: The Philosophy of Music*. Ed. Rolf Tiedeman, trans. Edmund Jephcott. Stanford: Stanford University Press, 1998.
—. *Notes to Literature*. Vol. 1. Ed. Rolf Tiedemann, trans. Shierry Weber Nicholsen. New York: Columbia University Press, 1991.

Agamben, Giorgio. *The End of the Poem: Studies in Poetics*. Trans. Daniel Heller-Roazen. Stanford: Stanford University Press, 1999.
—. *Homo Sacer: Sovereign Power and Bare Life*. Trans. Daniel Heller-Roazen. Stanford: Stanford University Press, 1998.
—. *Remnants of Auschwitz: The Witness and the Archive*. Trans. Daniel Heller-Roazen. New York: Zone Books, 1999.
Alexander, Arch. B. D. *A Short History of Philosophy*. Glasgow: James Maclehose and Sons, 1907.
Albright, Daniel. *Beckett and Aesthetics*. Cambridge: Cambridge University Press, 2003.
Aldington, Richard. 'Charles Péguy and His Work.' *The Egoist: An Individualist Review* 20.1 (Oct 1914): 386–7.
Alfano, Mark, Michael P. Lynch and Alessandra Tanesini (eds). *The Routledge Handbook of the Philosophy of Humility*. Abingdon: Routledge, 2020.
Allen, William S. *Aesthetics of Negativity: Blanchot, Adorno, and Autonomy*. New York: Fordham University Press, 2016.
Andrewes, Lancelot. *Seventeen Sermons on the Nativity*. London: Griffith Farran Okeden and Welsh, 1887.
Anonymous. *The Cloud of Unknowing*. Ed. James Walsh. New York: Paulist Press, 1981.
Antelme, Robert. *The Human Race*. Trans. Jeffrey Haight and Annie Mahler. Evanston: The Marlboro Press, 1998.
Arendt, Hannah. *The Human Condition*. 2nd edn. Chicago: The University of Chicago Press, 1958.
Aristotle. *The 'Art' of Rhetoric*. Trans. John Henry Freese. London: William Heinemann, 1926.
—. *Nicomachean Ethics*. Trans. and ed. Roger Crisp. Cambridge: Cambridge University Press, 2004.
Armitage, P. D., P. S. Cranston, and L. C. V. Pinder. *The Chironomidae: Biology and Ecology of Non-Biting Midges*. Dordrecht: Springer-Science and Business Media, 1995.
Arnold, Matthew. *Culture and Anarchy*. Oxford: Oxford University Press, 2006.
—. 'Review of Objections to *Literature and Dogma*, I.' *The Contemporary Review* XXIV (1874): 794–818.
Atik, Anne. *How It Was: A Memoir of Samuel Beckett*. London: Faber and Faber, 2001.
Auden, W. H. 'Dingley Dell & The Fleet'. *The Dyer's Hand and Other Essays*. New York: Random House, 1962, 407–28.
—. 'The Prince's Dog'. *The Dyer's Hand and Other Essays*. New York: Random House, 1962, 182–208.

Auerbach, Erich. *Mimesis: The Representation of Reality in Western Literature*. Fiftieth Anniversary Edition. Trans. Willard R. Trask. Princeton: Princeton University Press, 2003.

Augustine. *Confessions*. Trans. E. B. Pusey. Oxford: John Henry Parker, 1938.

—. *Responses to Miscellaneous Questions: Miscellany of Eighty-Three Questions; Miscellany of Questions in Response to Simplician; and Eight Questions of Dulcitius*, Part I, Vol. 12. Intro. and trans. Boniface Ramsay. Ed. Raymond Canning. New York: New City Press, 2008.

Ayers, Robert W. '*Murder in the Cathedral*: A Liturgy Less Divine.' *Texas Studies in Literature and Language* 20.4 (1978): 579–98.

Babbitt, Irving. *Democracy and Leadership*. Boston: Houghton Mifflin Company, 1962.

—. *Rousseau and Romanticism*. Boston: Houghton Mifflin, 1919.

Badiou, Alain. *On Beckett*. Ed. and trans. Alberto Toscano and Nina Power. Manchester: Clinamen Press, 2003.

—. *Saint Paul: The Foundation of Universalism*. Trans. Ray Brassier. Stanford: Stanford University Press, 2003.

Bailey, Iain. *Samuel Beckett and the Bible*. London: Bloomsbury, 2014.

Baillie, James. *Hume on Morality*. New York: Routledge, 2000.

Baker, Phil. *Beckett and the Mythology of Psychoanalysis*. London: Macmillan Press, 1997.

Banerjee, Ria. 'From Humiliation to Epiphany: The Role of Onstage Spaces in T. S. Eliot's Middle Plays.' *South Atlantic Review* 82.2 (2017): 59–77.

Bataille, Georges. *Death and Sensuality: A Study of Eroticism and the Taboo*. New York: Walker and Co., 1962.

Baudelaire, Charles. *Baudelaire: His Prose and Poetry*. Trans. and ed. T. R. Smith. New York: Boni and Liveright, 1919.

Beja, Morris, S. E. Gontarski and Pierre Astier (eds). *Samuel Beckett: A Humanistic Perspective*. Columbus: Ohio State University Press, 1983.

Benedict of Nursia. *The Rule of St Benedict*. London: SPCK, 1931.

Benjamin, Walter. *One-Way Street and Other Writings*. Trans. Edmund Jephcott and Kingsley Shorter. London: NLB, 1979.

Ben-Ze'ew, Aaron. 'The Virtue of Modesty.' *American Philosophical Quarterly* 30.3 (1993): 235–46.

Bergson, Henri. *Time and Free Will: An Essay on the Immediate Data of Consciousness*. Trans. F. L. Pogson. Mineola, NY: Dover Publications, 2001.

Bernard of Clairvaux. *The Steps of Humility and Pride*. Trans. M. Ambrose Conway. Kalamazoo, MI: Cistercian Publications, 1989.
Bersani, Leo. *Is the Rectum a Grave, and Other Essays*. London: The University of Chicago Press, 2010.
Bersani, Leo and Ulysse Dutoit. *Arts of Impoverishment: Beckett, Rothko, Resnais*. Cambridge, MA: Harvard University Press, 1993.
Blake, William. *Poetical Works*. Intro. W. B. Yeats. London: George Routledge & Sons, 1910.
Blamires, Harry. *Word Unheard: A Guide through Eliot's* Four Quartets. London: Methuen and Co., 1969.
Blanchot, Maurice. *The Infinite Conversation*. Trans. Susan Hanson. Minneapolis: University of Minnesota Press, 2003.
Blanton, C. D. *Epic Negation: The Dialectical Poetics of Late Modernism*. Oxford: Oxford University Press, 2015.
Blissett, William. 'T. S. Eliot and Catholicity.' *T. S. Eliot and Christian Tradition*. Ed. Benjamin Lockerd. Madison: Fairleigh Dickinson University Press, 2014, 33–52.
Bloom, Harold. *The Anxiety of Influence: A Theory of Poetry*. New York: Oxford University Press, 1973.
Bolin, John. *Beckett and the Modern Novel*. New York: Cambridge University Press, 2013.
Booth, Wayne C. *A Rhetoric of Irony*. Chicago: The University of Chicago Press, 1974.
Borradori, Giovanna. *Philosophy in a Time of Terror: Dialogues with Jürgen Habermas and Jacques Derrida*. Chicago: The University of Chicago Press, 2003.
Bradley, F. H. *Appearance and Reality*. London: Swan Sonnencschein and Co., 1899.
—. *Ethical Studies*. London: Henry S. King and Co., 1876.
—. *The Principles of Logic*. New York: G. E. Stechert and Co., 1912.
Brooker, Jewel Spears (ed.). *T. S. Eliot: The Contemporary Reviews*. Cambridge: Cambridge University Press, 2004.
Brooks, Cleanth. 'Irony as a Principle of Structure.' *The Critical Tradition: Classic Texts and Contemporary Trends*. Ed. David H. Richter. Boston: Bedford / St. Martin's, 2007.
Browne, Edward Harold. *An Exposition of the Thirty-Nine Articles, Historical and Doctrinal*. 14th edn. London: Longmans, Green, and Co., 1894.
Browne, Martin E. *The Making of T. S. Eliot's Plays*. Cambridge: Cambridge University Press, 1969.

Bryden, Mary. *Samuel Beckett and the Idea of God*. New York: St. Martin's Press, 1998.

—. *Women in Samuel Beckett's Prose and Drama*. Lanham: Barnes & Noble Books, 1993.

Burt, E. S. 'Regard for the Other: Embarrassment in the "Quatrième promenade".' *L'Esprit Créateur* 39.4 (1999): 54–76.

Bush, Ronald. *T. S. Eliot: A Study in Character and Style*. Oxford: Oxford University Press, 1983.

—. (ed.). *T. S. Eliot: The Modernist in History*. Cambridge: Cambridge University Press, 1991.

Button, Mark. '"A Monkish Kind of Virtue"? For and Against Humility.' *Political Theory* 22 (2005): 840–68.

Caputo, John D. *Cross and Cosmos: A Theology of Difficult Glory*. Bloomington: Indiana University Press, 2019.

—. *How to Read Kierkegaard*. New York: W.W. Norton & Company, 2007.

Casanova, Pascale. *Samuel Beckett: The Anatomy of a Literary Revolution*. Trans. Gregory Elliott. London: Verso, 2006.

Caselli, Daniela. *Beckett's Dantes: Intertextuality in the Fiction and Criticism*. Manchester: Manchester University Press, 2005.

—. 'Belacqua's Shadows in "Dream of Fair to Middling Women" and "How It Is".' *Samuel Beckett Today / Aujourd'hui* 11 (2001): 461–68.

Catalano, Joseph S. *Reading Sartre*. New York: Cambridge University Press, 2010.

Chevalier, Haakon M. *The Ironic Temper: Anatole France and His Time*. New York: Oxford University Press, 1932.

Childs, Donald J. *From Philosophy to Poetry: T. S. Eliot's Study of Knowledge and Experience*. London: The Athlone Press, 2001.

Chinitz, David, E. *T. S. Eliot and the Cultural Divide*. Chicago: The University of Chicago Press, 2003.

Cioran, E. M. *A Short History of Decay*. Trans. Richard Howard. London: Penguin Books, 1975.

—. *The Temptation to Exist*. Trans. Richard Howard. Chicago: Chicago University Press, 1968.

Clarke, James Freeman. *Vexed Questions in Theology: A Series of Essays*. Boston: Geo. H. Ellis, 1886.

Clement of Alexandria. *The Writings of the Fathers: Clement of Alexandria*. Vol. 2. Ed. Alexander Roberts and James Donaldson. Edinburgh: T. and T. Clark, 1869.

Clement, Jennifer. *Reading Humility in Early Modern England*. New York: Routledge, 2015.

Coetzee, J. M. 'What is a Classic?' *Current Writing: Text and Reception in Southern Africa* 5.2 (2011): 7–24.
Cohn, Ruby. *A Beckett Canon*. Ann Arbor: University of Michigan Press, 2001.
Collini, Stefan. *Absent Minds: Intellectuals in Britain*. Oxford: Oxford University Press, 2006.
Connor, Steven. *Giving Way: Thoughts on Unappreciated Dispositions*. Stanford: Stanford University Press, 2019.
—. 'How He Was: Samuel Beckett's Lives.' *Bullán: An Irish Studies Journal* 4.1 (1998): 121–26.
—. *Samuel Beckett: Repetition, Theory and Text*. Oxford: Basil Blackwell, 1988.
—. '"Was That a Point?": Beckett's Punctuation.' *The Edinburgh Companion to Samuel Beckett and the Arts*. Ed. S. E. Gontarski. Edinburgh: Edinburgh University Press, 2014, 269–81.
Cook, Eleanor. *Against Coercion: Games Poets Play*. Stanford: Stanford University Press, 1998.
Cooper, David E. *The Measure of Things: Humanism, Humility, and Mystery*. Oxford: Oxford University Press, 2002.
Cooper, John Xiros. *T. S. Eliot and the Ideology of* Four Quartets. Cambridge: Cambridge University Press, 1995.
Cooper, Julie E. *Secular Powers: Humility in Modern Political Thought*. Chicago: The University of Chicago Press, 2013.
Cooper, William. *Flagellation and the Flagellants: A History of the Rod in All Countries from the Earliest Period to the Present Time*. London: William Reeves, 1877.
Corcoran, Neil. *Shakespeare and the Modern Poet*. Cambridge: Cambridge University Press, 2010.
Cordingley, Anthony. *Samuel Beckett's* How It Is: *Philosophy in Translation*. Edinburgh: Edinburgh University Press, 2018.
Crawford, Robert. *Young Eliot: From St Louis to* The Waste Land. London: Jonathan Cape, 2015.
Critchley, Simon. *On Humour*. London: Routledge, 2002.
—. *Very Little . . . Almost Nothing: Death, Philosophy, Literature*. London: Routledge, 1997.
Cronin, Anthony. *Samuel Beckett: The Last Modernist*. London: Flamingo, 1997.
Crozier, W. Ray. *Blushing and the Social Emotions: The Self Unmasked*. New York: Palgrave Macmillan, 2006.
Cuda, Anthony. *The Passions of Modernism: Eliot, Yeats, Woolf, and Mann*. Columbia: University of South Carolina Press, 2010.

Curzer, Howard J. 'Aristotle's Much Maligned Megalopsychos.' *Australasian Journal of Philosophy* 69.2 (1991): 131–51.
Dante Alighieri. *Convivio*. London: J. M. Dent, 1903.
—. *The Divine Comedy*. Trans. Allen Mandelbaum. New York: Knopf, 1995.
—. *The Divine Comedy of Dante Alighieri: The Italian Text with a Translation in English Blank Verse and Commentary, Volume 1: Inferno*. Trans. Courtney Langdon. Cambridge, MA: Harvard University Press, 1918.
—. *The Divine Comedy of Dante Alighieri: The Italian Text with a Translation in English Blank Verse and Commentary, Volume 2: Purgatorio*. Trans. Courtney Langdon. Cambridge, MA: Harvard University Press, 1920.
—. *The Divine Comedy of Dante Alighieri: The Italian Text with a Translation in English Blank Verse and Commentary, Volume 3: Paradiso*. Trans. Courtney Langdon. Cambridge, MA: Harvard University Press, 1921.
Darwin, Charles. *The Expression of the Emotions in Man and Animals* 2nd edn. Ed. Francis Darwin. Cambridge: Cambridge University Press, 2009.
—. *On the Origin of Species*. Ed. Gillian Beer. Oxford: Oxford University Press, 2008.
Davie, Donald. 'T. S. Eliot: The End of an Era.' *T. S. Eliot: A Collection of Critical Views*. Ed. Hugh Kenner. Englewood Cliffs: Prentice Hall, 1962, 192–206.
Davies, William. 'A New Occasion, a New Term of Relation: Samuel Beckett and T. S. Eliot.' *Beckett and Modernism*. Ed. Olga Beloborodova, Dirk van Hulle and Pim Verhulst. New York: Palgrave Macmillan, 2018, 111–28.
Dearlove, J. E. *Accommodating the Chaos: Samuel Beckett's Nonrelational Art*. Durham, NC: Duke University Press, 1982.
De Man, Paul. *Aesthetic Ideology*. Ed. and Intro. Andrzej Warminski. Minneapolis: University of Minnesota Press, 1996.
Derrida, Jacques. *The Animal that Therefore I Am*. Ed. Marie-Louise Mallet, trans. David Wills. New York: Fordham University Press, 2008.
—. *The Gift of Death*. Trans. David Wills. Chicago: The University of Chicago Press, 1995.
—. 'How to Avoid Speaking: Denials.' *Derrida and Negative Theology*. Ed. Harold Coward and Toby Foshay. Albany: State University of New York Press, 1992, 73–142.

Descartes, René. *A Discourse on the Method of Correctly Conducting One's Reason and Seeking Truth in the Sciences*. Trans. Ian Maclean. Oxford: Oxford University Press, 2006.
—. *Meditations on First Philosophy: With Selections from the Objections and Replies*. Trans. Michael Moriarty. Oxford: Oxford University Press, 2008.
De Villiers, Rick. 'Banishing the Backward Devils: Eliot's Quatrain Poems and "Gerontion".' *The New Cambridge Companion to T. S. Eliot*. Ed. Jason Harding. New York: Cambridge University Press, 2017, 55–70.
Dilks, Stephen John. 'Samuel Beckett's Samuel Johnson.' *The Modern Language Review* 98.2 (2003): 285–98.
Docherty, Thomas. 'On Critical Humility.' *Textual Practice* 23.6 (2009): 1029–43.
Doctrine in the Church of England: The Report of the Commission on Christian Doctrine Appointed by the Archbishops of Canterbury and York in 1922. London: Society for Promoting Christian Knowledge, 1938.
Donne, John. *Biathanatos*. Ed. Ernest W. Sullivan II. Newark, DE: University of Delaware Press, 1984.
Donoghue, Denis. *Words Alone: The Poet T. S. Eliot*. New Haven: Yale University Press, 2000.
Dostoevsky, Fyodor. *Notes from Underground* and *The Double*. Trans. Jessie Coulson. London: Penguin Books.
Douay-Rheims Bible, or *The Holy Bible: Faithfully Translated into English out of the Authentical Latin, diligently conferred with the Hebrew, Greek, & Other Editions in Divers Languages*. Rouen: John Cousturier, 1636.
Driver, Julia. 'The Virtues of Ignorance.' *The Journal of Philosophy* 86.7 (1989): 373–84.
Droge, Arthur J. and James D. Tabor. *A Noble Death: Suicide and Martyrdom among Christians and Jews in Antiquity*. New York: HarperSanFrancisco, 1992.
Durkheim, Émile. *Elementary Forms of Religious Life*. Trans. Joseph Ward Swain. London: George Allen & Unwin, 1915.
—. *Suicide: A Study in Sociology*. Trans. John A. Spaulding and George Simpson. London: Routledge, 1952.
Eagleton, Terry. *Sweet Violence: The Idea of the Tragic*. Oxford: Blackwell, 2003.
Earle, John. *Micro-Cosmography, Or, A Piece of the World Characterized in Essays and Characters*. London: Salisbury, 1786 [1650].

Ellis, Steve. *British Writers and the Approach of World War II*. New York: Cambridge University Press, 2015.

Ellman, Maud. *The Poetics of Impersonality: T. S. Eliot and Ezra Pound*. Cambridge, MA: Harvard University Press, 1987.

Empson, William. *Some Versions of Pastoral*. Harmondsworth: Penguin. 1966.

—. 'The Style of the Master.' *T. S. Eliot: A Symposium*. Ed. Tambimuttu and Richard Marsh. London: Frank and Cass, 1965, 35–7.

Engelberts, Matthijs, Everett Frost and Jane Maxwell Engel (eds). *Samuel Beckett Today / Aujourd'hui: Notes diverse holo: Catalogues of Beckett's Reading Notes and Other Manuscripts at Trinity College Dublin, with Supporting Essays*. Amsterdam: Rodopi, 2006.

Epictetus. *The Discourse of Epictetus with the Encheiridion and Fragments*. Trans. George Long. New York: A. L. Burt, 1877.

Euripides. *Iphigenia in Aulis*. The Complete Greek Drama. Vol. 2. Ed. Whitney J. Oates and Eugene O'Neill, 289–350. New York: Random House, 1938, 289–350.

Fawcett, Edward Douglas. *The World as Imagination*. London: Macmillan and Co., 1916.

Federman, Raymond and John Fletcher. *Samuel Beckett: His Works and His Critics: An Essay in Bibliography*. London: University of California Press, 1970.

Feldman, Matthew. *Beckett's Books: A Cultural History of the Interwar Notes*. London: Continuum, 2006.

—. *Falsifying Beckett: Essays on Archives, Philosophy, and Methodology in Beckett Studies*. Fwd. Erik Tonning. Stuttgart: Ibidem-Verlag, 2015.

Fifield, Peter. *Late Modernist Style in Samuel Beckett and Emmanuel Levinas*. New York: Palgrave Macmillan, 2013.

Flood, Gavin. *The Ascetic Self: Subjectivity, Memory and Traditions*. Cambridge: Cambridge University Press, 2004.

Foerster, Norman. *American Criticism: A Study of Literary Theory from Poe to the Present*. Boston: Houghton Mifflin Company, 1928.

Foucault, Michel. *The Courage of the Truth (The Government of Self and Others II): Lectures at the Collège de France, 1983–1984*. Ed. Frédéric Gros. Trans. Graham Burchell. Basingstoke: Palgrave Macmillan, 2011.

—. 'Technologies of the Self.' *Technologies of the Self: A Seminar with Michel Foucault*, Ed. Luther H. Martin, Huck Gutman and Patrick H. Hutton. Amherst: University of Massachusetts Press, 1988, 16–49.

Foulcher, Jane. *Reclaiming Humility: Four Studies in the Monastic Tradition*. Collegeville, MN: Liturgical Press, 2015.
Franke, William. 'Apophasis and the Turn of Philosophy to Religion: From Neoplatonic Negative Theology to Postmodern Negation of Theology.' *International Journal for Philosophy of Religion* 60.1 (2006): 61–76.
—. (ed.). *On What Cannot Be Said: Apophatic Discourses in Philosophy, Religion, Literature, and the Arts*. Notre Dame, IN: University of Notre Dame Press, 2007.
Frankl, Victor E. *Man's Search for Meaning*. Revised edn. New York: Washington Square Press, 1959.
Fretz, Leo. 'Individuality in Sartre's Philosophy.' *The Cambridge Companion to Sartre*. Ed. Christina Howells. Cambridge: Cambridge University Press, 1992, 67–100.
Frye, Northrop. 'Yeats and the Language of Symbolism.' *University of Toronto Quarterly* 17.1 (1946): 1–17.
Gallagher, Shaun and Dan Zahavi. *The Phenomenological Mind: An Introduction to Philosophy of Mind and Cognitive Science*. Abingdon: Routledge, 2007.
Gallup, Donald. *T. S. Eliot: A Bibliography*. London: Faber and Faber, 1952.
Garber, Marjorie. *Shakespeare's Ghost Writers: Literature as Uncanny Causality*. New York: Routledge, 2010.
Gardner, Helen. *The Composition of* Four Quartets. London: Faber and Faber, 1978.
Geulincx, Arnold. *Ethics: With Samuel Beckett's Notes*. Trans. Martin Wilson. Ed. Han van Ruler, Anthony Uhlmann and Martin Wilson. Leiden: Koninklijke Brill NV, 2006.
Gibson, Andrew. *Samuel Beckett*. London: Reakton Books, 2010.
Gide, André. *Dostoevsky*. Trans. and Intro. Arnold Bennett. New York: New Directions, 1961.
—. *The Vatican Cellars*. Trans. Dorothy Bussy. London: Penguin, 1952.
Girard, René. *The Scapegoat*. Trans. Yvonne Freccero. Baltimore: Johns Hopkins University Press, 1986.
Goffman, Erving. *Interaction Ritual: Essays on Face-to-Face Behavior*. New York: Pantheon Books, 1967.
Goodheart, Eugene. *The Failure of Criticism*. Cambridge, MA: Harvard University Press, 1978.
Graver, Lawrence and Raymond Federman (eds). *Samuel Beckett: The Critical Heritage*. London: Routledge, 2005.

Grenberg, Jeanine. *Kant and the Ethics of Humility: A Story of Dependence, Corruption and Virtue*. Cambridge: Cambridge University Press, 2005.

Habib, M. A. R. *The Early T. S. Eliot and Western Philosophy*. Cambridge: Cambridge University Press, 1999.

—. 'The Prayers of Childhood: T. S. Eliot's Manuscripts on Kant.' *Journal of the History of Ideas* 51.1 (1990): 93–114.

Haecker, Theodor. *Virgil, Father of the West*. Trans. A. W. Wheen. New York: Sheed and Ward, 1934.

Halliwell, Martin and Andy Mousley. *Critical Humanisms: Humanist/Anti-Humanist Dialogues*. Edinburgh: Edinburgh University Press, 2003.

Harding, Jason. *The Criterion: Cultural Politics and Periodical Networks in Interwar Britain*. Oxford: Oxford University Press, 2002.

Harding, Jason and John Nash. 'An Introduction to Modernist Non-Translation.' *Modernist Non-Translation*. Ed. Jason Harding and John Nash. Oxford: Oxford University Press, 2019, 1–18.

Harmon, Maurice (ed.). *No Author Better Served: The Correspondence of Samuel Beckett and Alan Schneider*. Cambridge, MA: Harvard University Press, 1998.

Harpham, Geoffrey Galt. *The Ascetic Imperative in Culture and Criticism*. Chicago: The University of Chicago Press, 1987.

Harré, Rom. 'Embarrassment: A Conceptual Analysis.' *Shyness and Embarrassment*. Ed. W. Ray Crozier. Cambridge: Cambridge University Press, 1990, 181–204.

Harries, B. A. 'The Rare Contact: A Correspondence between T. S. Eliot and P. E. More.' *Theology* 75.136 (1972): 136–43.

Harton, F. P. *The Elements of the Spiritual Life: A Study in Ascetical Theology*. London: SPCK, 1932.

Harvey, Lawrence E. *Samuel Beckett: Poet and Critic*. Princeton: Princeton University Press, 1970.

Hatch, David A. '"I AM MISTAKEN": Surface and Subtext in Samuel Beckett's "Three Dialogues".' *Samuel Beckett Today / Aujourd'hui* 13 (2003): 57–71.

Hawkins, Peter S. *Dante's Testaments: Essays in Scriptural Imagination*. Stanford: Stanford University Press, 1999.

Heady, Chene. *Worlds of Common Prayer: Liturgical Time and Poetic Re-enchantment, 1827–1935*. Vancouver: Fairleigh Dickenson University Press, 2019.

Heft, James L., Reuven Firestone and Omid Safi (eds). *Learned Ignorance: Intellectual Humility among Jews, Christians and Muslims*. Oxford: Oxford University Press, 2011.

Hill, Geoffrey. *Collected Critical Writings*. Ed. Kenneth Haynes. Oxford: Oxford University Press, 2008.
—. 'Dividing Legacies.' *Collected Critical Writings*. Ed. Kenneth Haynes. Oxford: Oxford University Press, 2008, 366–79.
—. 'Poetry as "Menace" and "Atonement.' *Collected Critical Writings*. Ed. Kenneth Haynes. Oxford: Oxford University Press, 2008, 3–20.
Holland, Nancy J. *Ontological Humility: Lord Voldemort and the Philosophers*. New York: State University of New York Press, 2013.
Horner, Robyn. *Jean-Luc Marion: A Theo-logical Introduction*. Aldershot: Ashgate, 2005.
Hulme, T. E. *Speculations: Essays on Humanism and the Philosophy of Art*. Ed. Herbert Read. London: Routledge and Kegan Paul, 1924.
Hume, David. *An Enquiry Concerning the Principles of Morals*. Chicago: The Open Court Publishing Company, 1912.
—. *A Treatise of Human Nature*. 2nd edn. Ed. L. A. Selby-Bigge. Oxford: Oxford University Press, 1978.
Hutchings, William. '"Shat into Grace" Or, A Tale of a Turd: Why It Is How It Is in Samuel Beckett's *How It Is*.' *Papers in Language and Literature* 21.1 (1985): 64–87.
Hutchinson, Ben. *Lateness & Modern European Literature*. Oxford: Oxford University Press, 2016.
Hutchinson, Phil. *Shame and Philosophy: An Investigation in the Philosophy of Emotions and Ethics*. New York: Palgrave Macmillan, 2008.
Jain, Manju. *T. S. Eliot and American Philosophy: The Harvard Years*. Cambridge: Cambridge University Press, 1992.
Jameson, Fredric. *The Modernist Papers*. London: Verso, 2007.
—. *A Singular Modernity: Essay on the Ontology of the Present*. London: Verso, 2002.
John of the Cross. *The Dark Night of the Soul*. Trans. David Lewis. London: Thomas Baker, 1908.
Jones, Alun R. *The Life and Opinions of T. E. Hulme*. London: Victor Gollancz, 1960.
Jones, Ernest. *Papers on Psycho-Analysis*. London: Baillière, Tindall and Cox, 1913.
Jones, Terry (dir.). *Monty Python's Life of Brian*. 1979; UK: Paramount Home Entertainment, 2003. DVD.
Julian of Norwich. *The Writing of Julian of Norwich: A Vision Showed to a Devout Woman and A Revelation of Love*. Ed. Nicholas Watson and Jacqueline Jenkins. University Park, PA: Pennsylvania State University Press, 2005.

Juliet, Charles. *Conversations with Samuel Beckett and Bram van Velde*. London: Dalkey Archive Press, 1995.
Kant, Immanuel, *Grounding of the Metaphysics of Morals*. Trans. and ed. Mary Gregor. Cambridge: Cambridge University Press, 1997.
Keegan, Paul. 'Emily of Fire & Violence.' *London Review of Books* 42.20 (22 Oct 2020). https://www.lrb.co.uk/the-paper/v42/n20/paul-keegan/emily-of-fire-violence (accessed 1 December 2020).
Kenner, Hugh. *The Invisible Poet: T. S. Eliot*. London: Methuen, 1965.
—. *Samuel Beckett: A Critical Study*. Berkeley: University of California Press, 1968.
Kierkegaard, Søren. *The Concept of Irony: With Continual Reference to Socrates*. Ed., trans. and intro. Howard V. Hong and Edna H. Hong. Princeton: Princeton University Press, 1989.
—. *Concluding Unscientific Postscript to the Philosophical Crumbs*. Ed. and trans. Alastair Hannay. Cambridge: Cambridge University Press, 2009.
—. *Either/Or, Part II*. Ed. and trans. Howard V. Hong and Edna H. Hong. Princeton: Princeton University Press, 1987.
—. *Fear and Trembling* and *The Book on Adler*. Trans. Walter Lowrie. New York: Everyman's Library, 1994.
—. *The Sickness unto Death: A Christian Psychological Exposition for Upbuilding and Awakening*. Trans. and ed. Howard V. Hong and Edna H. Hong. Princeton: Princeton University Press, 1980.
Kilgore-Caradec, Jennifer. 'T. S. Eliot and Charles Péguy.' *T. S. Eliot, France, and the Mind of Europe*. Ed. Jayme Stayer. Newcastle-upon-Tyne: Cambridge Scholars Publishing, 2015, 129–45.
Kim, Sharon. *Literary Epiphany in the Novel, 1850–1950: Constellations of the Soul*. New York: Palgrave Macmillan, 2012.
Kleinberg-Levin, David. *Beckett's Words: The Promise of Happiness in a Time of Mourning*. London: Bloomsbury, 2015.
Koestenbaum, Wayne. *Humiliation*. London: Notting Hill Editions, 2011.
Knowlson, James. *Damned to Fame: The Life of Samuel Beckett*. New York: Simon & Schuster, 1996.
Knowlson, James and John Pilling. *Frescoes of the Skull: The Later Prose and Drama of Samuel Beckett*. New York: Grove Press, 1980.
Kristeva, Julia. *Powers of Horror: An Essay on Abjection*. Trans. Leon S. Roudiez. New York: Columbia University Press, 1982.
Kurtz, Paul (ed.). *The Humanist Alternative: Some Definitions of Humanism*. London: Pemberton Books, 1973.

Lacoue-Labarthe, Philippe and Jean-Luc Nancy. *The Literary Absolute: The Theory of Literature in German Romanticism*. Trans. Barnard, Philip and Cheryl Lester. New York: State University of New York Press, 1988.

La Rochefoucauld, Francois (de). *Collected Maxims and Other Reflections*. Trans., annotated and intro. E. H. Blackmore, A. M. Blackmore and Francine Giguère. Oxford: Oxford University Press, 2007.

Law, David R. *Kierkegaard's Kenotic Christology*. Oxford: Oxford University Press, 2013.

Lawlor, Seán. 'Making a Noise to Drown an Echo: Allusion and Quotation in the Early Poems of Samuel Beckett: 1929–1935.' PhD thesis, University of Reading, 2008.

Leacock, Stephen. *Essays and Literary Studies*. Toronto: S. B. Bundy, 1916.

Leland, Blake. '"Siete Voi Qui, Ser Brunetto?": Dante's *Inferno 15* as a Modernist Topic Place. *ELH* 59.4 (1992): 965–86.

Levinas, Emmanuel. *Entre Nous: Thinking of the Other*. Trans. Michael B. Smith and Barbara Harshav. New York: Columbia University Press, 1998.

—. *Proper Names*. Trans. Michael B. Smith. Stanford: Stanford University Press, 1996.

—. *Totality and Infinity*. Trans. Alphonso Lingis. Boston: Martinus Nijhoff Publishers, 1979.

Li, Victor P. H. '"The poetry does not matter": *Four Quartets* and the Rhetoric of Humility.' *T. S. Eliot Annual* 1 (1990): 63–86.

Longenbach, James. *Modernist Poetics of History: Pound, Eliot, and the Sense of the Past*. Princeton: Princeton University Press, 1987.

Luther, Martin. *The Annotated Luther, Volume 4: Pastoral Writings*. Ed. Mary Jane Haemig. Minneapolis: Fortress Press, 2016.

McDonald, Peter D. 'Calder's Beckett.' *Publishing Samuel Beckett*. Ed. Mark Nixon. London: The British Library, 2011, 153–70.

MacGreevy, Thomas. *Thomas Stearns Eliot: A Study*. London: Chatto and Windus, 1931.

MacIntyre, Alasdair. *After Virtue: A Study in Moral Theory*. 3rd edn. Notre Dame, IN: University of Notre Dame Press, 2007.

MacKay, Marina. *Modernism and World War II*. Cambridge: Cambridge University Press, 2007.

Magessa O'Reilly, Édouard. 'Preface.' *How It Is*. Ed. Édouard Magessa O'Reilly. London: Faber and Faber, 2009, vii–xv.

Malamud, Randy. *T.S. Eliot's Drama: A Research and Production Sourcebook*. Westport: Greenwood Press, 1992.
Mallinson, Jane Elizabeth. *T. S. Eliot's Interpretation of F. H. Bradley*. Dordrecht: Kluwer Academic Publishers, 2002.
Mander, W. J. *An Introduction to Bradley's Metaphysics*. Oxford: Clarendon Press, 1994.
Marcel, Gabriel. *Being and Having*. Trans. Katharine Farrer. Westminster: Dacre Press, 1949.
Marchesi, Serena M. *Eliot's Perpetual Struggle: The Language of Evil in Murder and the Cathedral*. Florence: Olschki, 2009.
Margalit, Avishai. *The Decent Society*. Trans. Naomi Goldblum. Cambridge, MA: Harvard University Press, 1996.
Marston, John. The Malcontent *and Other Plays*. Ed. Keith Sturgess. Oxford: Oxford University Press, 1997.
Matthews, Steven. *T. S. Eliot and Early Modern Literature*. Oxford: Oxford University Press, 2013.
May, Todd. 'Humanism and Solidarity.' *Parrhesia* 18 (2013): 11–21.
Merrin, Jeredith. *An Enabling Humility: Marianne Moore, Elizabeth Bishop, and the Uses of Tradition*. New Brunswick: Rutgers University Press, 1990.
Mersch, Peter Paul A., Martin Hildebrand, Edith H. Lavy and Ineke Wessel. 'Somatic Symptoms in Social Phobia: A Treatment Method Based on Rational Emotive Therapy and Paradoxical Interventions.' *Journal of Behavior Therapy and Experimental Psychology* 23.3 (1992): 199–211.
Middleton, Thomas and William Rowley. *The Changeling*. Ed. N. W. Bawcutt. Manchester: Manchester University Press, 1977.
Miller, Ian and Kay Souter. *Beckett and Bion: The (Im)Patient Voice in Psychotherapy and Literature*. London: Karnac Books, 2013.
Miller, James E. Jr. *T.S. Eliot: The Making of an American Poet, 1888–1922*. University Park: The Pennsylvania State University Press, 2006.
Miller, William Ian. *Humiliation: And Other Essays on Honor, Social Discomfort, and Violence*. New York: Cornell University Press, 1993.
Milligan, Tony. 'Murdochian Humility.' *Religious Studies* 43.2 (2007): 217–28.
Milton, John. *Paradise Lost*. Ed. and intro. Stephen Orgel and Jonathan Goldberg. Oxford: Oxford University Press, 2004.
Modigliani, André. 'Embarrassment and Embarrassability.' *Sociometry* 31.3 (1968): 313–26.
Monk, Ray. *Bertrand Russell: The Spirit of Solitude, 1872–1921*. New York: The Free Press, 1996.

Moody, A. David. *Tracing T. S. Eliot's Spirit: Essays on His Poetry and Thought*. Cambridge: Cambridge University Press, 1996.
Moore, Marianne. 'Humility, Concentration, and Gusto.' *The Complete Prose of Marianne Moore*. Ed. and intro. Patricia C. Willis. New York: Viking, 1986, 420–6.
Moorjani, Angela. 'Beckett's *Molloy* in the French Context.' *Samuel Beckett Today / Aujourd'hui* 25.1 (2013): 93–108.
More, Paul Elmer. *Aristocracy and Justice: Shelburne Essays*. Ninth Series. Boston: Houghton Mifflin, 1915.
Morin, Emilie. *Beckett's Political Imagination*. Cambridge: Cambridge University Press, 2017.
Mulhall, Stephen. *Heidegger and* Being and Time. Abingdon: Routledge, 2005.
Murdoch, Iris. *Existentialists and Mystics: Writings on Philosophy and Literature*. New York: Penguin, 1997.
—. *The Sovereignty of Good*. London: Routledge, 2014.
Murray, Rachel. *The Modernist Exoskeleton: Insects, War, Literary Form*. Edinburgh: Edinburgh University Press, 2020.
Nashef, Hania A. M. *The Politics of Humiliation in the Novels of J.M. Coetzee*. New York: Routledge, 2009.
Ngai, Sianne. *Ugly Feelings*. Cambridge, MA: Harvard University Press, 2005.
Nichols, Ashton. *The Poetics of Epiphany: Nineteenth-Century Origins of the Modern Literary Moment*. Tuscaloosa, AL: The University of Alabama Press, 1987.
Nieland, Justus. *Feeling Modern: The Eccentricities of Public Life*. Urbana and Chicago: University of Illinois Press, 2008.
Nietzsche, Friedrich. *The Anti-Christ, Ecce Homo, Twilight of the Idols*. Ed. Aaron Ridley and Judith Norman. Trans. Judith Norman. Cambridge: Cambridge University Press, 2005.
—. *Daybreak: Thoughts on the Prejudices of Morality*. Ed. Maudemarie Clark and Brian Leiter. Trans. R. J. Hollingdale. Cambridge: Cambridge University Press, 1997.
—. *Human, All Too Human*. Trans. R. J. Hollingdale. Cambridge: Cambridge University Press, 1996.
Nixon, Mark. *Samuel Beckett's German Diaries 1936–1937*. London: Continuum, 2011.
Nobel, Alfred. 'Testament', 27 November 1895. https://www.nobelprize.org/alfred-nobel/full-text-of-alfred-nobels-will-2/ (accessed 5 October 2020).

Nordau, Max. *Degeneration*. Trans. Max Simon. London: Heinemann, 1913.

North, Michael. 'The Dialect in/of Modernism: Pound and Eliot's Racial Masquerade.' *American Literary History* 4.1 (1992): 56–76.

Nussbaum, Martha. *Hiding from Humanity: Disgust, Shame, and the Law*. Princeton: Princeton University Press, 2004.

—. 'Pity and Mercy: Nietzsche's Stoicism.' *Nietzsche, Genealogy, Morality: Essays on Nietzsche's* On the Genealogy of Morals. Ed. Richard Schacht. Berkeley: University of California Press, 1994, 139–67.

Origen. *Prayer* and *Exhortation to Martyrdom*. Trans. John J. O'Meara. New York: Newman Press, 1954.

Oser, Lee. *The Ethics of Modernism: Moral Ideas in Yeats, Eliot, Joyce, Woolf, and Beckett*. Cambridge: Cambridge University Press, 2007.

Österling, Anders. 'Yttrande av Herr Österling.' 'Utlåtande av Svenska Akademiens Nobelkommitté, 1969', compiled by Anders Ryberg. Swedish Academy Archive, 10–11. https://www.svenskaakademien.se/sites/default/files/nobelkommittens_utlatande_1969.pdf (accessed 2 March 2021).

Paden, William E. 'Theaters of Humility and Suspicion: Desert Saints and New England Puritans.' *Technologies of the Self: A Seminar with Michel Foucault*. Ed. Luther H. Martin, Huck Gutman and Patrick H. Hutton. Amherst: University of Massachusetts Press, 1988, 64–79.

Pascal, Blaise. *Pensées and Other Writings*. Trans. Honor Levi. Ed., intro. and annotated by Anthony Levi. Oxford: Oxford University Press, 1995.

Péguy, Charles. 'De Jean Coste.' *Oeuvres Complètes de Charles Péguy, 1873–1914: Oeuvres de Prose*. Intro. Maurice Barrès. Paris: Nouvelle Revue Française, 1920.

—. 'Préface de L'Éditeur.' Antonin Lavergne, *Jean Coste: ou l'instituteur de village*. Paris: Éditions des Cahiers, 1902, v–vii.

Perl, Jeffrey M. *Skepticism and Modern Enmity: Before and After Eliot*. Baltimore: Johns Hopkins University Press, 1989.

Perl, Jeffrey M. and Andrew P. Tuck. 'The Hidden Advantage of Tradition: On the Significance of T. S. Eliot's Indic Studies.' *Philosophy of East and West* 35.2 (1985): 115–31.

Pessoa, Fernando. *The Book of Disquiet*. Ed. and trans. Richard Zenith. London: Penguin Books, 2011.

Philippe, Charles-Louis. *Bubu of Montparnasse*. Intro. T. S. Eliot. New York: Shakespeare House, 1951.

Piette, Adam. 'Torture, Text, Human Rights: *Comment C'est / How It Is* and the Algerian War.' *Around 1945: Literature, Citizenship, Rights*. Ed. Allan Hepburn. Montreal and Kingston: McGill-Queen's University Press, 2016, 151–74.

Pilling, John. *A Companion to 'Dream of Fair to Middling Women'*. Tallahassee, FL: Journal of Beckett Studies Books, 2004.

—. '"For Interpolation": Beckett and English Literature.' *Samuel Beckett Today / Aujourd'hui* 16 (2006): 203–35.

—. *Samuel Beckett's 'More Pricks than Kicks': In a Strait of Two Wills*. London: Continuum, 2011.

Plato. *Protagoras. Plato: Complete Works*. Ed. and intro. John M. Cooper. Indianapolis: Hackett Publishing Company, 1997.

Porter, H. Abbott. 'Beginning Again: The Post-Narrative Art of *Texts for Nothing* and *How It Is*.' *The Cambridge Companion to Beckett*. Ed. John Pilling. Cambridge: Cambridge University Press, 1994, 106–23.

Pothast, Ulrich. *The Metaphysical Vision: Arthur Schopenhauer's Philosophy of Art and Life and Samuel Beckett's Own Way to Make Use of It*. New York: Peter Lang, 2008.

Potter, Rachel and David Trotter. 'Low Modernism: Introduction.' *Critical Quarterly* 46.4 (2004): iii–iv.

Pound, Ezra. *Collected Poems*. London: Faber and Faber, 1975.

—. 'Hugh Selwyn Mauberley.' *Collected Poems*. London: Faber and Faber, 1975, 98–118.

Pound, Ezra and Stanley Nott. *One Must Not Go Altogether with the Tide: The Letters of Ezra Pound and Stanley Nott*. Ed. Miranda B. Hickman. Montreal: McGill-Queen's University Press, 2011.

Pusey, E. B. *'Blessed Are the Meek': A Sermon, Preached at the Opening of the Chapel of Keble College*. London: Rivingtons, 1876.

Rabaté, Jean-Michel. *Think, Pig!: Beckett at the Limit of the Human*. New York: Fordham University Press, 2016.

Rashdall, Hastings. *Conscience and Christ: Six Lectures on Christian Ethics*. New York: Charles Scribner's Sons, 1916.

—. *The Theory of Good and Evil: A Treatise on Moral Philosophy, Volume 1*. Oxford: Clarendon Press, 1907.

Reckford, Kenneth. 'Recognizing Venus (I): Aeneas Meets His Mother.' *Arion* 3.2 (1996): 1–42.

—. 'Recognizing Venus (II): Dido, Aeneas, and Mr. Eliot.' *Arion* 3.2 (1996): 43–80.

Reeves, Gareth. *T.S. Eliot: A Virgilian Poet*. New York: St. Martin's Press, 1989.

Richards, Norvin. *Humility*. Philadelphia: Temple University Press, 1992.
Ricks, Christopher. *Allusion to the Poets*. Oxford: Oxford University Press, 2002.
—. *Beckett's Dying Words*. Oxford: Oxford University Press, 1993.
—. *Decisions and Revisions in T. S. Eliot*. London: British Library and Faber and Faber, 2003.
—. *Keats and Embarrassment*. London: Oxford University Press, 1974.
—. *T. S. Eliot and Prejudice*. London: Faber and Faber, 1994.
Riquelme, John Paul. 'Staging the Modernist Monologue as Capable Negativity: Beckett's "A Piece of Monologue" between and beyond Eliot and Joyce.' *The Edinburgh Companion to Samuel Beckett and the Arts*. Ed. S. E. Gontarski. Edinburgh: Edinburgh University Press, 2014, 379–408.
Robinson, Ben. 'State of Embarrassment: Kafka's "*In der Strafkolonie*".' *The Germanic Review: Literature, Culture, Theory* 90.2 (2015): 101–22.
Rose, Arthur. *Literary Cynics: Borges, Beckett, Coetzee*. London: Bloomsbury, 2017.
Roth, Sabine. 'Eliot Comforted: The Yeatsian Presence in "Four Quartets".' *Journal of Modern Literature* 18.4 (1993): 411–20.
Royce, Josiah. *Studies of Good and Evil: A Series of Essays upon the Problems of Philosophy and of Life*. New York: D. Appleton and Co., 1898.
Russell, Henry M. W. 'Beyond the Will: Humiliation as Christian Necessity in *Crime and Punishment*.' *Dostoevsky and the Christian Tradition*. Ed. George Pattison and Diane Oenning Thompson. Cambridge: Cambridge University Press, 2001, 226–36.
Said, Edward. *On Late Style: Music and Literature Against the Grain*. Fwd. Mariam C. Said. Intro. Michael Wood. London: Bloomsbury, 2006.
Saint-Amour, Paul. 'Weak Theory, Weak Modernism.' *Modernism/modernity* 25.3 (2018): 437–59.
Salisbury, Laura. *Samuel Beckett: Laughing Matters, Comic Timing*. Edinburgh: Edinburgh University Press, 2012.
Salvato, Nick. *Obstruction*. Durham, NC: Duke University Press, 2016.
Sartre, Jean-Paul. *Being and Nothingness: An Essay on Phenomenological Ontology*. Trans. Hazel E. Barnes. London: Routledge, 2003.
—. *Existentialism is a Humanism*. Trans. Carol Macomber. New Haven: Yale University Press, 2007.

Saurette, Paul. *The Kantian Imperative: Humiliation, Common Sense, Politics*. Toronto: University of Toronto Press Incorporated, 2005.
Savile, Anthony. *Leibniz and the 'Monadology'*. London: Routledge, 2000.
Scheler, Max. 'Humility'. Trans. Barbara Fiand. *Aletheia. An International Journal of Philosophy*, 2 (1981): 210–19.
—. *Person and Self-Value: Three Essays*. Ed. and trans. M. S. Frings. Dordrecht: Martinus Nijhoff Publishers, 1987.
—. *Ressentiment*. Ed. and intro. Lewis A. Coser. Trans. William W. Holdheim. New York: The Free Press of Glencoe, 1975.
Schopenhauer, Arthur. *The World as Will and Representation*. Vols 1 and 2. New York: Dover Publications, 1969.
Schuchard, Ronald. *Eliot's Dark Angel: Intersections of Life and Art*. New York: Oxford University Press, 1999.
Schueler, G. F. 'Why IS Modesty a Virtue?' *Ethics* 109.4 (1999): 835–41.
Scofield, Martin. *T. S. Eliot: The Poems*. Cambridge: Cambridge University Press, 1988.
Sencourt, Robert. *T. S. Eliot: A Memoir*. London: Garnstone Press, 1971.
Shakespeare, William. *The Complete Sonnets and Poems*. Ed. Colin Burrow. Oxford: Oxford University Press, 2002.
—. *Coriolanus*. Ed. Lee Bliss. Cambridge: Cambridge University Press, 2010.
—. *Measure for Measure*. Updated edn. Ed. Brian Gibbons. Cambridge: Cambridge University Press, 2006.
Sheehan, Paul. *Modernism, Narrative and Humanism*. Cambridge: Cambridge University Press, 2002.
—. 'A World without Monsters: Beckett and the Ethics of Cruelty.' *Beckett and Ethics*. Ed. Russell Smith. London: Continuum, 2008, 86–101.
Sheils, Barry and Julie Walsh. *Shame and Modern Writing*. New York: Routledge, 2018.
Shepherd-Barr, Kirsten. *Theatre and Evolution from Ibsen to Beckett*. New York: Columbia University Press, 2015.
Sherry, Vincent. *The Great War and the Language of Modernism*. Oxford: Oxford University Press, 2003.
Shklovsky, Victor. *Victor Shklovsky: A Reader*. Ed. and trans. Alexandra Berlina. New York: Bloomsbury, 2017.
Shusterman, Richard. *T. S. Eliot and the Philosophy of Criticism*. London: Duckworth, 1988.
Sidgwick, Henry. *The Methods of Ethics*. 7th edn. London: Macmillan and Co., 1907.

Sinha, G. Alex. 'Modernising the Virtue of Humility.' *Australasian Journal of Philosophy* 90.2 (2012): 259–74.
Sloterdijk, Peter. *You Must Change Your Life*. Trans. Wieland Hoban. Cambridge: Polity Press, 2013.
Smith, Grover. *T. S. Eliot's Poetry and Plays: A Study in Sources and Meaning*. Chicago: The University of Chicago Press, 1956.
Snow, Nancy. 'Humility.' *The Journal of Value Inquiry* 29 (1995): 203–16.
—. 'Theories of Humility: An Overview.' *The Routledge Handbook of the Philosophy of Humility*. Ed. Mark Alfano, Michael P. Lynch and Alessandra Tanesini. Abingdon: Routledge, 2020, 9–25.
Sontag, Susan. *Styles of Radical Will*. New York: Picador, 1966.
Soper, Kate. *Humanism and Anti-Humanism*. London: Hutchinson, 1986.
Sorel, Georges. *Reflections on Violence*. Trans. and intro. T. E. Hulme. London: George Allen & Unwin, 1916.
Spanos, William V. *On the Ethical Imperatives of the Interregnum: Essays in Loving Strife from Soren Kierkegaard to Cornel West*. Cham: Palgrave Macmillan, 2016.
Spoo, Robert. *Without Copyrights: Piracy, Publishing, and the Public Domain*. Oxford: Oxford University Press, 2013.
Spurr, Barry. *'Anglo-Catholic in Religion': T. S. Eliot and Christianity*. Cambridge: Lutterworth, 2010.
—. 'Liturgical Anachronism in *Murder in the Cathedral*.' *Yeats-Eliot Review* 15 (1998): 3–7.
Statman, Daniel. 'Modesty, Pride and Realistic Self-Assessment.' *The Philosophical Quarterly* 42.169 (1992): 420–38.
Steiner, George. *The Death of Tragedy*. New York: Oxford University Press, 1980.
—. *On Difficulty and Other Essays*. Oxford: Oxford University Press, 1978.
Stephen, Karin. *Psychoanalysis and Medicine: A Study of the Wish to Fall Ill*. Cambridge: Cambridge University Press, 1960.
Stevenson, Kay Gilliland. 'Belacqua in the Moon: Beckett's Revisions of "Dante and the Lobster".' *Critical Essays on Samuel Beckett*. Ed. Patrick A. McCarthy. Boston: G. K. Hall, 1986, 36–46.
Stillman, Anne. '*Prufrock and Other Observations*.' *The New Cambridge Companion to T. S. Eliot*. Ed. Jason Harding. New York: Cambridge University Press, 2017, 41–54.
Tajiri, Yoshiki. *Samuel Beckett and the Prosthetic Body: The Organs and Senses in Modernism*. New York: Palgrave Macmillan, 2007.

Tanner, Stephen L. *Paul Elmer More: Literary Criticism as the History of Ideas*. New York: State University of New York Press, 1987.
Tate, Allen. 'Irony and Humility.' *Contemporary Reviews*. Ed. Jewel Spears Brooker. Cambridge: Cambridge University Press, 2004, 188–92.
Taylor, Charles. *A Secular Age*. Cambridge, MA: Belknap Press of Harvard University Press, 2007.
Taylor, Gabriele. *Pride, Shame, and Guilt: Emotions of Self-Assessment*. Oxford: Clarendon Press, 1985.
Taylor, Jeremy. *Holy Living and Dying: With Prayers Containing the Whole Duty of a Christian, and the Parts of Devotion Fitted to All Occasions, and Furnished for All Necessities*. London: G. Bell and Sons, 1913.
Tennyson, Alfred. *Becket*. London: Macmillan and Co., 1884.
Thaventhiran, Helen. *Radical Empiricists: Five Modernist Close Readers*. Oxford: Oxford University Press, 2015.
Thomas á Kempis. *The Imitation of Christ*. Trans. William Benham. *The Harvard Classics: The Confessions of St Augustine* and *The Imitation of Christ by Thomas Á Kempis*. New York: P. F. Collier and Son, 1909.
Tomkins, Silvan S. *Affect Imagery Consciousness: The Complete Edition*. New York: Springer Publishing Company, 2008.
Trilling, Lionel. *The Liberal Imagination: Essays on Literature and Society*. New York: Anchor Books, 1953.
—. 'On the Teaching of Modern Literature.' *The New York Intellectuals Reader*. Ed. Neil Jumonville. New York: Routledge, 2007, 223–42.
Tucker, David. *Samuel Beckett and Arnold Geulincx: Tracing 'a Literary Fantasia'*. London: Continuum, 2012.
Tucker, David, Mark Nixon and Dirk van Hulle (eds). *Samuel Beckett Today / Aujourd'hui: Revisiting* Molloy, Malone Meurt / Malone Dies *and* L'Innommable / The Unnamable. Amsterdam: Rodopi, 2014.
Tucker, Shawn. R. *Pride and Humility: A New Interdisciplinary Analysis*. New York: Palgrave Macmillan, 2016.
Uhlmann, Anthony. *Samuel Beckett and the Philosophical Image*. Cambridge: Cambridge University Press, 2006.
Underhill, Evelyn. *Mysticism: A Study in the Nature and Development of Man's Spiritual Consciousness*. London: Methuen and Co. Ltd, 1977.
Unger, Leonard. *Eliot's Compound Ghost: Influence and Confluence*. University Park: Pennsylvania State University Press, 1981.
Van Hulle, Dirk. *The Making of Samuel Beckett's* Krapp's Last Tape / La Dernière Bande. Antwerp: University Press Antwerp, 2015.

—. 'Publishing "The End": Beckett and *Les Temps modernes*.' *Publishing Samuel Beckett*. Ed. Mark Nixon. London: The British Library, 2011, 73–82.
—. 'Samuel Beckett's *Faust* Notes.' *Samuel Beckett Today / Aujourd'hui* 16 (2006): 283–97.
Van Hulle, Dirk and Mark Nixon. *Samuel Beckett's Library*. Cambridge: Cambridge University Press, 2013.
Van Hulle, Dirk, Mark Nixon and Vincent Neyt (eds). *The Beckett Digital Library: A Digital Genetic Edition*. Brussels: University of Antwerp (ASP/UPA), 2016. http://www.beckettarchive.org.ezphost.dur.ac.uk/library/home/welcome (accessed 30 October 2020).
Vattimo, Gianni. *The End of Modernity: Nihilism and Hermeneutics in Post-modern Culture*. Trans. Jon R. Snyder. Cambridge: Polity Press, 1988.
Vattimo, Gianni and Santiago Zabala. '"Weak Thought" and the Reduction of Violence: A Dialogue with Gianni Vattimo.' Trans. Yaakov Mascetti. *Common Knowledge* 8.3 (2002): 452–63.
Virgil. *Aeneid*. Trans. Robert Fagles. New York: Penguin, 2006.
Walsh, James (ed.) 'Introduction', *The Cloud of Unknowing*. New York: Paulist Press, 1981.
Wasson, Richard. 'T. S. Eliot's Antihumanism and Antipragmatism.' *Texas Studies in Literature and Language* 10.3 (1968): 445–55.
Waugh, Patricia. *Metafiction: The Theory and Practice of Self-Conscious Fiction*. London: Routledge, 2001.
Weil, Simone. *An Anthology*. Ed. and intro. Siân Miles. London: Penguin Books, 2005.
—. *Gravity and Grace*. Trans. Emma Crawford and Mario von der Ruhr. New York: Routledge, 2002.
Weiss, Katherine. '". . . Humanity in Ruins . . .": The Historical Body in Samuel Beckett's Fiction.' *Samuel Beckett: History, Memory, Archive*. Ed. Seán Kennedy and Katherine Weiss. New York: Palgrave Macmillan, 2009, 151–68.
Weller, Shane. '"Gnawing to be Naught": Beckett and Pre-Socratic Nihilism.' *Samuel Beckett Today / Aujourd'hui* 20 (2008): 321–33.
—. *A Taste for Nothing: Beckett and Nihilism*. London: Legenda, 2005.
Wengst, Klaus. *Humility: Solidarity of the Humiliated: The Transformation of an Attitude and Its Social Relevance in Graeco-Roman, Old Testament-Jewish and Early Christian Tradition*. Trans. John Bowden. London: SCM Press Ltd, 1988.

West, Rebecca. *Ending in Earnest*. New York: Books for Libraries Press, 1967.
Wetzel, James. 'Predestination, Pelagianism, and Foreknowledge.' *The Cambridge Companion to Augustine*. Ed. Eleonore Stump and Norman Kretzmann. Cambridge: Cambridge University Press, 2001, 49–58.
Whiteside, George. 'T. S. Eliot's Dissertation.' *English Literary History* 34.3 (1967): 400–24.
Williams, James. 'Beckett between the Words: Punctuation and the Body in the English Prose.' *Samuel Beckett Today / Aujourd'hui* 24 (2012): 249–59.
Williams, Linda. 'Darwin and Derrida on Human and Animal Emotions: The Question of Shame as a Measure of Ontological Difference.' *New Formations* 76 (2012): 21–37.
Wilson, James Matthew. '"The Rock" against Shakespeare: Stoicism and Community in T. S. Eliot.' *Religion and Literature* 43.3 (2011): 49–81.
Wimbush, Andy. 'Hey Prestos and Humilities: Two of Beckett's Christs.' *Journal of Beckett Studies* 25.1 (2015): 78–95.
—. 'Humility, Self-Awareness, and Religious Ambivalence: Another Look at Beckett's "Humanistic Quietism".' *Journal of Beckett Studies* 23.2 (2014): 202–21.
—. *Still: Samuel Beckett's Quietism*. Stuttgart: Ibidem-Verlag, 2020.
Windelband, Wilhelm. *A History of Philosophy with Special Reference to the Formation and Development of its Problems and Concepts*. 2nd edn, revised and enlarged. Trans. James H. Tufts. New York: The Macmillan Company, 1921.
Winstanley, Adam. 'A "Whispered Disfazione": Maurice Blanchot, Leonardo da Vinci and *Three Dialogues with Georges Duthuit*.' *Journal of Beckett Studies* 22.2 (2013): 135–60.
Wolf, A. *The Philosophy of Nietzsche*. London: Constable and Co., 1915.
Wolfe, Thomas. 'Go Forget Me.' *The Prose and Poetry of Europe and America*. Ed. G. P. Morris and N. P. Willis. New York: Leavitt and Allen, 1845, 360.
Wolosky, Shira. *Language Mysticism: The Negative Way of Language in Eliot, Beckett and Celan*. Stanford: Stanford University Press, 1995.
Yang, Carol L. 'Revisiting the *Flâneur* in T. S. Eliot's "Eeldrop and Appleplex – I".' *Orbis Litterarum* 66.2 (2011): 89–120.
Yeats, W. B. *The Collected Letters: Electronic Edition*. http://pm.nlx.com.ezphost.dur.ac.uk/xtf/view?docId=yeats_c/yeats_c.04.xml;chunk.

id=div.el.yeats.unpublished.1;toc.depth=1;toc.id=div.el.yeats. unpublished.1;brand=default (accessed 8 September 2020).
—. *Essays and Introductions*. London: Macmillan, 1961.
—. 'Modern Poetry.' *Essays and Introductions*. London: Macmillan, 1961, 491–508.
—. (ed.). *The Oxford Book of Modern Verse: 1892–1935*. Oxford: Oxford University Press, 1936.
—. 'Introduction.' *The Oxford Book of Modern Verse: 1892–1935*. Oxford: Oxford University Press, 1936, v–xlii.
—. *The Poems*. Ed. and intro. Daniel Albright. London: Everyman's Library, 1992.
Zahavi, Ben. 'Shame and the Exposed Self.' *Reading Sartre: On Phenomenology and Existentialism*. Ed. Jonathan Webber. Abingdon: Routledge, 2011, 211–26.
Žižek, Slavoj. *The Fragile Absolute Or, Why Is the Christian Legacy Worth Fighting for?* 2nd edn. London: Verso, 2008.

Index

Adorno, Theodor W., 61, 84, 86, 161, 181, 183–5
Agamben, Giorgio, 32, 49, 199
Aiken, Conrad, 27
Aldington, Richard, 56n
Andrewes, Lancelot, 11, 17, 95–104, 109, 119n
Anglo-Catholicism, 94, 96, 116–17; see also Church of England
Aquinas, Thomas, St, 7
Aristotle, 6–9, 34, 142
Arnold, Matthew, 35, 109–111, 112, 122n
Auden, W. H., 151, 152
Auerbach, Erich, 120n
Augustine, St, 102, 103, 109, 208n
Authorized Version, 103; see also King James Bible

Babbitt, Irving, 11, 57n, 109–12
Badiou, Alain, 203
Beauvoir, Simone de, 125
Beckett, Samuel (works)
   'Calmative, The', 204
   'Capital of Ruins, The', 143–4
   Comment C'est, 180, 183, 193
   Company, 82, 130–1, 144
   Disjecta, 6, 12, 196
   Dream Notebook, 13, 19, 189, 208n
   Dream of Fair to Middling Women, 18–19, 60, 185, 189, 190, 191–2

'Echo's Bones', 197
Eleutheria, 128
'End, The', 63, 145, 205
Endgame, 64, 84, 126, 143, 183, 204
'Enough', 199
'Expelled, The', 68
'First Love', 64
Happy Days, 63, 85, 194, 212–13
How It Is, 18, 126, 178–206
'Humanistic Quietism', 141
Krapp's Last Tape, 60, 126, 194
Malone Dies, 71, 148n, 204
Mercier et Camier, 128
Molloy, 18, 126, 127–45, 199, 204, 205, 208n
More Pricks than Kicks, 5, 17, 60–1, 62, 68, 72, 73, 78, 79–80, 86, 185; 'A Wet Night', 202; 'Dante and the Lobster', 73–80; 'Ding-Dong', 69–70, 72; 'Fingal', 66; 'Love and Lethe', 80–4; 'Walking Out', 86–7, 211; 'Wet Night, A', 67–8; 'Yellow', 87
Murphy, 13, 56n, 64, 126, 128, 133, 142, 197
Proust, 71, 84, 133, 137, 138, 189
'Psychology Notes', 71
Rough for Theatre I, 142
Rough for Theatre II, 61

Beckett, Samuel (works) (cont.)
   'Serena III', 91n
   'Text 3', 75–6
   Texts for Nothing, 128, 181, 204–5
   Three Novels, 127–8
   Unnamable, The, 12, 71, 127, 128, 133, 137, 181, 187, 199, 203, 204, 205
   Waiting for Godot, 12, 14, 85–6, 142, 195, 200–1, 205, 211
   Watt, 9–10, 14, 78, 133, 136, 137–8, 143, 182, 197
   Worstward Ho, 15, 150, 211
Benedict of Nursia, St, 14
Benjamin, Walter, 32
Bernard of Clairvaux, St, 133
Blake, William, 157, 162, 163, 165, 167, 174n, 176n
Blanchot, Maurice, 181–2, 186
Bloom, Harold, 156, 180–1
bovarysme, 16, 46, 48, 51, 57n, 68, 86, 100, 155
Bradley, F. H., 17, 43, 95, 104–5, 109–14, 153
Brooks, Cleanth, 152
Burton, Robert, 13
Bush, Ronald, 174n

Calvin, John, 111–12, 113
Church of England, 93, 102, 108–9; *see also* Anglo-Catholicism
Cioran, Emil, 132, 139, 140
Cloud of Unknowing, The, 15
Copeland, Charles Townsend, 152
Costello, Nuala, 62–3, 64–5

Dante Alighieri, 39–40, 42, 43, 48–9, 75–7, 134–5, 147n, 159–60, 189, 191–2, 195–6, 201–2, 204, 206
Darwin, Charles, 182, 196–7, 198
De Man, Paul, 153, 171
Democritus, 188
Donne, John, 51

Dostoevsky, Fyodor, 11, 40–1, 56n, 67, 130, 147n
Douay-Rheims Bible, 95, 101–4

Earle, John, 88
El Greco, 192
Eliot, Henry Ware, 93–4
Eliot, T. S.
   Poems and plays
      Ara Vos Prec, 28
      'Ash-Wednesday', 153
      'Aunt Helen', 34–5
      Burnt Norton, 158, 162, 163
      'Choruses from *The Rock*', 108
      Cocktail Party, The, 53–4, 82, 212–13
      Complete Poems and Plays, 101
      'Cooking Egg, A', 163–6
      Coriolan, 158, 162, 164
      'Cousin Nancy', 34–5
      'Cultivation of Christmas Trees, The', 98
      Dry Salvages, The, 150
      East Coker, 18, 118, 138, 149–50, 151–4, 157–72, 181
      Elder Statesman, The, 50
      Family Reunion, The, 52–3, 72, 176–7n
      'Gerontion', 98–9, 108, 163, 167–70,
      'Hollow Men, The', 80
      'Hysteria', 32–3
      'Journey of the Magi', 98
      'La Figlia Che Piange', 163, 165
      Little Gidding, 19, 108, 150, 151, 168, 174
      Murder in the Cathedral, 5, 17, 40, 51, 93–119
      Poems 1920, 28
      'Portrait of a Lady', 32
      Prufrock and Other Observations, 163
      Sweeney Agonistes, 48–9, 52, 116
      'Sweeney Erect', 11, 35–6

Waste Land, The, 3, 43, 153,
    162, 163
Prose works
  After Strange Gods, 94
  'Catholicism and International
    Order', 101, 105, 116–17
  Criterion, The, 118, 153, 161,
    166, 175n,
  Eeldrop and Appleplex, 16,
    28–31, 32, 33–4, 36,
    37–54, 211
  'Elementary Forms of the
    Religious Life, The', 36
  For Lancelot Andrewes, 94, 96
  'Francis Herbert Bradley', 105
  *Idea of a Christian Society,
    The*, 101, 170
  'Introduction to *Nightwood*',
    37, 4
  *Knowledge and Experience
    in the Philosophy of F. H.
    Bradley*, 38, 43
  'Modern Dilemma, The', 101,
    115–16, 117–18
  'Political Theorists', 119n
  'Report on the Ethics of Kant's
    Critique of Practical Reason',
    106–7, 108, 118
  'Search for Moral Sanction,
    The', 115
  'Second Thoughts on
    Humanism', 12
  'Seneca in Elizabethan
    Translation', 46
  'Shakespeare and the Stoicism
    of Seneca', 46–7
  'Thomas Middleton', 44–5
  'To Criticise the Critic', 173n
  'Tradition and the Individual
    Talent', 156
Elyot, Thomas, 172
embarrassment, 16, 17, 27, 28, 32,
  33, 36–7, 60–87, 156
Emerson, Ralph Waldo, 11, 35, 111
Empson, William 23n
Esslin, Martin, 180

Faber, Geoffrey, 94, 105, 113,
Foerster, Norman, 10–11
Foucault, Michel, 22n, 47
Frankl, Victor, 67

Geulincx, Arnold, 7, 12–13, 16,
  86, 132, 133–4, 136, 147n,
  203, 210n
Gide, André, 69, 70, 89n
Goethe, von, Johann Wolfgang, 154
Gray, Thomas, 19

Haigh-Wood, Vivien, 28, 37, 105
Hale, Emily, 44
Hill, Geoffrey, 151–2, 160, 166
Huber, Pierre, 197, 198
Hulme, T. E., 12, 111, 129n
humanism, 6, 10–13, 95, 105–6,
  109–12, 116, 123n
Hume, David, 34

Joachim, Harold, 22n
John of the Cross, St, 116, 140
Jones, Ernest, 63, 66, 70–1
Joyce, James, 23–4n, 78, 126,
  139, 180
Julian of Norwich, 19, 212

Kant, Immanuel, 58n, 106–7, 110,
  111, 118, 121n, 149
kenosis, 14, 97, 181
Kierkegaard, Søren, 14, 49–50,
  136, 150–1, 152
King James Bible, 13, 103
Kipling, Rudyard, 152, 154

Laforgue, Jules, 154
Latimer, Hugh, 175n
Les Temps modernes, 125
Lewis, Wyndham, 158
Little Review, The, 30
Luther, Martin, 21n, 111–12

MacGreevy, Thomas, 12, 25, 63,
  191, 196
Magee, Pat, 183, 186

Marcel, Gabriel, 21n
Masefield, John, 155
Middleton, Thomas, 44–6
Milton, John, 154, 185–6, 194
modernity, 2–3, 5, 35, 52,
modesty, 8–9, 22n, 23n, 27, 41, 160, 162,
Monty Python's Life of Brian, 1, 211
Moore, Marianne, 20n, 162
More, Paul Elmer, 11, 55n, 57n, 172
Munich Agreement, 17, 101, 176n,
Murdoch, Iris, 87

New English Weekly, 155
Nietzsche, Friedrich, 6, 21n, 47–8
Nobel Prize, 3, 19n
Nordau, Max, 81–2
Nussbaum, Martha, 10–11, 31

Pascal, Blaise, 11, 132, 133, 143, 171, 185, 208n
Paul, St, 111–12, 118, 185, 190
Péguy, Charles, 41–3
Pessoa, Fernando, 139
Plato, 10
Pound, Ezra, 4, 50–1, 52, 55n, 57n, 94
Proust, Marcel, 18

Rashdall, Hastings, 8, 23n, 57n
Ricks, Christopher, 29, 74, 88n, 127, 149, 172
Rochefoucauld, Francois de La, 141
Russell, Bertrand, 104

Said, Edward, 181
Scheler, Max, 47, 86, 121n
Schopenhauer, Arthur, 132
Shakespeare, William, 45–7, 48, 167, 168–9, 176n, 194
Sidgwick, Henry, 7–8
Spender, Stephen, 94, 119n
Steiner, George, 3, 52, 59n
Stephen, Karin, 65–6, 70–1, 79

Tate, Allen, 153
Taylor, Charles, 4, 121n, 56n, 147n
Taylor, Jeremy, 15, 132, 133
Thomas à Kempis, 14, 132, 133, 182, 189–91, 192
Tomkins, Silvan, 66–7
Treaty of Versailles, 17
Trilling, Lionel, 5

Unitarianism, 8, 27, 37, 57n, 106, 115–16, 123n
Updike, John, 180, 206

via negativa, 3, 167
Villon, François, 16
Virgil, 159–60

weakness, 4, 15, 46, 86, 126, 139, 142, 153, 168, 178–9, 182
Weil, Simone, 15, 140
Wells, H. G., 11
Windelband, Wilhelm, 133
Woods, J. H., 22n

Yeats, W. B., 152, 154–5, 157–63, 166, 167–8, 171, 172, 174n

EU representative:
Easy Access System Europe
Mustamäe tee 50, 10621 Tallinn, Estonia
Gpsr.requests@easproject.com

www.ingramcontent.com/pod-product-compliance
Lightning Source LLC
Chambersburg PA
CBHW052048220426
43663CB00012B/2487